THIS DOG'LL HUNT

Wallace O. Chariton

Introduction by Ann Richards

Illustrations by Wayde Gardner

Wordware Publishing, Inc.

Library of Congress Cataloging-in-Publication Data

Chariton, Wallace O.
   This dog'll hunt.

   Includes index.
   1. English language—Provincialisms—Texas—Dictionaries
   2. English language—Texas—Slang—Dictionaries.
   3. Texas—Social life and customs—Dictionaries.
   I. Title.
   PE3101.T4C48   1989   427'.9764   88-33865
   ISBN 1-55622-126-6 (hardbound)
   ISBN 1-55622-125-8 (pbk.)

1506 Capital Ave.
Plano, Texas 75074

ISBN 1-55622-126-6 (hardbound)
ISBN 1-55622-125-8 (pbk.)

10 9 8 7 6 5 4 3
8908

All inquiries for volume purchases of this book should be
addressed to Wordware Publishing, Inc., at the above address.
Telephone inquiries may be made by calling:

(214) 423-0090

dog'll \dog-ul\ Of rural origin from Texas and the deep South. It is actually a contraction for the phrase "dog will." Thus the phrase "this dog'll hunt" translates into "this dog will hunt" which means it will work.

Contents

Introduction
by Ann Richards, Texas State Treasurer

This Dog'll Hunt is the latest and perhaps most complete effort to catalog that which will never be completely cataloged: the metaphors, similes, and word pictures of everyday speech. The trouble with cataloguing them is that before you can complete the list, some farmer out on the High Plains is saying he's mad enough to eat bees (a new one I heard recently), or a high school kid in Houston is calling his best friend his "dog" as in Jim is my Dog (another one I read about in a recent newspaper article, which means it is no longer current).

The author of this tome, Wally Chariton, is to be commended for his heroic attempt. I always enjoy thumbing through these compilations because they bring back memories of listening to my relatives in the country. Growing up, as I did, in rural Central Texas, I heard some of the most colorful spoken language extant. Long before I knew what a metaphor was, I knew that if you "talked a blue streak" you talked too much.

Of course it was country and rural and it was occasionally crude. But mostly it was humorous. It added the sparkle of a slight smile to common talk.

My father, Cecil Willis, is one of the true geniuses of Texas talk. His speech is unique. Had he been a more literary man and had the inclination to fuse words to paper, he could have written wonderfully colorful stories. His metaphors are always clear and always contain the hint of a man who doesn't take life too seriously. There is the suggestion of the belly laugh, of guffaws around a potbellied stove. A touch of the ribald is there, too.

When a reporter interviewed him after my Democratic Keynote speech, he asked daddy if he ever thought that his daughter would ever be doing something like "this."

"I didn't even know there was a 'this'," he replied truthfully and matter of factly.

I've always wondered what makes a people, especially the unlettered and perhaps unsophisticated folk around the rural areas of Texas, speak in such sophisticated language.

I doubt if many of my parents' station and generation could have told you what a simile was and if asked to make one up, they would have been as speechless as a tongue-tied hog.

Yet, their everyday speech used as many figures of speech as a couple of acts of "Hamlet." Shakespeare would be proud.

Such colorful language is less apparent today, although it is still there and it still grows. It seems to me, however, that the most inventive minds in this field have moved to the city, where there has always been a rich stew-pot of language entrepreneurs milling out images of their hard experience.

Teenagers are especially inventive. The argot of youthful urban blacks has always bubbled with savory language and in Texas, as elsewhere, where there is a mixture of Spanish and English, the lilting accents and images of other cultures is especially exciting.

I am saddened that generations of English classes have had their effect of standardizing English. True, good standard English doesn't have to be lifeless and colorless. And true, good standard English brings a precision to language that is often missing from non-standard versions.

But what saddens me is the homogeneity. Good grey language is fine for an obituary or the instructions manual for a word processor (how apt the name!) but it is too often as bland as beans without salt pork.

I think that our great communications industry, from long distance telephones to radio and television, has been largely responsible. Clearly, not an original thought, but true nonetheless.

We all learn our language now not on the back porch but on the Cosby Show.

We may understand one another better now, but I do miss knowing a stranger's roots by the expression in his or her speech.

And sometimes, late in the evening after one of those grueling evenings at the office or (worse) on the stump, I look at myself in the mirror as I get ready for bed and recall my daddy. I ache and I'm tired and I know what he'd be saying to momma. "That ole girl looks like she was rode hard and put up wet."

And that about says all that needs to be said.

Preface

A Dallas newspaper columnist once used the analogy that something or other happened as frequently "as a new book on how to talk Texan appeared in the book stores." The implication was that there have been a lot of books on the language of Texas, which is certainly true. The reasons are simple - Texans talk with a colorful, often unique, usually interesting, and always entertaining sort of homespun language.

Unfortunately, most of the books on Texas talk have been little more than collections of Texasisms, which are the sayings that find their way into the everyday language of the people in the Lone Star state. While such books may be interesting and entertaining to read, they stop far short of being useful except for people with exceptional memories. If you are looking for a particular saying or phrase in one of those collections, you generally have to scan the entire book to find it. That problem is precisely the idea behind this book.

As a fifth generation native Texan, I've always been infatuated with the state, its people, and customs. When I was about knee-high to a 6-oz. Dr Pepper bottle, I resolved to someday write about Texas and, who knows, I may achieve that goal yet. I also realized at a tender age that if I was going to write Texan, I had to talk Texan. Toward achieving that objective, at about age 10, I started dutifully recording the clever sayings and descriptions that I heard in everyday conversation. Thirty years later, I'm still writing down all the sayings I hear. Old habits are sure enough hard to break.

Thanks to a wide variety of family, friends, associates, and casual acquaintances, I have been exposed to Texasisms from almost every corner of the state. My travels have taken me from Amarillo to Austin, Pampa to Palacious, Bovina to Beaumont, Muleshoe to Mission, Fort Worth to Fort Sam Houston, Dallas to Dalhart and most everywhere in between. Wherever I went, when I wasn't talking I was listening - to waitresses, cowboys, farmers, bell hops, seed salesmen, and anyone else who talked Texas. The more I listened, the more I wrote, until my little notebook of sayings grew to roughly the size of a rough draft of *Gone With the Wind*.

When I finally decided to try my hand at writing, I felt I had enough sayings to get me through three novels, a screen play, and half a dozen magazine articles. I was probably correct in that assumption but there was one enormous hair in the butter. My large collection of sayings was just that, a large collection. The material was not categorized or classified, which meant finding a certain saying for a particular purpose required considerable reading. Generally, before I found what I was looking for, I had forgotten why I was looking for it in the first place. It was sort of like having a shoe box full of baseball cards and having to look through the entire collection to find one Mickey Mantle.

After several frustrating attempts to find some certain thing in my notebook, I decided my lifelong hobby had been a waste of time. I resolved to break down and purchase some commercial dictionary of Texas sayings and forget about trying to write down what I heard. Like that Dallas newspaper columnist, I knew there were lots of books out on talking Texas and I assumed at least one of them would be useful for my purpose. I was wrong.

All the books I reviewed fell into one of two categories. Most were just published collections that, like my notebook, where not categorized and thus useless for someone looking for a particular phrase. Category two was the dictionaries which attempted to explain what the Texas sayings meant but offered no help unless you already knew a particular phrase. What I needed was a sort of English-to-Texas conversion dictionary but, after turning over every rock and half the cow patties in Texas looking for one, I became convinced such a critter did not exist.

I gave fleeting thoughts to creating my own English-to-Texas dictionary, but every time I picked up my notebook to get started, I'd get half a hernia and an entire heartache. My collection was just too big to handle manually, especially for someone like myself who is, at best, only a fair to middlin' hunt 'n pecker when it comes to typing. I was on the verge of giving up my infant writing career and enrolling in barber college when a friend introduced me to a new fangled invention called the personal computer. Now there's an invention that ranks right up there with sliced bread and the Weedeater as far as being useful to mankind.

After reading through my first printout, it seemed possible that other people might enjoy having a useful dictionary that could be used to quickly find a good ol' Texas saying for a particular purpose or need. I decided to edit my material as best I could, correct as many spelling errors as possible, and see if I could interest any publisher in the project. The fact that you are reading this book is testimony to the success of that mission.

The title, *This Dog'll Hunt* actually came from Austin via Atlanta, Georgia with the help of television. When Texas State Treasurer Ann Richards gave the keynote address at the 1988 Democratic convention, she propelled herself into the limelight with genuine Texas talk. Naturally, being a collector of Texas phrases, I listened to every word and made several entries in my notebook as Ms. Richards spoke. She used the phrase "that dog won't hunt" when referring to Republican policies, and when I entered that into my computer, it dawned on me that my little dictionary was something that "will hunt," meaning it will work, because it would be useful to anyone wishing to talk Texan.

This Dog'll Hunt is a perfect title for the book for several reasons. First, it is a Texasism in itself. Second, the interpretation of the phrase fits the book perfectly. A dog that'll hunt is useful while one that won't is just another mouth to feed. An English-to-Texas conversion dictionary is useful while a simple collection of sayings is just another book on the shelf. Third, a name like *This Dog'll Hunt* has more appeal than Conversion Dictionary.

Once I had the name, another bolt from the blue struck. Since Ms. Richards had indirectly contributed to the name, I wondered if she might be willing to write the foreword for the book. Knowing full well that people in the public eye are frequently busier than a one-armed fry cook in a truck stop, I still decided to risk the cost of a postage stamp and send her a letter with a formal request -- more of a bent-knee plea for help, actually -- and see what would happen. Being a writer I was accustomed to rejection and was prepared for a polite "don't have time" response. To my absolute surprise she said yes, which, in my book, qualifies her for a Nobel prize for friendliness.

Once I had the material, the title, and an interesting foreword, I had myself a book. Now, since you're reading this, it can be assumed you have a copy. Before you dive headlong into the material, some cautions are perhaps in order. You should bear in mind that this is a simple dictionary, not an in depth study of language. To qualify for inclusion in this book, a particular word or phrase had to be simply used in Texas, not necessarily invented in the state. The population of Texas is comprised of a mixed herd of all sorts of folks which means the language is equally mixed. It is entirely possible that you could hear some of the material from this book in places like California, Montana, or Florida. About all I did was weed out the phrases that didn't seem even remotely associated with Texas which probably meant they came from some place like New York.

Another necessary caution is that, unlike mathematics, the language of Texas is not an exact science. A lot of Texasisms have many meanings and uses. Take the saying "plow around the stump" as an example. That could be used to mean avoid trouble. A very large person could be "too large too plow around" while a mean person could be one who "plows through stumps." A pretty girl could be worth "plowing through a stump" for.

To keep this book from being longer than the Bible, only the more popular uses of most phrases were included, but you can still use your imagination. Also, bear in mind that some phrases mean different things to different people.

As a parting shot, be aware that this book is not all-inclusive. It is not possible for one person to get a loop on all the Texasisms, although I tried. Without doubt some old sayings slipped through the cracks and several new ones have been invented since this book went to press. If you have some favorite sayings that didn't get included, you are welcome to send them along to: Wordware Publishing, Inc., 1506 Capital Avenue, Plano, Texas 75074; Attention Wallace O. Chariton. If you are the first one to send in material that gets used in any next edition, I'll include your name in the book so you can show the neighbors. That ought to be a fair trade, right?

As you read this book, remember it was designed to be more useful than ornamental. The whole idea is that you will use the material either to better talk like a Texan, or to understand what a Texan is saying. Either way, the wonderful language of

Texas is preserved and that, after all, is the most important point.

Till we meet again, keep the fireflies out of the buttermilk and your wagon between the ditches.

On a plain ol'   Wallace O. Chariton
creek near
Plano, Texas

Special Dedication

This Dog'll Hunt is specially dedicated to two of the bravest dogs in the history of Texas - both veterans of the second battle of Adobe Walls.

In the late 1800's buffalo hunting was big business in Texas. It has been estimated that perhaps ten million of the critters were slaughtered for their hides in a twenty year period between 1870 and 1890. The great southern herd of buffalo was all but exterminated.

In 1874 a group of hunters that included Billy Dixon and Bat Masterson were camped out near some abandoned ruins beside the East Adobe Walls Creek in present Hutchinson County. In the early morning hours of June 27th, 1874 a noise awakened some of the men. They feared a rig pole had snapped and they wanted to be sure their lodgings didn't come tumbling down around them. At just about dawn, as the men were finishing shoring up the roof, Chief Quanah Parker and several hundred Comanches attacked the buffalo hunters.

The battle lasted three days with heavy losses on both sides. On the third day Billy Dixon, using a Sharps "Big 50" buffalo rifle, managed to pick off an Indian at a distance later measured to be over 1,500 yards. Quanah Parker decided to withdraw his men saying they couldn't compete against the white man's guns which "shoot today and kill tomorrow."

After the fighting ceased, members of the hunting party discovered that the list of casualties included two freighters, Mike and Charlie Shiedler, and their big black Newfoundland dog. All three had been killed and scalped. The fact that the dog had been scalped was a sure sign he had put up quite a fight, before he was killed, trying to protect his masters. Billy Dixon also discovered that his dog, a female setter named Fannie, was missing. It was presumed she had either been killed or was scared off and would surely starve to death on the harsh prairie.

A couple of months following the battle, Billy Dixon and another party of hunters returned to the area. To everyone's amazement, they discovered that Fannie was still alive. Not only had she survived her ordeal, but she had a new litter of four pups whose father was the Shiedler's Newfoundland dog. According to Billy Dixon, when they broke camp and left the next day, "Fannie and her babies were given a snug place in the mess wagon." The story of the dogs of Adobe Walls was so popular among the people of the Panhandle that for years when a really good dog came along, it was said to be a descendent of the litter produced by Fannie and the big Newfoundland.

Considering the title of this book, we decided to use a dog character to illustrate some of the sayings. Naturally, we needed a name for the character, and even though he isn't exactly a descendent of one of Fannie's litter, we named him Adobe in honor of the dogs of Adobe Walls.

Acknowledgements

If you read much at all, you have undoubtedly come across authors who go to great lengths to acknowledge all the people who helped on his or her project. I'd like to do the same thing but it simply isn't possible because a great many people who helped with this project didn't even know they were helping, and I have no idea who they are.

Over the years I picked up most of the material for this dictionary simply by listening to other Texans talk. For example, I once rode an elevator to the top floor of the Driskill Hotel in Austin. Two strangers were also in that elevator and one of them remarked to the other that his blind date the night before had been ugly enough "to make a freight train take a dirt road." I used the saying but have no way of knowing who the man was to acknowledge his help. Most of the sayings in the collection were collected in similar fashion so, perhaps, I should simply say, "Thanks, Ya'll," to all of the many Texans who inadvertently contributed.

One inadvertent contributor who does deserve special mention is Darrell Royal, the former head football coach at the University of Texas. Coach Royal took over the reins at Texas about the time I started recording sayings. Since I was already a Longhorn fan, I naturally listened to what Royal had to say - and he always seemed to have a lot to say. Many of the sayings he used have found their way into this book. Thanks, Coach.

Thanks, also, to John Connally, Davy Crockett, John Nance Garner, Sam Houston, Lyndon and Lady Bird Johnson, Tom Landry, Bobby Layne, Bum Phillips, Sam Rayburn, Allan Shivers, and a host of other Texans who contributed to this work simply by talking.

I'd like to offer a special thanks to Glen P. Owen, a sure 'nuff old-Texan if there ever was one. He's responsible for the first Texasism I ever collected and he's also my uncle. When I was about 10 years old, I happened to say something particularly stupid which caused my uncle some embarrassment. He quickly replied that I was "like a catfish, all mouth and no brains." I'm reminded of that saying every time my mouth starts working before my brain is in gear.

Joe "Redneck" Reynolds, a West Texas country boy and old friend, deserves special recognition. Not only did Redneck contribute a tremendous number of sayings to this collection, but he also provided encouragement and moral support. He'd be the first to say no thanks was necessary, but I want to say it anyway. Thanks, my friend.

I would be remiss if I didn't say thanks to the staffs of the Dallas Public Library, Texas History Division and the Gladys Harrington Public Library in Plano. Every writer owes his soul to cooperative library staffs and, for my money, the folks in the Dallas and Plano libraries are among the best.

Finally, I have to acknowledge the help of Judy, Gage, and Jennifer. They stood by me through some really hard times and were always supportive. No question about it, they deserve the biggest thanks of all.

A

ACTIVE — as an egg suckin' dog

ABANDONED As last year's bird nest ❏ left high and dry ❏ as a dry well

ABLE He's still got some snap in his garters ❏ she still has a rustle in her dress *See also Capable*

ABOUT TIME High time, as in "It's high time we painted the barn."

ABOUT Near bout, as in "It's near bout four miles to town."

ABOUT TO Fixin' to, as in "He's fixin' to mow the lawn."

ABSOLUTELY Bet your boots ❏ sure as shooting ❏ dead certain guaranteed fact *See also Certain, Fact*

ABSENT MINDED Sent his wife to the bank and kissed his money good-bye ❏ he scratched his watch and wound his hair

ACCEPT What can't be cured must be endured ❏ bite the bullet, which is a reference to the days before anesthetic was invented when old west doctors offered patients a bullet to bite while being operated on ❏ hump up and take it like an old bull in a blue norther ❏

stand your watch ❏ take your medicine

ACCEPTABLE That dog'll hunt ❏ that'll do for me and any old gal I'd go out with ❏ tolerable for my needs ❏ suits me to a fare-thee-well ❏ I can sit still for that ❏ I can live with that ❏ in the oilpatch, that'll drill means acceptable ❏ close enough for government work, which refers to the general belief that when you are working for the government, any government, close is considered acceptable *See also Agree*

ACCEPTABLE, BARELY It beats a poke in the eye with a sharp stick ❏ It'll do till something better comes along.

ACCIDENT PRONE He could fall up a well (or tree) ❏ he could cut his finger with an electric razor ❏ he's a train wreck looking for a place to happen ❏ he's got a rubber-lined bathroom, which is a reference to most accidents in the home occurring in the bathroom ❏ if his windmill breaks down, his cows go thirsty. Since windmills were often out in a pasture by themselves, falling off a windmill while trying to fix it was one of the most dangerous accidents that could happen to a cowboy

3

because it might be some time before help arrived. Anyone prone to accidents would not even attempt the repairs.

ACCOMPANY You might as well come go with me.

ACCOUNTANT Pencil pusher ❑ bean counter ❑ figure fanatic ❑ book balancer ❑ debit and credit man ❑ tax wrangler

ACCOUNTED FOR All the horses are in the corral ❑ the cattle ain't a hoof shy ❑ the deck's full ❑ all the beans are in the pot.

ACCURATE That hit the nail on the head ❑ that hit in the black, which is a reference to hitting a target in the center, which is usually black ❑ that rang the bell

ACCURATE AS A weather vane. No matter which way the winds blows, the weather vane will always be right.

ACCUSATION That's the pot calling the kettle black. ❑ He's a fox calling a coyote a chicken thief. ❑ He's a horse thief callin' a cattle rustler a criminal.

ACE (PLAYING CARD) Bullet ❑ arrow head

ACHIEVEMENT He's earned his spurs, place at the fire, or spot at the bar

ACQUAINTED We've howdied and shook. ❑ I've known him for years in all kinds of weather.

ACQUAINTED, CASUALLY We've howdied but we ain't ever shook. ❑ We've watered our horses at the same trough. ❑ I've seen him in the mirror behind the bar.

ACQUAINTED, WELL I'd know his ashes in a whirlwind. ❑ I'd know him if he was BBQ'd and served for lunch. ❑ I'd know him if he'd been through a meat grinder and made into a sausage.

ACQUIESCED He broke down and caved in

ACT Play possum

ACT INTELLIGENT It's one thing for people to think you're stupid but it's another matter all together for them to have proof. Former Houston coach Bum Phillips once commented that he didn't want to trade any players who might hurt his team later. He explained, "I don't mind people thinking I'm stupid but I don't want to give them any proof."

ACT NOW Quick stitches save britches ❏ Strike while the iron is hot because it's hard to brand with a cold iron.

ACT PREMATURE He kicks and jumps before he's spurred ❏ He broke the barrier, which refers to rodeo cowboys leaving too early and breaking the barrier resulting in penalty time being added to their score.

ACTIVE A used key is the one that shines ❏ he's full of spit and vinegar ❏ his axles stay hot ❏ he plays a frisky fiddle ❏ grass don't grow on a busy street ❏ a goin' Jesse ❏ he moves around so much you'd swear he was twins. Editor's Note: A real active person would move around so much you'd swear he was triplets.

ACTIVE AS A bobcat tied up in a tow sack ❏ as a fox in a hen house ❏ as an egg-sucking dog in a chicken coop ❏ lightning in a jug ❏ as a blind dog in a packin' plant ❏ as a worm on a BBQ grill ❏ as a henpecked husband with a harem ❏ as a stump-tailed bull at fly time, which implies that a bull's main defense against biting flies is a swish of his tail. A bull with a stump tail will be very active during fly season. *See also Busy As*

ADEQUATE It'll do till something better comes along ❏ it'll do in a pinch ❏ up to snuff *See also Acceptable*

ADMIRE He's a legend in my mind ❏ I'll take my hat off to him Texan Bob Wills, the King of Western Swing, was known for never taking off his hat. One exception was at his induction into the Country Music Hall of Fame when he took of his hat in admiration of his many fans around the world.

ADVANTAGE He's playing with a deck he stacked. ❏ He's got the cavalry on his side. ❏ He's paying the right preacher. ❏ He built his teepee inside the fort.

ADVICE When you're up to your neck in manure, don't open your mouth. ❏ never play leap frog with a unicorn ❏ When your hand is in a bobcat's mouth, don't pull his tail. Sam Houston used a variation when he said, "My rule is when my hand is in a lion's mouth never to strike him on the nose." ❏ sometimes the squeaking wheel gets replaced, which is a variation of the old saying "the squeaking wheel gets the grease" ❏ a worm is the only animal that can't fall down ❏ keep your

5

wagon between the ditches ❑ don't change horses in the middle of the stream,

AFFIRMATIVE I reckon. If someone asks if you'd like to go to a honky tonk, "I reckon" would be a strong answer in the affirmative. *See also Yes*

AFRAID Scared half out of my wits ❑ scared half (or plumb) to death ❑ has cold feet no matter how hot the country ❑ spends most of his time in the shadow of mamma's apron ❑ my insides are boogered ❑ Texan Audie Murphy once said, "Seems to me if you're afraid or living with some big fear, you're not really living, you're only half alive." *See also Scared, Scary*

AFTER Gunning for ❑ got my sights on ❑ got 'em in my cross hairs ❑ lookin' to find ❑ stalkin' some game ❑ drawing a bead on it

AFTERNOON Shank of the day ❑ cow time, which means cows generally come home late in the day.

AFTERNOON, LATE Dark thirty, which is an expression that means thirty minutes before dark. In the days before daylight savings time, dark was considered the end of the

afternoon. Parents used dark thirty as a way of telling kids to before home before dark. Editor's Note: Some people use dark thirty to mean thirty minutes after dark.

AGAINST Agin ❑ that goes against my raising ❑ that goes against my grain ❑ dead set not in favor of ❑ I can't sit still for that ❑ powerful opposed to

AGAINST THE ODDS Sawing against the grain ❑ swimming against the tide ❑ bucking the odds

AGGRESSIVE He's hornin' the bush ❑ he's eatin' fire ❑ he's smokin' his wheels

AGGRESSIVE AS A snake oil salesman ❑ as a used car salesman ❑ as an old time Methodist circuit rider ❑ as an insurance peddler ❑ as a condo time-share salesman ❑ as a television evangelist

AGILE Loose jointed ❑ nimble footed ❑ fragile footed

AGILE AS A champion cuttin' horse ❑ as a snake on a hot concrete road ❑ as a kid in a cactus patch

AGING Getting on in years ❑ the spring has gone out of his chicken ❑ getting long in the tooth, which is a reference to the gums in older horses receding, giving the appearance that their teeth grow longer as they get older *See also Elderly, Old*

AGITATED AS A pack mule in a hailstorm ❑ as a frog under a milk bucket ❑ as a short dog in tall grass

AGITATOR He's stirring the fire with a sabre ❑ he's forking manure into the well ❑ he's rocking the boat ❑ he's raising waves on the sea of tranquility.

AGREE I can dance to that tune ❑ I can ride on that range ❑ I'd vote for that and lend a hand stuffing the ballot box ❑ I'd do the same thing if I was in his boots ❑ we're seein' eye to eye ❑ we're chewing off the same plug of tobacco *See also In Agreement*

AGREEABLE I'd as soon do that as not ❑ might as well since it's too wet to plow and the hogs are too small to kill

AIM, GOOD He's got prayerful aim. ❑ He shoots seein' eye bullets.

AIM, POOR Couldn't hit the side of an outhouse if he fired from inside it ❑ couldn't hit the side of a barn with a scatter gun at 10 paces ❑ couldn't hit a bull in the butt with a base fiddle

ALCOHOL *See Whisky, Liquor, Champagne, Tequila*

ALCOHOLIC, REFORMED *See Drunk, Reformed*

ALCOHOLICS ANONYMOUS Soberness refinery

ALERT He never missed a bet or overlooked a blonde ❑ eagle eyed ❑ on the ball ❑ he knows the sound opportunity makes when it comes knocking ❑ keep your ear to the ground and your eyes peeled ❑ you don't get kicked in the backside by someone who is in front of you, which basically means don't let the enemy sneak up behind you. *See also Be Alert*

ALIKE Poured out of the same mold ❑ squeezed from the same udder ❑ drained from the same crankcase ❑ poured out of the same milk bucket ❑ cut from the same hide ❑ two peas in a pod ❑ mixed in the same bowl ❑ cut from the same bolt ❑ punched out of the same die ❑ not a nickle's worth of difference between 'em ❑ cut from the same herd

7

❏ out of the same flock *See also Identical*

ALL Everybody and the dog (or cook)

ALL THE WAY Clear (or clean) to, as in "He went clear to the county line tryin' to outrun the sheriff," or "He was cut clean to the bone" ❏ plumb, as in "He went plumb to Florida looking for a job."

ALMOST Close but no cigar ❏ like to, as in "I like to forgot" ❏ pert near, as in "I pert near forgot my anniversary."

ALMOST FINISHED In the short rows, which is derived from the days when cotton choppers considered the job almost done when they made it to the short rows.

ALONE Stewing in his own juice ❏ playing solitaire ❏ playing a lone hand ❏ on his own hook ❏ Lone Rangerin' it ❏ lone wolfin' it

ALOOF High headed ❏ hifalutin' ❏ uppity as a mountain goat ❏ he can strut sitting down, which is how attorney Temple Houston once described the prosecutor in a case he was defending.

ALTERNATE Change about ❏ swap around ❏ turn about is fair play ❏ take turns dancin' on both feet

ALTERNATIVE More than one way to break a dog (or a mother-in-law) from sucking eggs ❏ more than one way to skin a cat or win a pretty girl's heart ❏ every coin has two sides ❏ every record has a flip side except a prison record

AMARILLO, TEXAS Pronounced Am-a-rill-a, a city in the Texas Panhandle which is often called the helium capital of the world. Amarillo means yellow.

AMATEUR Jake leg ❏ tinhorn ❏ greenhorn *See also Tenderfoot*

AMAZED (OATH) I'll be dipped in snuff (or tobacco juice) ❏ I'll be switched (or jiggered) ❏ well shuck me nekkid (naked)

AMAZING That'll blow your dress up ❏ that'll blow your hat in the creek ❏ it'll pop your eyeballs right out of their sockets far enough to get a rope on 'em ❏ that'll snap your girdle ❏ a real whistle bringer, which is derived from the fact that a lot of people whistle when something amazing happens ❏ that'll cock your pistol ❏ that'll melt your butter *See also Astonishing, Exciting*

AMBITIOUS He's always looking for new ranges to ride (or fields to plow) ❏ a real barn burner ❏ he thinks he can break every ornery brono in Texas ❏ he'll take on all comers if the big ones will line up and the little ones will bunch up.

AMERICAN A real Texas pronunciation is Murkin. Texan Lyndon Johnson, while serving as President, often opened his speeches with, "Ma fella Murkins." In Spanish it's Americano or gringo. Of course, most Americans from north of the Red River are Yankees.

AMONG Amongst ❏ in the thick of ❏ in the heat of ❏ in the heart of

AMOUNT, LARGE *See Large Amount*

AMOUNT, SMALL *See Small Amount*

ANAHUAC, TEXAS Usually pronounced Anny-ock or Anna-wack, the small town, on Trinty Bay near Houston,

where the Texas revolution took seed.

ANGERS That chaps my hide (or butt) ❏ that boils my water ❏ that pops my cork ❏ that fries my patience ❏ that gets my dander (dandruff) up ❏ that gets a rise out of me quicker than a snake can stick out his tongue

ANGRY AS A preacher with the devil camped out in his back yard ❏ as a rooster in an empty hen house ❏ as a buzzard who circled a sick mule for half a day before he discovered the mule was only asleep ❏ as a teased rattlesnake (or cotton mouth water moccasin)

ANGRY FEMALE Her fangs are flashing and her nails are twitchin' ❏ she's gettin' ready to throw a hissey fit ❏ she's wearing war paint instead of makeup ❏ her purr has turned to a growl ❏ she's stoked up hotter than the coals in a depot stove

ANGRY MALE Ready to pit his bird, which is a reference to cock fighting ❏ riled up ❏ foaming at the mouth ❏ he's gettin' ready to burn some powder (shoot someone) ❏ putting on his raking spurs ❏ got his holster tied down ❏ got

9

his eyes pulled up like BBs ❑ bellerin' and pawing the dirt ❑ he's got his hat set at a fighting angle ❑ he's got his teeth set like a stubborn mule *See also Mad*

ANGRY WORDS War words

ANIMALS Critters, if they are friendly, varmints if they ain't.

ANNOUNCE Put it on a billboard ❑ tell it to someone going to a ladies' club meeting (or a church social) ❑ tell somebody it's a secret

ANXIOUS Sittin' on the well, which means he is anxious to bring it in ❑ raring to go ❑ pawing the dirt ❑ got buck fever

ANXIOUS AS A kid on Christmas eve ❑ as a dry steer scenting fresh water. On a trail drive, cattle had to have water at least once a day, and preferably twice. During dry spells, the head often had to go two, three, or more days without drinking. When they finally got near water, they would catch the scent and become anxious, even stampede.

APPEALING Strikes my fancy ❑ tickles my fancy

APPEARANCE, BAD Looks like he was inside the outhouse when lightning struck it ❑ looks like an unmade bed ❑ looks like he was rode hard and put up wet ❑ looks like he spent the night in a dishwasher ❑ looks like he was shot out of a cannon and missed the net, which refers to circus performers who are shot out of a cannon and are supposed to land in a net ❑ looks like the mill ends of hell, which refers to the mill ends produced in sawmills ❑ looks like he was pulled through a knot hole backwards *See also Looks*

APPEARANCE, DECEIVING Just because someone looks like they are in the fast lane, it don't mean they ain't just hitchhiking ❑ just because a chicken has wings don't mean he can fly ❑ he's like a duck, what you can see looks calm but underneath he's paddling as fast as he can

APPEARANCE, GOOD Looks like he ought to be entering a plea, which refers to the fact that most people dress up when appearing in court ❑ he always looks like he just stepped out of an air conditioned room ❑ looks like a picture out of a wish book (mail order catalog) ❑ looks good enough to give a sermon ❑ looks good enough to marry a banker's daughter *See also Looks*

APPETITE, LARGE Eats more than a roundup crew ❑ if he was a pissant, he could eat a bale of hay

APPETITE, SMALL Eats like a hummingbird on a buttermilk diet ❑ don't eat enough to stoke a sparrow

APPLY Dab it on

APPRECIATION Never looking a gift horse in the mouth. Looking a horse in the mouth refers to checking the teeth to determine approximate age. Looking a gift horse in the mouth would show very little appreciation.

APPREHENSIVE As a crippled fly in a spider's web ❑ as a pregnant woman in her tenth month

APPROXIMATELY Pert near, as in "He's got pert near 500 head of cattle."

APRIL Shearin' time, which is when sheep are sheared for their wool.

ARDUOUS *See Difficult, Hard To Do*

AREA, LARGE Big as all of hell and half of Texas. No one knows for sure how big hell is but it is assumed to be larger than Texas, say about the size of Alaska.

ARGUMENT Cuss fight ❑ a fallin' out ❑ a hen fight

ARGUMENTATIVE He'd argue with a sign post, lamp post, goal post, fence rail, or wooden Indian

ARID LAND Got about as much water as a secretarial pool ❑ it'd take 50 acres to support one middlin'-sized jack rabbit ❑ steamboats would rise a cloud of dust in the riverbed ❑ birds build their nests out of barbed wire ❑ the only swimming hole is the water left in a cow track after a thunder storm. Hondo Crouch, the folk legend who owned Luckenback, was also an accomplished swimmer on the University of Texas swim team. He claimed he learned to swim in cow tracks around Hondo, Texas. *See also Drought, Dry*

ARMADILLO Pronounced arm-a-dill-a. The nine banded armadillo is an official mascot of the state of Texas. Also referred to as opossum on the half shell and

11

Hoover Hog, which is derived from the fact that during the depression, a lot of Texans couldn't afford pork so they often ate armadillos, which aren't all that tasty. The nickname is a slur against former President Herbert Hoover.

ARRIVED Blew in with the weather (or tumbleweeds) ❑ struck town ❑ lit and stayed

ARROGANT Riding a high horse ❑ too big for his britches (or overalls) ❑ snot nosed ❑ beggety ❑ biggedy *See also Aloof*

ARTIST, POOR He couldn't draw a conclusion

ASKEW Totally haywire ❑ all cattywhampus ❑ scattered every which way

ASSEMBLED, POORLY Put together with spit and baling wire ❑ Southern engineered ❑ jerry-rigged, which, in Texas, is pronounced jury-rigged

ASSISTANT Right-hand hand ❑ range boss, which was the ranch owner's assistant ❑ hazer, which is a rider who assists a calf roper or steer wrestler in a rodeo.

ASSOCIATED In cahoots with ❑ they're in the same hitch ❑ they're eatin out of the same feed bag ❑ they're singing off the same song sheet ❑ they're riding on the same range ❑ they're marching to the same beat ❑ they're dipping ink from the same bottle *See also Involved*

ASTONISHED (OATH) You could a knocked me over with a hummingbird's tailfeather.

ASTONISHING Beats all I ever saw or heard tell of ❑ a sight to behold ❑ takes the cake *See also Amazing, Exciting*

ASTRODOME Miracle on Main Street, because it was built on Main Street in Houston. ❑ The Reverend Billy Graham said it was "the 8th wonder of the world." According to Bud Adams, the Owner of the Houston Oilers, the rent on the Astrodome is "the 9th wonder of the world." ❑ When the stadium first opened, a Houston sportswriter claimed it was something God might build if he had the money. *See Also New Orleans Super Dome*

ASYLUM Booby hatch ❑ looney bin ❑ nut cracker suite ❑ the loco motel ❑ the Holler

Day Inn, which is a takeoff on Holiday Inn ❏ loco lockup ❏ the Terrell Hilton, which refers to the state hospital located in Terrell, Texas ❏ The La Cain't A, which is a takeoff on La Quinta motor hotels.

AT ALL A Texan pronounces it atall.

AT RISK See Risky

ATHLETE, INEPT He plays like he ought to be in a game where the mothers make the uniforms.

ATTACK Plow into 'em ❏ crawl his hump ❏ try 'em on for size ❏ give 'em both barrels, which refers to a double-barreled shotgun ❏ lit into 'em ❏ Also: bomb primary, which is a reference to a quote from Texan Claude Eatherly. During WWII, he piloted the Straight Flush, which was the scout plane for the Enola Gay that carried the first atomic bomb. After surveying the target area, Eatherly reported, "Cloud cover less than three tenths at all altitudes. Advise bomb primary." The rest is history.

ATTACKED Like grandma after a chicken snake with a chunk of firewood ❏ like conventioneers on a free buffet ❏

like grasshoppers on a corn field ❏ like a chicken hawk on a fat fryer ❏ like a horned toad on a bed of red ants

ATTEMPT Like a steer, I can try, which refers to the fact that even though a steer has been castrated he can still try ❏ try your hand at, as in "I'm gonna try my hand at writing a novel someday."

ATTENTIVE *See Alert, Be alert*

ATTIRE *See Clothes*

ATTRACTED TO Like a hawk to a prairie dog ❏ like lightning to a lightning rod ❏ like a bug to a light ❏ like steel to a magnet ❏ like a pig to slop ❏ like flies to molasses (or honey) ❏ took a liking to ❏ took a shining to ❏ like a kid to a horse ❏ like a pack mule to a bell-mare

AUTOMOBILE DEALERSHIP House, as in Pontiac House or Chevrolet house. Generally used only for American-made brands since Toyota House or Porsche House just don't sound right.

AVERAGE Run of the mill ❏ fair to middlin' ❏ nothing to write home to mamma about ❏

13

everyday wash ❏ just one of
the herd *See also Common*

AVOID Plow around the stump
❏ dance around it ❏ take a
different trail ❏ ride around
the swamp ❏ Stay away from
that like you would a swamp if
you were drunk.

AVOIDED You slipped the
noose ❏ you dodged a bullet.
Editor's Note: If you avoided
big trouble, you didn't just
dodge a bullet, you dodged a
mortar round (or cannon
ball).

AWESOME A rolling ball of
butcher knives. Darrell Royal
once said his Texas team was
not a rolling ball of butcher
knives after they lost to Texas
Tech.

AWHILE A spell, such as "Sit
a spell and take a load off."

AWKWARD As a crippled
cow ❏ as a duck out of water

AWKWARD SITUATION In-
laws on a honeymoon trip ❏ a
mother-in-law that's a bad
cook ❏ a father-in-law that's a
good shot

B

BE SURE YOU'RE RIGHT — 'cause once you cut off a dog's tail you can't sew it back on

BACHELOR Been saved by the bell but never the wedding bell ❑ he'd shuck his hide to get out of a wedding date ❑ he's one fly that won't ever get caught in a spider's web ❑ a lone ranger that never gets in a marryin' mood ❑ he'll never take time to put up a clothesline, which is a reference to the days when wash was usually hung on a line to dry and members of the fairer sex would require a clothesline before they'd agree to get married.

BACHELOR, CONFIRMED He'd chew off his own arm to get out of a matrimonial trap, which is a reference to a coyote that will chew off his own leg to get out of a steel trap ❑ the only way he'll ever get married is under the influence of a shotgun. ❑ the only ring you'll ever get from him is one around your tub.

BACK IT UP Put your money where your mouth is ❑ put your cash where your crower is

BACKSLIDER *See Sinful Person*

BACKWARDS Often pronounced bassackwards ❑ you got the tail waggin' the dog ❑ you got your wagon before your horse

BAD That would drive a preacher to cuss (or to the bottle.)

BAD DAY If today was a fish, I'd throw it back.

BAD PERSON He needs to turn over an entire book, not just a new leaf. The "entire book" is, of course, the Bible. ❑ they ought to jack up the jail and put him under it ❑ he's lower than a snake's belt buckle (or navel) ❑ he's got a reserved seat in hell and he's headed that way in the devil's hand basket ❑ J. Frank Dobie once described a bad person when he said someone was, "mean enough to suck eggs and cunning enough to hide the shells." *See also Evil Person, Mean Person, Wicked*

BAFFLED Buffaloed ❑ ain't got a clue ❑ bumfuzzled ❑ in a fog

BALD HEADED Hitch-headed, which means he has about as much hair as a ball on a trailer hitch ❑ chrome dome, because many bald heads shine like they were chrome plated ❑ Some bald-headed men claim anyone can grow hair but it takes a real man to keep it worn off, implying they wear it off on the headboard. There may be something to that when you consider that grass don't grow on a busy street. It is also widely believed that God made a few perfect heads and then put hair on the rest. It should also be pointed out that they don't put marble tops on cheap furniture.

BANGING Like an outhouse door with the latch broke ❏ like a gate with one hinge rusted off ❏ like a screen door in an orphanage

BANKRUPT Been run over by the plowshare of financial ruin ❏ stuck my boot into the stirrup of financial ruin and got drug all the way to the poor house ❏ lost everything but my name and my conscience *See also Went Broke*

BAPTIST Dipper, dunker, or plunger, referring to the Baptist practice of immersing for Baptism.

BAPTIST, FUNDAMENTALIST Hardshell Baptist

BAR Booze parlor ❏ drinking resort ❏ booze bungalow ❏ saloon ❏ beer (or wine) shed

BAR, CONCEALED A Baptist bar. This refers to a belief, widely held by proponents of liquor by the drink, that many Baptists will go to the polls to vote against liquor by the drink, then go home, open their concealed bar and have a drink to celebrate their victory. This belief gave rise to the phrase "closet-drinking Baptist."

BARBECUE One of the big three in Texas, along with chili and chicken fried steak. It's been said Texans will barbecue everything except ice cream and watermelon, which may be true since there was once a restaurant which specialized in barbecued lobster.

BARBED WIRE Pronounced bobbed war or bob war ❏ the Devil's necklace ❏ Satan's necktie ❏ sticker wire ❏ When barbed wire was first sold, it was advertised as being "steer strong, feather light, and dirt cheap."

BARGAIN Dicker ❏ do a little horse tradin'

BARREN Not enough top soil to make a good dirt dauber's nest ❏ not enough trees to make a wooden penny, much less a nickel *See also Arid Land*

BARTENDER Beer (or drink) wrangler ❏ bar dog ❏ he stays on the sober side of the bar ❏ snake charmer, which is a reference to some people seeing snakes when they have too much to drink.

BARTENDER, GOOD Lead-fisted drink slinger, which implies his hand is so heavy he can't help but pour strong drinks.

BATH A dipping

BATH, QUICK A soiled-dove shower (or whore bath.) Instead of actually taking a shower or bath, you simply load up with deodorant and perfume. Works every time.

BATH TUB Dipping vat

BE ALERT Keep one eye on the cow's tail. This is a reference to the days when cows were milked by hand. About the time you had the bucket full of fresh, foamy white milk, the old cow would swish her tail through a pile of manure and half of it would land in your milk bucket. The only way to prevent that is to keep your eye on the cow's tail. ❏ keep the cows milling so they won't stampede. Being killed while trying to turn a stampede was a leading cause of death among old-time cowboys. The cattle were generally kept milling in an effort to prevent stampedes ❏ keep a weather eye on 'em ❏ keep your eyeballs peeled *See also Alert*

BE BRIEF Just give me the bare bones ❏ give me the bacon without the sizzle

BE CAREFUL Don't plow too close to the cotton ❏ don't throw out the baby with the bath water ❏ if you hook an unbroken horse to a wagon, you are liable to lose a wagon ❏ keep the powder dry ❏ keep your skirts clean ❏ don't sit with your back to the window, which was a common caution for old-time gunfighters since a back to an open window presented an easy target to backshooters and bushwhackers ❏ you were too hard to raise to take chances ❏ always whistle some before drifting into a strange camp, which refers to the days of the old west when a man could turn up dead if he went unannounced in a strange camp ❏ don't dig up more snakes than you can kill *See also Advice, Careful, Caution*

BE CREATIVE *See Innovative*

BE DISCREET Don't hang your dirty wash on someone

else's line ❏ don't make love by the garden gate because even if love is blind, the neighbors ain't ❏ If you kiss an ugly girl, she will tell the world.

BE ON TIME If you are late to church, you have to sit on the front row.

BE PATIENT A watched clock moves slower than molasses in January ❏ you can't catch a pop fly till it comes down ❏ a watched pot never boils ❏ every bell you hear ain't the dinner bell ❏ don't cross the river till you come to it ❏ hot will cool if greedy will let it, which refers to sampling cooked food before it is cool enough to eat ❏ don't count your chickens till they hatch ❏ Don't count the crop till it's in the barn, which was a favorite saying of Texan Sam Rayburn, former Speaker of the United States House of Representatives.

BE PREPARED You can't sell from an empty wagon ❏ keep your ducks in a row ❏ keep your saddle oiled and your gun greased ❏ if you're gonna run with the big dogs, be prepared to hike your leg in tall grass ❏ keep your gun loaded and the safety on *See also Plan Ahead*

BE QUIET Hobble your lip ❏ don't rattle your spurs ❏ a closed mouth gathers no foot ❏ you don't have to explain what you don't say ❏ every fish ever caught had his mouth open ❏ When Lyndon Johnson was in the U.S. Senate, he had a sign in his office proclaiming, "You ain't learning nothing when you're talking."

BE SPECIFIC Scrape off the scab and get to the meat ❏ don't dance all over the floor ❏ don't ride all over the range ❏ cut to the quick ❏ When Bubbles Cash, renowned stripper and Dallas Cowboy fan, was asked what it was she did, she replied, "I'm not an exotic dancer. And not exactly a stripper either. All I do is take my clothes off." That's specific.

BE STILL Get your nest built. This is generally used for sleeping partners who are thrashing around in bed trying to get comfortable. It can, however, be used in any instance where someone is moving around too much to suit you.

BE SURE YOU'RE RIGHT Once you cut off a hound dog's tail you can't sew it back on. Davy Crockett, the frontiersman who died in the Alamo, left this piece of advice for those who followed him, "Be sure you're right, then go ahead."

BE THOROUGH Whitewash don't poison termites.

BEANS The thundering herd ❏ Mexican strawberries ❏ frijoles ❏ shrapnel, when cooked with chili; motherless, when cooked without pork.

BEANS IN THE POD Snap beans

BEANS, PINTO Red beans ❏ Rock beans, which refers to the fact that tiny rocks often get mixed in with the beans when harvested.

BEAT Whip him like a redheaded stepchild ❏ like a farmer would a stubborn mule ❏ tie his ears in a bow knot ❏ knock the stuffing out of him ❏ take the starch out of him ❏ collect his tail feathers ❏ burn his barn ❏ knock him cold enough to skate on ❏ sheer his pin ❏ nail his hide to the barn (or outhouse) wall

BEATABLE The bigger they are, the harder they fall so make sure they don't fall on you ❏ even the meanest bull can be dehorned

BEATEN Feel like someone got after me with a hoe handle ❏ he knocked the enamel loose from my eye teeth ❏ feel like I was whipped with a slippery elm (or bois d'arc) fence post ❏ all my nuts, bolts, and screws are loose ❏ a fat lip never bolstered anyone's confidence ❏ feel like I was whipped with a windmill wrench. A windmill wrench is a large, heavy, and cumbersome tool used to repair windmills. Because of its size and weight, the windmill wrench found its way into much of the language of older Texans who had to contend with those particular tools when the need arose.

BEATEN, SEVERELY They had to pick me up with a sponge ❏ got beat so hard, the wax popped out of my ears (or my ears started smoking) ❏ got licked in spades, which is a reference to spades being the highest ranking playing cards, thus anything in spades is the best or worst it can be ❏ beat so bad it took a week to get the sawdust out of my beard, which is a reference to the practice of putting sawdust on the floor of honky tonks, where fights are not that uncommon.

BEDTIME Roosting time

BEER Cowboy Koolaid ❏ Colorado Koolaid (Coors) ❏ belly fertilizer, which implies that if you drink beer you will grow a big belly ❏ Lone Star is the National Beer of Texas.

BEER, DISGUISED Baptist tea, which is beer served without the foam in an iced tea glass. Baptist tea is most frequently served in dry areas of Texas where beer is illegal.

BEER FOAM Calf slobber, which is also used for meringue on pie.

BEGIN "Take it away, Leon," which is a reference to Bob Wills. When he was ready to get started playing a tune, he would ask Leon McAuliffe to "take it away, Leon." ❏ commence to ❏ cut loose with ❏ pop the cork ❏ break the ground ❏ scratch a fiddle, which means begin playing ❏ open fire ❏ throw out the first pitch *See also Start*

BEGINNING The get-go ❏ first rattle out of the box ❏ when the ball opened

BEHIND You better put on a postage stamp and mail yourself to catch up ❏ you're coming up short in the keeping up department

BELIEVE ME If I say a flea can pull a plow, you can hitch him up. ❏ If I say a katydid can pull a freight train, you can hitch him up and clear the tracks. ❏ If I say a jackass can lay an egg, you can start gathering twigs for a nest. ❏ If I say it's Christmas, you can hang up your stocking. ❏ If I say a hen dips snuff, you'll find the can under her wing. *See also Guaranteed, Fact, Trustworthy*

BELIEVED They lapped it up like it was the gospel. ❏ They took it, hook, line, sinker, and bobber.

BEND OVER Hunker down ❏ rest on your haunches

BEST Pick of the litter ❏ top rung on the ladder ❏ nickle plated ❏ cream of the crop ❏ top drawer ❏ on the blue chip list

BET Risk, as in "I'd risk all my egg money on you not being able to eat six saltine crackers in a minute."

BETRAYED Sold 'em down the river ❏ sold the horse right out from under him

BETWEEN Betwixt

BEWARE Something that sounds too good to be true is probably illegal ❑ a dead hornet can still sting ❑ a dead snake can still bite

BEXAR Pronounced Bear, a county in South Texas. *See also San Antonio*

BIG Big un ❑ big as a barn or the side of a barn ❑ bigger 'n Dallas ❑ big as Texas ❑ big as a number three washtub ❑ big as an oak tree ❑ big as a soup dish ❑ big as a saddle blanket ❑ big enough to shade an elephant ❑ big as a windmill ❑ big as a number three grain scoop *See also Large*

BIG AS A Brazos riverboat, a barn, a killing hog, a four-bit cigar, the capitol dome, or an athlete's ego. *See also Large*

BIG BUILDING The rough riders could have held maneuvers inside it ❑ all you need is the airplane, you got the hangar

BIG PERSON He fills up a room like he was wearing it ❑ looks like half of him ought to be rotating over an open spit, which refers, of course, to BBQing a side a beef for a party ❑ Big Tex wears his hand-me-down jeans. (Big Tex is the giant cowboy who greets visitors to the Texas State Fair in Dallas. His jeans size is 256.) *See also Large Person*

BIG SPRING, TEXAS Texans usually add an "s" to convert the name of this town in West Texas to Big Springs. It has been rumored that school teachers will accept either spelling.

BINOCULARS Bring-'em-up-close glasses ❑ cheaters

BISCUIT Sourdough bullet ❑ hot rock

BLACK As the inside of a pocket (or coffin) ❑ as a cow's tongue ❑ as bois d' arc root ❑ as the ace of spades ❑ as the devil's riding boots ❑ as the bottom of a dry well

BLAME Tie the can on him ❑ put the saddle on him ❑ tie the knot in his tail

BLANKET Lap robe ❑ soogan

BLEEDING Like a stuck pig ❑ like a chicken with his head cut off. On a farm, chickens are generally killed by chopping off their head and it isn't uncommon for blood to squirt like water from a patio fountain.

BLIND AS A bat ❏ as a fence post ❏ as a post hole ❏ as a snubbin' post ❏ as a coil of bobbed war

BLINK Bat an eyelash

BLONDE Palomino ❏ straw haired

BLUE As pinkeye medicine

BLUE, LIGHT Like underwear washed with a new pair of jeans

BLUFF Rattling his sabre or the more modern version, rattling his rockets ❏ While serving as President, Lyndon Johnson said, "I am not going to rattle our rockets. I am not going to bluff with our bombs. I am going to keep our guard up at all times and our hand out."

BODY, SQUATTY Built like a rain barrel ❏ built like an apartment refrigerator ❏ Built like a deep freeze chest ❏ built like a refrigerator up to the handle

BOIS D'ARC Pronounced bow-dark. The wood from the bois d'arc tree is very hard and very straight, which makes it perfect for fence posts if you can find a way to cut the trees down. In the early days of Texas, before concrete was in-

vented, bricks made of bois d'arc wood were used to pave streets. They became obsolete when someone discovered they became very slick when wet.

BOIS D'ARC FRUIT Horse apples

BOOTLESS Sock-footed

BOOTS, REPAIRED Had my boots retreaded, which means they got new half soles.

BOOTS, WORN Could stand on a dime and tell if heads or tails was up

BOOZE *See Beer, Champagne, Liquor, Tequila, Whiskey*

BORED Enjoyed about all this I can stand ❏ a frog in a skillet would have more fun ❏ a wooden Indian in a forest fire would have more fun

BORING As a fishing trip with a game warden ❏ as a school play your kid isn't in ❏ as the unemployment line ❏ This is about as exciting as scraping dead flies off fly paper

BOSS Arena director, which is the person in charge of the arena where a rodeo is held ❏ lead steer ❏ big auger ❏ range manager ❏ ramrod ❏ honcho ❏ big biscuit in the pan ❏ roost ruler ❑ wagon boss ❑ When the big boss is around, it's good advice to work hard, look worried, and keep a hobble on your lip. *See also Important Person, Leader*

BOTHER *See Pester*

BOWLEGGED Saddle warped ❑ banjo legged ❑ couldn't catch a pig in a ditch ❑ as a barrel hoop ❑ a yearling calf could run under him without touching either leg ❑ warp legged ❑ he's so bowlegged he can't sit in an arm chair

BOY Hen wrangler ❑ whistle britches ❑ fryin' size ❑ muchacho

BRAGGART Big talker, little doer ❑ windbelly ❑ flannel-mouth ❑ all gurgle and no guts ❑ truth stretcher ❑ blows harder than a middlin' hurricane ❑ talked himself out of a place at the bar ❑ Texans have long been known as braggarts. One classic case was the Texan who went off to fight in the Civil War claiming "I can beat the damn Yankees with a broomstick." When he returned after the war, minus an arm and so much worse for the wear, someone asked him about his boast. "I could have beat 'em with a broom stick," he replied, "'cept I couldn't get

'em to fight with broomsticks."

BRASSIERE Flopper stopper ❑ over-the-shoulder boulder holder ❑ double-barrel slingshot or catapult ❑ marble pouch.

BRAVE Could win an Audie Murphy act-alike contest. Audie Murphy was a youngster from near Farmersville, Texas who became America's most decorated hero in World War II. Murphy also described bravery as "determination to do a job that you know has to be done." ❑ he can't be stampeded, which is how many early Texas Rangers were described and it probably holds true today ❑ not afraid to go to hell alone. One of the most famous Texas Rangers of all time was Jack Hayes and he was that brave. Chief Flaco of the Lipan Indians once said of Hayes, "Me and Red Wing not afraid to go to hell together. Captain Jack Hayes brave, not afraid to go alone." ❑ Perhaps the best description of brave is he's kin to Bill Travis. William B. Travis was the acting commander of the Alamo. In his famous letter, called the most patriotic in American history, Travis said, "I shall never surrender or retreat." He didn't.

BRAVE AS A rodeo clown ❑ as a first grade teacher ❑ as the man that ate the first oyster (or egg) ❑ as a bigamist. Surely any man with more than one wife is the bravest of them all.

BRAVE ENOUGH TO Eat in a boomtown cafe, which were notorious for serving food that wasn't exactly pleasing to the palate. In *Roundup: A Texas Kid's Companion,* David Kaplan credits Ned Alvord with saying, "They're building monuments to Sam Houston, when all he ever done was to face Mexican bullets on the battlefield. I ate in the cafes of Longview during the oil boom."

BRAZOS RIVER Pronounced braz ess, one of the most popular rivers in Texas. The name is of Spanish origin and means arms or arms of God.

BREASTS Bobbers ❑ begonias ❑ kitties

BREASTS, LARGE Bra busters ❑ quite a pair to draw to ❑ carrying a big rack

BREASTS, SMALL Chicken breasted ❑ like BBs on the kitchen table (or ironing board) ❑ no bigger than moles on a chigger ❑ she could put her bra on backwards and not notice the difference

BREATH, STRONG As strong as gasoline, kerosene, No. 2 diesel, turpentine, or Clorox ❑ strong enough to use as a clothesline and hang all the wash in Texas on it ❑ as if he had supper in a coyote den

BREATHING HARD Puttin' out enough air to run a gin whistle

BRIGHT As a new penny

BRING Fetch that with you ❑ tote that along for the ride

BROKE More than all Ten Commandments put together ❑ down to my last chip ❑ couldn't take the first hand in a penny ante game ❑ couldn't change my mind or pay attention ❑ I'd scrape the bottom of the barrel if I could reach it ❑ If a trip around the world cost a dollar, I wouldn't have enough to get to the Texas state line. *See also Destitute, Poor*

BROKEN Broke down ❑ out of whack ❑ out of kilter

BRUSH, THICK So thick the snakes had to crawl around it ❑ so thick a starving coyote wouldn't go in there after a wounded rabbit

BUCK Referring to the jumping action of a horse, most Texans say pitch, as in, "That old nag can pitch with the best of 'em."

BUCK TOOTHED Could eat corn through a picket fence

BUDGET, SMALL Poor boying it

BULLY Big behaver ❑ got a carload of big behavior ❑ they don't make britches as big as he behaves

BUMPKIN He just arrived on a load of watermelons (or cantaloups)

BUMPY As a 25-pipe cattle guard (See Handy)

BUNCHED UP Like wild turkeys in a hailstorm ❑ like hogs at a trough ❑ like cows in a thunderstorm

BURDENED Saddled with ❑ he's got an anvil in his shorts ❑ his heart's heavier than a windmill wrench ❑ he's hitched with a dead mule ❑ got a dead chicken hanging around his neck. When Bill Clements ran for governor the first time, he said, "I'm gonna hang Jimmy Carter around John Hill's neck like a dead chicken." He did and it turned out to be more of a burden than Hill could handle.

BURLAP BAG Tow sack, feed sack ❑ gunny sack ❑ croker sack

BURNED Like a cockroach caught in an electric chair ❑ like an empty shuck

BURNING *See On Fire*

BURY Funeralize ❑ put to bed with a shovel ❑ plant ❑ move 'em into stone city

BUS (Greyhound) Dog (or grey dog) as in, "I'll come for a visit soon as I round up enough money to ride the dog." Some folks don't like riding the bus but it shore beats wearin' out boot leather and thumbs hitchhiking.

BUSINESS Bidness. In Texas, all commerce is bidness, as in the oil bidness, the cattle bidness, the printing bidness, etc.

BUSINESS ADVICE Never sign anything in the glow of a neon light. Neon lights generally glow in bars and honky tonks where people are prone to drink, which means if you use that light to sign something, such as a contract, you may wake up in the morning wishing you'd used invisible ink. *See also Good Business Practice*

BUSINESS, GOOD A land office bidness, which refers to the early days of Texas when there was lots of cheap available land and the land office was frequently the busiest around, except for the saloon ❏ doing better than a hotel in a boomtown. In boomtowns, bed space was generally very scarce and often rooms were rented in eight-hour shifts, which meant the hotel owners were cleaning up. This fact led Conrad Hilton to purchase his first hotel, the Mobley, in Cisco Texas. He said it was, "a cross between a flop house and a gold mine." Also doin' better than a boomtown cafe or saloon, either one of which probably did even better than a boomtown hotel.

BUSINESS PRACTICE Never try to out-trade a man and never let a man out-trade you if you can help it. That advice came from Texan Hugh Roy Cullen, who never was out-traded in his life.

BUSY Catching 'em faster than I can string 'em ❏ got weeds growing faster than I can hoe 'em ❏ the hens are laying eggs faster than I can gather 'em

BUSY AS A chicken drinking out of a pie pan. Pie pans are generally shallow so a chicken trying to drink out of one would be very busy and frustrated. ❏ as a pair of jumper cables at a Fourth of July picnic ❏ as a one-armed man (or woman) saddling a horse ❏ as a barefoot boy on a red ant bed ❏ as a bartender on pay day ❏ as a one-armed paper hanger ❏ as a one-legged man in a butt-kicking contest ❏ as a windsock (or windmill) in a whirlwind ❏ as a funeral home fan in July ❏ as a one-eyed dog in a smokehouse *See also Active As*

BUTTER Cow grease ❏ skid grease

BUTTOCKS *See Rear End*

C

CAUTIOUS — as a small dog with a big bone

This Dog'll Hunt

CAFE Feed lot ❏ chili joint ❏ feed trough ❏ eatin' ranch ❏ greasy spoon ❏ greasy sack outfit ❏ feed ground

CALCULATE Put a pencil to it ❏ cipher it

CALF, MOTHERLESS Dogie. Also used for orphan

CALM A hot bed of tranquility ❏ as the bottom of a dry well ❏ as a root cellar

CALM AS A pup sleeping in the spring sunshine ❏ as a horse trough in a drought ❏ as a post hole ❏ as a dry river bed in a drought

CALM DOWN Don't get your shorts in a knot ❏ don't bust your bloomers ❏ wash off the war paint ❏ reset your hat ❏ don't go off half cocked ❏ hold your horses ❏ ease up on the reins ❏ simmer down ❏ put the safety on ❏ choke your motor ❏ pull in your horns ❏ tap off your temper ❏ holster your gun ❏ set your hammer ❏ cool your heels

CAN'T BE DONE You can't unring a bell ❏ You can't take it back once you spit it out, which refers to not being able to take back something you said.

CAPABLE Could track a bumblebee blindfolded in a blizzard ❏ could milk a rattlesnake into a Dr Pepper bottle ❏ a good judge of horse flesh ❏ got a lot of arrows in his quiver ❏ up to snuff ❏ got plenty of notches on his gun *See also Competent*

CAPITOL Ranch building *See also XIT*

CARDBOARD Pasteboard

CARDS Devil's calling cards See also individual cards such as Ace, Two, Three, etc.

CARE FOR Take him under your wing

CAREFREE Footloose and fancy free ❏ don't give a hoot or a holler ❏ maintains a spit and whittle attitude, which refers to those who have nothing to do in life but spit tobacco juice and whittle on limbs. Generally, members of the spit and whittle club are found on park and courthouse benches.

CAREFUL He never lets his alligator mouth overload his mockingbird behind ❏ watches his step when the (cow) chips are down ❏ he never rides more than one horse at a time ❏ plays his cards close to the vest ❏ he

31

don't get his wing feathers wet, which, for birds, would mean they could not fly until the feathers dried, making them vulnerable to predators *See also Advice, Be Careful, Caution*

CAREFUL AS A toupee wearer in a windstorm ❑ as a welder in a gasoline refinery ❑ as a frog in a thumbtack factory

CARELESS Shoots from the hip, which means he doesn't take time to aim ❑ shoots first and asks questions later if he has the time

CARRY Pissant it. This is a reference to having to carry something heavy using brute force and small, pissant sized steps, as in "We had to pissant the piano down the hall to the bedroom" ❑ tote, as in "You tote the watermelon."

CARRY THROUGH Stay on till you hear the buzzer, which refers to rodeo riders who must stay on the bull or bucking bronc till they hear the buzzer signifying they have ridden for eight seconds. It is the longest eight seconds in history and a lot of cowboys don't carry through ❑ you don't get lard lessen (unless) you boil the hog ❑ the hooked fish ain't

caught till he's on the stringer ❑ follow the trail to the end

CASH ON DELIVERY Cash on the barrel head

CASTRATE Steeralize ❑ trim up the calves (or pigs)

CAT Mobile mouse trap ❑ mouse wrangler ❑ cheese wrangler ❑ just a ball of fur with fangs and claws

CATALOG Sheep herder's bible ❑ wish book ❑ outhouse bible

CATCH Hem 'em up ❑ set the hook ❑ throw a loop on 'em ❑ drop a loop on 'em ❑ corral 'em

CATFISH Tourist trout

CATTLE Mortgage on the hoof, which refers to the fact that many a rancher depends on cattle profits to pay the mortgage on the ranch.

CATTLE, POOR Would take half a dozen head to make one shadow ❑ nothing between the horns and the hooves but hide ❑ not much more than a backbone on four legs ❑ Ace Reid specials. Ace was an old Texas brush popper who was a pretty fair hand at drawing and most of his cartoon cows were poor and scrawny-looking critters.

CATTLE PROD Stingin' stick ❑ hot shot

CATTLE, WITHOUT HORNS Muley cows

CAUGHT Lassoed ❑ corralled ❑ fenced ❑ run to earth ❑ like a chicken snake in a picket fence, which refers to a chicken snake slithering through a picket fence to eat some eggs, then discovering he can't crawl back through until the eggs are digested. In other words, he is caught.

CAUSE That was the anvil our trouble was forged on.

CAUSED TROUBLE Stirred up a hornet's nest or a den of snakes ❑ woke up a bear, which refers to waking up a hibernating bear ❑ tipped over the outhouse

CAUTION Protect your nest ❑ keep the food in the wagon 'cause the dogs are loose ❑ be sure you're right, then go ahead, which was a favorite saying of Davy Crockett ❑ shoot low, they might be riding Shetlands ❑ keep an Indian ear to the ground or listen to the ground, which are references to Indians putting their

ear to the ground to determine if buffalo herds where near. In *The Raven,* Marquis James claimed Sam Houston knew the Alamo had fallen because he put his ear to the ground and did not hear the rumble of distant cannon fire. *See also Advice, Be Careful*

CAUTIOUS As a small dog with a big bone ❑ as a bobcat on a barbed wire fence

CELEBRATE Put the big pot in the little pot and fry the skillet ❑ shoot out the lights, which refers to the habit of cowpokes shooting out saloon and town lights when they were on the prod (celebrating) ❑ let's rodeo, which is an advertising line of Nocona Boot Company ❑ raise a little cane and pray for a crop failure ❑ kick up your heels ❑ honky tonk till you drop ❑ paint the whole town and the front porch ❑ shoot the anvil, which refers to the old habit of packing the blacksmith's anvil with powder and setting it off in celebration. This was usually done in towns too small to have a cannon.

CELEBRATE A LITTLE Hold the gunfire to a bare minimum.

CELEBRATED Hallelujahed all over the saloon, town, south forty or entire prairie.

CEMETERY Bone orchard ❑ stone city ❑ stone orchard ❑ grave pasture ❑ buryin' pasture

CENTER Smack dab (or square dab) in the middle

CERTAIN Lead pipe cinch ❑ sure as shootin' ❑ guaranteed natural fact ❑ If I'm not right I'll eat my hat, band, feathers, and all ❑ The only things that are certain are death, taxes, and Texas ❑ a lock nut gut cinch ❑ In Texas, as elsewhere, it is often said the only thing that is certain is that nothing is certain. That saying was used considerably when the price of oil and Texas real estate began falling like an ice cream cone dropped from the top of a Ferris Wheel. *See also Fact, Guaranteed, Positive, Reliable, That's A Fact*

CHALLENGE If you want it, come and take it. In 1835 when the Mexican army demanded the citizens of Gonzales return a small cannon, the demand was answered with "Come and take it." The Mexicans withdrew.

CHALLENGING As tryin' to mate a bobcat and a bob white quail (or a mockingbird and a buzzard) ❑ as trying to cross a wet prairie in a wide-wheeled buggy

CHAMPAGNE Bubble water ❑ whoopee water ❑ giggle water ❑ French firewater

CHANCE, SLIM As much as a grasshopper on a red ant hill ❑ as much as a steer in a packin' plant ❑ there are two chances, slim and none and slim is saddling up to leave town ❑ there are two chances, slim and fat

CHANGE (COINS) Egg money ❑ scalp money

CHANGEABLE It's chicken one day and feathers the next ❑ a drought usually ends with a flood

CHARGE Go a hornin' ❑ Remember the Alamo, which was the battle cry at the battle of San Jacinto.

CHARMING He could charm a bird out of a tree ❑ he could charm the gloss out of a photograph

CHASED Went after him with intent to BBQ

CHEAP COST As suntan oil in a snowstorm ❑ as a two-week-old newspaper ❑ as used chewing tobacco ❑ as used bubble gum ❑ as used toilet paper ❑ Dirt cheap, which refers to the days when Texas land sold for as little as fifty cents an acre.

CHEAPSKATE Wouldn't pay a nickel to see a pissant eat a bale of hay ❑ wouldn't pay a nickel to see a monkey make love to a football ❑ wouldn't a paid a dollar for a box seat at the battle of San Jacinto *See also, Frugal, Miser, Stingy*

CHEATED Been screwed, blued, and tattooed ❑ got the short end of the stick ❑ hornswoggled ❑ paid for an Indian and got a goat herder, which refers to the days when bounties were paid for dead Indians and some poor goat herders were passed off as Indians. In the 1920s the Texas Bankers Association offered a reward of $5,000 for DEAD bank robbers. Famous Texas Ranger Frank Hamer was convinced petty thieves were being set up and shot as bank robbers for the reward money. He claimed the bankers were, "paying for Apaches and getting sheep herders."

CHEATER He's on a first name basis with the bottom of the deck ❑ he always seems to know both sides of the cards ❑ when you play with him you have to play fair 'cause he knows what cards he dealt you ❑ he made his living selling swampland in Lubbock. Located on the south plains, Lubbock is so dry that even pictures of swamps shown on television tend to dry up quickly.

CHEST Brisket ❑ barrel

CHICKEN Cluckker ❑ settin' hen ❑ rooster bait ❑ Sunday dinner on the hoof, which refers to rural families splurging and having fried chicken after church on Sunday.

CHIGGERS Red bugs. Pound for pound, the Texas chigger is the meanest critter on the face of the earth.

CHILD Tricycle motor ❑ patch-seated kid ❑ little britches ❑ button cowboy ❑ towhead ❑ papoose ❑ little shaver ❑ pullet ❑ yard (or house) ape, rug rat ❑ curtain climber ❑ whipper snapper ❑ fryin' size ❑ short-tailed rooster

CHILD, INJURED It'll heal before you get married

CHILD, MEAN He's the only hell his folks ever raised ❑ he's the worst crop his daddy ever raised ❑ if he'd been twins, his folks would a killed themselves ❑ he was harder to raise than corn in a concrete field ❑ hate to have a litter of those

CHILD, UNDERAGE Still in warranty, which means parents are responsible for fixing anything they break. According to law, the warranty expires when the little darlings reach 18 years of age.

CHILDREN, SPOILED She raised three "only" children. Any number of children can be substituted.

CHILDREN, TWINS A matched pair of dueling pistols.

CHILI Bowl a red ❑ Texas red ❑ national dish of Texas. Contrary to popular belief, not all Texans enjoy chili. In the April, 1983 issue of *Esquire* magazine, Paul Burka quoted the following chili recipe from former Texas governor Allan Shivers: Put a pot of chili on the stove to simmer. Let it

simmer. Meanwhile, broil a good steak. Eat the steak. Let the chili simmer. Ignore it.

CHILI, HOT Sinus medicine, which refers to really hot chili having the ability to open clogged sinuses and make your nose run ❑ armor piercing ❑ could eat through a crowbar ❑ two- (or three- or four-) alarm warm ❑ would cauterize your hemorrhoids, which implies chili is just as hot coming out as it is going in ❑ had to keep it on a pile of cracked ice to keep the cast iron pot from melting ❑ will melt the fillings out of your eye teeth ❑ would melt the enamel off your molars ❑ The hottest chili could be freeze dried and used for gunpowder.

CHILI, MILD False-alarm chili

CHILI, WITH BEANS Chili with shrapnel ❑ Texas red with Mexican strawberries ❑ rocks in the red sea

CHOICE Druthers

CHORE, BIG Got a lot of cotton patch to hoe ❑ got a lot of calves to fix ❑ a lot of corn to shuck ❑ a big barn to raise ❑ a big hole in the fence

CHURCH GOER Steeple people ❏ bible thumpers

CHURCH GOER, INFREQUENT A two-fer, which implies he only goes to church twice a year, on Christmas and Easter. If married, he is generally a three-fer since he can't get out of going on Mother's Day also.

CHURCH MEETING Prayer meeting ❏ Sunday go to meetin'

CIGAR Sea-gar

CIGARETTE Cancer stick ❏ coffin nail

CITY BOY Raised on concrete

CIVIL WAR The fight. Northerners called it a war, Southerners called it a fight.

CLARIFY Cut the deck a little deeper ❏ put another log on the fire ❏ shuffle and re-deal ❏ throw a new loop ❏ run that flag a little higher up the pole ❏ stir that chili a little more ❏ chew it a little finer ❏ chew the bark off and get down to the wood

CLATTERING Like two skeletons making love on a sheet of galvanized iron ❏

like a skeleton dancing in a washtub *See also Noisy*

CLAWS Dinner hooks

CLEAN As a hounds tooth ❏ as a fresh boiled white shirt ❏ as a whistle ❏ his mother wouldn't know him by sight or smell ❏ as a new mirror

CLEAN SHAVEN Bald faced

CLEAR As mother's milk ❏ as glass ❏ as a bell

CLING Like East Texas black mud to a rusty shovel ❏ like a tick to a dogs (or mules) ear ❏ like manure to a boot *See also Hang On*

CLOSE Within hollerin' distance ❏ a holler and a half away ❏ just two whoops and a holler away ❏ just down the road apiece ❏ I could chunk a rock and hit it ❏ enough to share a snap (or button hole) ❏ enough to be Siamese twins ❏ within ear shot ❏ enough to raise a blister

CLOSE CALL Didn't lose nothing but some confidence ❏ Close only counts in horseshoes and hand grenades.

CLOSE FINISH Finished in the money but it wasn't top money ❏ we had to develop the picture to see who won ❏ He made the picture but he wasn't the star, implying he was in the photo finish but he didn't win.

CLOSE TO THE GROUND Could trip an ant (or caterpillar)

CLOSED Nailed shut ❏ like a covered coffin ❏ like a bank vault on the fourth of July ❏ as a judge's mind

CLOSED MIND Gathers no new ideas

CLOTHES Duds ❏ riggin'

CLOTHES, FANCY Sunday go-to-meeting outfit ❏ looks like a page out of a mail order catalog ❏ looks like the joker out of a deck of cards

CLOTHES, WORN Brush frazzled

CLOUDY Muddy skies

CLUB Big stick, hoe handle, or ax handle ❏ a Walker Colt, which refers to Texas Ranger Samuel Walker suggesting Samuel Colt made his hand guns heavier so they could be used as a club in an emergency. The improved and heavier models were referred to as Walker Colts.

CLUBS (PLAYING CARD SUIT) Dog foot ❏ dog track

CLUMSY Tangle-footed ❏ shot himself in the foot ❏ got two left feet ❏ an accident looking for a place to happen *See also Accident Prone*

CLUMSY AS A longhorn bull in a Neiman-Marcus china shop

COFFEE Belly wash ❏ up and at 'em juice ❏ muddy water

COFFEE, COOL Saucered and blowed, which refers to the cafe practice of pouring coffee into the saucer, blowing on it till cool and then drinking it straight out of the saucer.

COFFEE, STRONG It'll grow hair on your saddle (or chest) ❏ strong enough to float a horseshoe, anvil, windmill wrench, or Colt pistol. Very strong coffee doesn't have to be poured, it'll walk into the cup.

COFFEE, WITH CREAM With the socks on ❏ white-washed

COFFIN Dust bin ❏ dirt box ❏ pine overcoat ❏ eternity box, buryin' crate ❏ forever bed ❏ planter box

COLD AS An ex-wife's heart ❑ as a witch's teat in a brass bra in an Amarillo snow storm ❑ as a cast iron (or brass) commode in the shade of a glacier ❑ as a well digger's shovel in Dalhart ❑ as a witch's caress ❑ as a banker's heart ❑ as a mother-in-law's kiss ❑ as a frozen bullet ❑ as an outhouse seat in January ❑ as a dead snake in a deep freeze ❑ as a bartender's heart ❑ as hell with the furnace off ❑ as a pawn broker's smile ❑ as a week-old enchilada

COLD BLOODED As a frozen snake ❑ as a grand jury foreman ❑ as an ex-wife's lawyer ❑ one drop of his blood would freeze a cat. Almost any small animal can be substituted for cat. Sam Houston once said of Jefferson Davis, the president of the Confederacy, "He's as cold as Lucifer and one drop of his blood would freeze a frog."

COLD ENOUGH TO Freeze all the water outside the tea kettle ❑ make a 32nd degree Mason drop a degree ❑ to freeze the tail off a brass monkey ❑ freeze the stink out of manure ❑ freeze the horns off a billy goat (or longhorn steer) ❑ freeze ducks to a pond ❑ to make the eagle on a silver dollar shiver ❑ to make cows give ice cream ❑ to freeze boiling water so fast the ice will still be warm

COLLEGE Where your kids and your money are easily separated

COME BACK Ya'll come back now, ya hear.

COMEDIAN He does a 10-minute routine every time the refrigerator light comes on, which is derived from a quote by Texan Debbie Reynolds.

COMFORTABLE As an old boot ❑ snug as a bug in a deep-pile rug

COMMENCING The pot's beginning to simmer ❑ the chili's beginning to boil

COMMON As corn bread ❑ as dirt ❑ as rocks ❑ as cow (or pig) tracks ❑ run of the orchard ❑ everyday wash

COMMON-LAW MARRIAGE Hitched but not churched ❑ united with a cotton patch (or saw mill) license

COMMON SENSE Horse sense

COMMOTION Like a lizard in a pile of dry leaves ❑ like

there's a chicken snake in the coup

COMPATIBLE Goes together like red beans and ham hock ❑ like chili and beer ❑ like bourbon and Coca Cola ❑ like chili and pepper ❑ like biscuits and gravy ❑ like a gun and a holster ❑ like a kid and a candy store

COMPETENT Top hand ❑ could hunt a whisper in a whirlwind ❑ right smart of a windmill fixer ❑ could string ten miles of barbed wire blindfolded in a blizzard ❑ could track a hornet in a hurricane *See also Capable*

COMPLAIN Bellyache ❑ a hit dog hollers ❑ a squeaking wheel gets the grease ❑ a squeaking windmill (or gate hinge) gets the oil ❑ a banging gate gets the new latch

COMPLETE Lock, stock and barrel ❑ the whole shootin' match ❑ it takes eight bits to make a dollar ❑ hook, line, sinker, and bobber

COMPLICATION That muddied up the water ❑ that turned over the creek ❑ gummed up the windmill works ❑ there is more to this than meets the eye

COMPLIMENT *See Good Person*

COMPOSURE Whatever you do, never let 'em see you sweat.

COMPOSURE, LOST He come apart at the seams ❑ hot words lead to cold slabs

COMPUTER Brains in a box ❑ electric thinker

CON MAN Snake oil salesman ❑ lightning rod salesman ❑ condo time-share salesman ❑ he could talk you out of the shirt on your back and then convince you to buy it back

CONCEITED He thinks the sun comes up just to hear him crow ❑ he thinks the manure from his cows don't stink ❑ he hangs a mirror on the bathroom ceiling so he can watch himself gargle

CONCENTRATE Keep the cobwebs out of your head ❑ defog your brain ❑ unclutter your mind. In 1974, Dallas Cowboy rookie Clint Longley, from Abilene, Texas filled in for an injured Roger Staubach and led the team to one of the most memorable comebacks of all time against arch rival Washington. Fellow Cowboy

Blaine Nye said, "It was a triumph of an uncluttered mind."

CONCLUDED Put two and two together

CONCRETE To a Texan it's sea-mint

CONFERENCE Prayer meeting ❑ pow-wow ❑ making medicine ❑ treaty talks

CONFESS Let the cat out of the bag ❑ spill the beans (or your guts)

CONFIDENT He thinks he's bullet proof ❑ cock sure ❑ he'd take on Pecos Bill with one arm tied behind his back. Pecos Bill is the Texas equivalent to Paul Bunyon.

CONFIDENTIAL Keep it close to the vest ❑ keep it under your hat ❑ keep it between me and you and the gatepost (or snubbin' post)

CONFIRMED According to all accounts ❑ got it from the horse's (or mare's) mouth

CONFORM Walk the line ❑ toe the mark

CONFRONTATION A set to ❑ a prayer meeting without the preacher or the choir ❑ a

shootout. In 1969, when No. 1 Texas played No. 2 Arkansas for the National Championship of collegiate football, Longhorn coach Darrell Royal referred to the game as a shootout. Since then every major sports confrontation has been a shootout.

CONFUSED Buffaloed ❑ don't know if he's gettin' up or goin' to bed ❑ can't find the right wagon to load ❑ barking up the wrong tree ❑ driving the wrong herd to market ❑ getting your horse before your cart ❑ don't know if he's commode-hugging drunk or taking communion at church ❑ his mind is in a fog ❑ got his fingers in Chinese handcuffs. Chinese handcuffs are those little straw tubes designed to make it difficult to get out a finger once you stick it in. The confusing part is how a finger that went in so easy could be so hard to get out.

CONFUSED AS A woodpecker in a petrified forest ❑ as a goat on astroturf ❑ as a frog in a blender ❑ as a little kid who dropped his chewing gum in the chicken yard

CONFUSING Greek (or algebra) to me ❑ a rocket scientist couldn't figure it out ❑ it's a real mare's nest ❑ as

41

the flex defense to an NFL rookie. A flex defense, used for years by the Dallas Cowboys, requires that a player protect an area rather than going for the ball, which is what comes naturally. The defense is confusing to rookies and many veterans, because no college uses it, thus no player comes into the NFL prepared to run the flex.

CONSECUTIVELY Hand runnin', as in "He's been sick for four days hand runnin'."

CONSERVATIVE Never bites off more than he can chew ❏ never puts more on his plate than he can say grace over

CONSISTENT He never changes horses in the middle of a stream.

CONSPICUOUS As a pink saddle ❏ as fender skirts on a fire truck ❏ sticks out like a thumb mashed by a ball peen hammer, which is a Texas version of sticks out "like a sore thumb."

CONSPIRACY The big dogs are ganging up on the little dogs.

CONSTIPATED My plumbing's backed up ❏ got a peach pit in my plumbing

CONSTRUCTION, POOR *See Assembled, Poorly*

CONTENTED As a barbershop cat ❏ as a boardinghouse pup ❏ as a buffalo in a dirt wallow ❏ as a turtle on a log ❏ as a hog in mud

CONTEST A real rodeo ❏ a cuss off. In the old West, cowboys actually got together, on occasion, to hold cuss offs to determine who could sulphurize the air (cuss) the best. Although the winner wasn't held in as high esteem as, say, the best all around cowboy, he was still admired by his peers.

CONTINUE Meanwhile, back at the ranch

CONTINUED Went right ahead ❏ kept right on plowing

CONTROL Keep a tight hold on the whoa reins ❏ shorten the stake rope ❏ ride a close herd on ❏ keep the fences up 'cause a loose mare is always looking for a greener pasture ❏ hold down the fort ❏ take the slack out of the rope

CONTROL YOURSELF Keep the lid on your can ❏ keep

your buttons snapped ❏ hobble your emotions ❏ stake rope (or ground hitch) yourself

CONVENIENT *See Handy*

CONVERSATION Chin music ❏ squaw talk ❏ lip exercising *See also Talk*

CONVICTION Sticks to his guns ❏ tends to her knitting ❏ keeps his fields plowed

CONVINCE Bring 'em to your lick log, which infers to convince others your opinion is best.

CONVINCED Got him on my stringer ❏ got him on my hook ❏ got him singing off my song sheet

CONVINCING As a spade flush ❏ as the business end of a 45 ❏ could make a well believe it's a windmill ❏ could make a cow give up her calf without a beller

COOK Steak charmer ❏ bean masher ❏ belly cheater ❏ biscuit roller ❏ biscuit shooter ❏ pot wrangler ❏ oven boss ❏ One of the mysteries of life is which is worse a wife who can cook but won't or a wife who can't cook but does.

COOK, POOR If she'd been cooking for the North, the South would have won the war ❏ it takes her an hour and a half to cook minute rice ❏ never throw one of her biscuits at a cat unless you want a dead cat ❏ she can scorch water trying to boil it ❏ you could use one of her pancakes to patch an inner tube ❏ her chili tastes like is was cooked in an old boot

COOKING Kissing don't last, cooking does.

COOPERATE I'll sit still for that ❏ I'll help corral that horse ❏ I'll help plant that crop ❏ I'll help raise that barn

COORDINATION, POOR He has to pull over to the side of the road and come to a complete stop before he can blow the horn (or turn on the windshield wipers)

COPULATION Naval engagement

CORE The nubbin' ❏ the heart

CORPUS CHRISTI The name of this Texas Gulf coast town, which is Spanish for "body of Christ," is often shortened to simply Corpus.

43

CORRECT You hit the nail right on the head ❏ you hit the bull in the eye or you hit the bull's eye ❏ you got your saddle on the right horse ❏ you got your boots on the right feet

CORRECTIVE ACTION Get the train back on the track ❏ get the horses hitched to the right wagon ❏ pick up all the pieces of the puzzle ❏ buy a new deck of cards ❏ get the wagon (or ox) out of the ditch

COUNTERFEIT, POOR QUALITY Couldn't fool a blind man

COUNTRY BOY Redneck ❏ good ol' boy ❏ goat roper ❏ foaled in the country

COUNTRY GIRL Redneck girl ❏ good ol' girl

COUNTY PEOPLE Ranch-raised folks ❏ raised on dirt ❏ range folks

COURAGEOUS He works the high wire without a net ❏ he's got Brazos River water in his veins ❏ knows how to die standing up ❏ got more guts than you could hang on a fence ❏ got enough guts to fill a number three washtub ❏ got a double backbone ❏ he would fight a rattlesnake with one hand tied behind his back and give the snake three bites head start ❏ would go down the cliffs of hell without a safety rope ❏ his bullet don't have any more places left to bite ❏ Audie Murphy once said, "I don't know what bravery is. Sometimes it takes more courage to get up and run than to stay. You either just do it or you don't." *See also Brave, Fearless*

COVER IT Like green on grass ❏ like white on rice ❏ like stink on manure ❏ like fur on a cat ❏ Mother Hubbard it. A Mother Hubbard dress is one that covers everything but touches very little, generally worn by your less than dainty ladies.

COVERED Like a low water crossing in a flash flood ❏ like a dew on a lawn ❏ like it was under grandma's quilt ❏ like an anvil at the bottom of a stock tank, which would be covered with water ❏ like a hardwood floor under wall to wall carpet

COW DROPPINGS Cow chips ❏ meadow muffins ❏ prairie coal. The reference to coal is derived from the fact that when wood was scarce, as it often was on the plains, dried cow chips were used for cook fires on trail drives.

COWARD He's got hen house ways or his breath smells like hen feathers, both of which mean he's "chicken" ❑ if he was melted down, he couldn't be poured into a fight ❑ fraidy cat ❑ afraid of his own shadow or afraid of a worm's shadow ❑ paper backed ❑ yellow as mustard but without the bite ❑ He always wears white underwear 'cause he never knows when he might need a white flag. *See also Afraid, Scared*

COWARD, EXTREME In Texas, the supreme definition of coward is 1st cousin to Moses Rose. In 1836, as legend has it, William Barret Travis became convinced the Alamo would fall. He gave an impassioned speech to the men, then drew a line with his sabre and invited all who wanted to stand and fight to cross the line. All but Moses Rose crossed the line and died for Texas independence. *See also Afraid, Scared*

COWBOY Stands on his own two feet by sitting on a horse ❑ saddle warmer ❑ leather pounder ❑ bronc buster ❑ goat roper ❑ buckeroo ❑ kicker ❑ wrangler ❑ cow puncher ❑ cow chaser ❑ chuck wagon tailer ❑ brush popper ❑ wad- die ❑ a lover, a fighter, and a wild bull rider

COWBOY, FEMALE Wranglerette ❑ buckerooette ❑ kickerette ❑ a lover, a fighter, a wild barrel rider

COWBOY, GOOD Can ride anything with hair on it ❑ top hand ❑ he's an expert at the 3 rs. To a cowboy, the 3 rs are riding, roping, rangling ❑ a three-jump cowboy, which is one good enough to stay on a pitching horse for three jumps. ❑ he'd do to ride the rough string. Every ranch outfit had a string of rough horses that were barely broken, much less suited for everyday riding. The best cowboys had the job of getting the kinks out of horses in the rough string. *See also Good Person*

COWBOY, POOR A corral cowboy, which means he spends more time around the corral talkin' cows than he does cowboyin' ❑ couldn't ride a tame stick horse ❑ couldn't ride a charley horse ❑ couldn't ride a nightmare without getting thrown out of bed ❑ would get throwed by a good rocking chair (or wheel chair) *See also Tenderfoot*

CRAVE Got a hankerin' for ❑ got a hurtin' for

CRAZY A few bricks shy of a load ❑ he ain't playing with a full deck ❑ his guitar ain't tuned right ❑ his porch light's on but nobody is home ❑ been eatin' loco weed with his Wheaties ❑ got a screw loose in his thinker assembly ❑ the vertical hold is out on his television set ❑ his cinch is loose ❑ he's half a bubble out of plumb ❑ if he put his brain in a mockingbird it would fly backwards *See also Insane, Nutty*

CRAZY AS A bed bug ❑ as a loco'd calf ❑ as a lizard with a sunstroke

CRAZY LOOK Loco was camped out in his eyeballs ❑ his eyeballs are fogged over like a windshield

CREDIT Living on his jawbone ❑ tick, such as "He bought it on tick."

CREDIT, BAD The cork's been hammered into my bottle. This is a reference to the old bartenders who would set the bottle on the bar and let you drink until your credit ran out in which case he'd hammer the cork into the bottle with the ball of his hand. You didn't get any more to drink till the tab was paid.

CREEK BED, DRY Arroyo

CRIME, SMALL Chicken larceny

CRIMINAL High line rider ❑ rides a crooked trail ❑ desperado ❑ low lifer ❑ drygulcher ❑ backshooter *See also Crook*

CRIMINAL, SMALL TIME Chicken rustler ❑ Saturday night sinner, which means he leads a good life till he goes out on Saturday night and gets drunk ❑ if there was a bounty on his head, it wouldn't pay for a bullet to shoot him

CRITICIZE Badmouth ❑ sulphurize his reputation

CROOK His family tree has a lot of horse thieves hanging in it ❑ got more ways to take your money than a room full of lawyers

CROOKED If he swallowed a ten-penny nail, he spit up a corkscrew ❑ he'll have to be screwed into a coffin when he passes on ❑ he's so crooked he has to screw on his socks ❑ he's so crooked you can't tell from his tracks if he's a coming or a going ❑ a snake would break his back tryin' to follow his trail

CROOKED AS A barrel of snakes ❏ as a barrel of fish hooks ❏ as a dog's hind leg ❏ as the devil's backbone

CROSS CUT SAW Misery whip, which refers to the whip action that occurs when a cross cut saw becomes jammed and springs back into place, causing misery to the person working the saw. Anyone who spent any time in an East Texas saw mill learned first hand about a misery whip.

CROSS-EYED He can stand up in the middle of the week and see two Sundays.

CROWDED You can't swing a dead cat without hitting someone ❏ as a Baptist revival ❏ the barn's full and the corral is fillin' up fast ❏ packed to the rafters ❏ thick as yellow jackets on a spring nest ❏ there's an hour wait for the bathroom ❏ the dance floor is full ❏ somebody left the gate open, which implies that the pasture is full of cows because someone left the gate to the pen open.

CRUDE Rough hewn

CRUEL He'd tie two cats together by their tails and hang 'em on a clothesline ❏ he'd steal a kid's candy and eat it

in front of him ❏ he d steal pencils from a blind beggar

CRY Bawl ❏ squall ❏ catterwall

CUERO, TEXAS Pronounced kwa' ro, this Dewitt County town is the turkey capital of Texas.

CUNNING As a repossessing wrecker driver

CUSS WORDS, CLEAN Heck fire ❏ shoot fire ❏ goldarn ❏ consarned ❏ dad blast it ❏ bull pucky ❏ hell's bells ❏ son of a buck ❏ dad blamed ❏ fiddlesticks ❏ consarn

CUSSED A LOT Ran out a string of profanity so hot it would a fried bacon ❏ cussed enough to singe all the grass within ten yards ❏ cussed enough to melt the ears off a Baptist preacher ❏ made the air sulphurous with profanity ❏ fluent in the bull whacker's language ❏ could outcuss a veteran mule skinner on his best day. Bull whackers, men who drove oxen teams in the early days of freighting, and mule skinners were known to be among the most proficient cussers in the world, next to sailors, of course.

CUSSER Naughty tongued ❑ tough mouthed ❑ flannel tongued ❑ keeps a Civil War tongue in his mouth, which refers to the fact that many of the soldiers in that fight were notorious cussers. For confederate soldiers, if they didn't cuss before they joined up, they sure did by the time the fight was over.

CUSSING Airing out his lungs ❑ taking the strain off his liver

CUT IT SHORT Scissor it off some ❑ trim the fat and get to the meat ❑ bob tail it ❑ take a short cut to the main point

CUT OFF Geld it

CUT UP Required more stitches than a patchwork quilt ❑ got himself fricasseed ❑ got himself skewered

CUTE Darlin'

CUTE AS A bugs ear ❑ as a white-faced calf ❑ as a speckled pup ❑ a paint horse ❑ as a newborn colt (or puppy)

CUTTING HORSE, GOOD Could cut the bakin' powder out of a biscuit without breaking the crust ❑ could cut fly specks out of a pepper shaker ❑ could cut a prairie dog out of

his hole ❑ could cut the eye teeth out of a rattlesnake

D

A GOOD DOG — is hard to keep under the porch

DAINTY As a June bride ❑ as a blown glass bell

DALLAS Big D ❑ Manhattan of the West. It's been said that Dallas is where the East peters out, which means Fort Worth is where the West begins. No one is dead solid positive about who Dallas was named for but the word is Scottish for place on the plains.

DANCE (NOUN) Wing ding ❑ shindig ❑ hoe down ❑ hoe dig ❑ daince

DANCE (VERB) Hugging to music ❑ boot scooting ❑ shake a hoof ❑ rubbin' bellies ❑ scratching belt buckles

DANCE A LOT Smoke your boots

DANCE CLOSE Hog rasslin'

DANCE FAST Movin' to a frisky fiddle ❑ smoke your boots

DANCER Hoofer ❑ two stepper ❑ boot scooter ❑ buckle polisher

DANCING Like a bobber on a line

DANGER SIGN The horse is running with an empty saddle, which in the old West usually meant the rider had either been thrown or shot off ❑ the flag is flying upside down. A Texas flag flown upside down is supposed to be a danger or help-needed signal but most people don't realize that. Usually when the Texas flag is flying white stripe down, it means some Yankee didn't know how to fly it.

DANGEROUS As opening the latch on a wire gate. In less modern times, gates in Texas were constructed by attaching barbed wire to a stick or pole. The gate would be closed by stretching the wire taut and latching the pole in loops of wire on a fence post. If you let the pole slip when opening the gate, it would whip back and strike you, usually in the chest or belly. Although no one ever got killed opening a gate, it was still a dangerous proposition. In his book *Western Words,* Ramon F. Adams says that Texans referred to the pole on the gate as a "belly buster." ❑ dangerous as lightning striking your zipper ❑ wetting on a 'lectric fence. Any male who has ever made that mistake knows just how dangerous and painful it can be. *See also Hazardous*

51

DANGEROUS PERSON A skunk (or scorpion) with his tail up ❏ a hornet (or yellow jacket) with his tail down ❏ he's bad medicine ❏ he's due a wide berth ❏ he'll whip or tree anyone who gets in his way ❏ a very good person not to mess with

DANGEROUS SITUATION You're smoking in a fireworks factory ❏ you're using rocket fuel in your coal oil lamp ❏ you're pouring gasoline on a fire ❏ a bad time to have your gun jam ❏ you're running out of room on the dance floor ❏ the cattle are getting mighty thirsty, which is a reference to cattle being hard to control when they are thirsty ❏ you're driving on black ice. Black ice is a layer of ice on a busy highway that is thin, almost invisible, and extremely dangerous to drive on, especially if it happens to be on North Central Expressway in Dallas.

DARING He'd play basketball in a mine field ❏ he'd shoot craps with the devil himself ❏ ain't afraid of hell, high water, or a pretty girl ❏ he'd arm wrestle King Kong ❏ he's a fugitive from the law of averages, which is how Audie Murphy, one of the most daring Texans of all time,

once described himself when signing an autograph for an admirer.

DARK AS A pile of black cats on a moonless night ❏ as the bottom of a well ❏ as a lighthouse with the bulb burned out ❏ as night under a wash pot (or skillet) *See also Black*

DARK, NIGHT So dark, if you lit a match you'd have to light a second one to see if the first one was burning ❏ so dark the bats are flying on auto pilot ❏ you couldn't see your hand in front of your face ❏ you couldn't find your nose with both hands

DARLING Darlin'

DAWN Rooster time ❏ crack of day ❏ break of day ❏ newborn day ❏ first light

DAWN, CLOUDY The new day was stillborn

DAY SHIFT Day herding

DEAD Shook hands with eternity ❏ morgue-aged ❏ on a stoney lonesome ❏ just coyote bait ❏ pushing up bluebonnets ❏ don't have the pulse of a pitchfork ❏ ready for a cold slab ❏ answered the last roll call ❏ turned up his toes or turned belly up, which refers to the fact that many animals turn up their belly when dead. *See also Died, Died Suddenly*

DEAD AS Hell in a preacher's back yard (or a parson's parlor) ❑ as a 6-card poker hand ❑ as Santa Anna ❑ as a lightning bug in the cream pitcher ❑ as a drowned cat in a goldfish bowl ❑ as a rotten stump ❑ as a doornail or door knob *See also Died, Died Suddenly*

DEAF As a cow skull ❑ as a snubbin' post. On a ranch, wild horses were tied to a snubbin' post so they could be saddled. The reference to deaf is just that a wooden post can't hear anything.

DECEIVED Pulled the wool over their eyes ❑ hoodwinked

DEDICATED Goes the whole hog ❑ he'll stay with you till the last drop of sweat, as long as it's your sweat ❑ married to, as in "He's married to his job."

DEDICATED AS A preacher tracking sin ❑ an Aggie football fan

DEEP Goes all the way to bedrock ❑ goes all the way to the bottom of the well ❑ goes so far down the other end of the hole could be a cup on a Chinese golf course ❑ In Terlingua, Texas, where the world championship chili cook-offs are held, the outside toilets were said to be so deep you could listen in on Chinese conversations while using the facilities.

DEEP WELL The water comes out boiling, which implies the well is deep enough for hell to heat the water ❑ you have to strain the rice before using the water, implying the well goes all the way to China.

DEFEATED Got saucered and blowed ❑ got blown plumb out of the tub ❑ got my tail feathers trimmed

DEFUNCT As aunt Bessie's corset ❑ as ethyl gasoline *See also Obsolete*

DELAY Put it on the back burner ❑ put it on the back shelf ❑ drag you feet a while

DELICATE SITUATION Got a fly in the ointment ❑ got a blonde hair in the butter

DELICIOUS Larrupin' good ❑ powerful good ❑ sets your lips to rejoicing ❑ better than mesquite grass to a longhorn steer ❑ better than cow's milk to a newborn calf ❑ best I ever wrapped a lip around

DELIRIOUS Got snakes in his boots ❑ got spiders in his shorts

DEMOTE Put him on the haying crew, fence crew, or thrashing crew, all of which are jobs a real cowpoke considers a demotion.

DENTIST Enamel driller ❑ tooth doctor ❑ tooth fairy ❑ jaw breaker ❑ jaw cracker. A dentist's office is a jaw cracker suite.

DEPARTED Left out for parts unknown ❑ left out in a hurry ❑ cut a hole in the atmosphere ❑ took off for some high riding ❑ high tailed it *See also Leave*

DEPARTING If you don't think I'm leaving, you just count the days I'm gone.

DEPENDABLE Solid as bedrock ❑ plows a straight row all the way to the end ❑ her gravy is always good

DEPRESSED My heart is as heavy as a bucket of hog livers, which refers to the fact that when hogs were killed, the livers were generally saved

in one bucket. If you had a lot of hogs to kill, the bucket got heavy to tote ❑ my heart is as heavy as a bushel basket full of ball bearings ❑ It's been said the most depressing thing that can happen to a woman is to run into a baldheaded man who was two or three years behind her in high school.

DERANGED *See Crazy, Insane*

DESIRABLE It's better than a fifty-yard-line ticket to the Cotton Bowl ❑ as a snowcone in hell ❑ I'd give one half the King Ranch for it. The King Ranch is one of the world's largest, occupying 850,000 acres in Texas alone, not to mention the foreign holdings.

DESIRE Want that so bad I could spit (or taste it) ❑ got a yearn for ❑ got a hankerin' for ❑ When asked why he purchased the town of Luckenback, Texas, Hondo Crouch replied, "I wanted it for the same reason a dog buries a bone, so no other dog'll get it."

DESOLATE Looks like hell with all the inmates out to lunch ❑ where rattlesnakes wouldn't pitch their tent

DESPERATE Playing dead to call buzzards ❏ grabbing at strings (or straws) ❏ I need that more than a dry land farmer needs rain, which is something a farmer always needs ❏ grabbing at sunbeams

DESTINATION Jumping off place ❏ gettin' off place ❏ halting place

DESTITUTE The bank won't let me draw breath ❏ ain't got a tailfeather left ❏ scraping the bottom of my last barrel ❏ my boot soles are so thin, if I scratched a match on 'em I'd set my socks on fire ❏ if eagles were a dollar a pound, I couldn't afford a hummingbird drumstick ❏ I grew up so hard we had to take turns eating, and my turns came on Monday, Wednesday, and Friday ❏ if money was leather, I couldn't half sole a katydid *See also Broke, Poor*

DETERIORATED Gone to the dogs, to hell, to pot, or to seed

DETERMINATION Come hell or high water ❏ the good Lord willing and the creeks don't rise, which means you will do something if He is willing and the water in the creek don't rise so high you

can't cross it. A feminine variation is the good Lord willing and the wash don't fall off the line, which means she can do it if her wash don't fall off the line so she wouldn't have clean clothes to wear. We all know that women, unlike cowboys, don't go anywhere unless their clothes are clean.

DETERMINED Shore 'nuff means business ❏ hell bent for leather ❏ he'll do it if it means hairlipping the governor and every mule in Texas

DEVELOPING Something's brewing, cooking, or stewing ❏ it's taking shape like a growing girl ❏ the coffee is getting ready to boil

DEVICE Contraption ❏ thingamajig ❏ dofunny

DEVIL Boogerman ❏ old heck ❏ old scratch

DIAGONALLY Catty corner ❏ cattywhampus ❏ antigogglin ❏ antigodlin

DIAMONDS (PLAYING CARD SUIT) Glass cutter. In some cases the "gl" in glass is dropped, especially if you have a winning hand in diamonds.

DIARRHEA Aztec two step ❏ Montezuma's revenge

DIBOLL, TEXAS Pronounced Dye-ball, a small town in East Texas.

DICE Bones ❏ devil's play bones ❏ painted rocks or marbles

DIED Woke up shoveling coal for the furnaces of hell ❏ gave up the ghost ❏ went over the river ❏ fed the buzzards ❏ quit the earth ❏ gave up his guitar for a harp ❏ headed for the last roundup in the sky ❏ finished his branding ❏ loped off into the sunset ❏ cashed in his chips

DIED HAPPY It took the undertaker and his helper three days to get the smile off his face

DIED SUDDENLY Bit the dust and got too large a mouthful ❏ lit a shuck for the pearly gates and didn't have time to get a passport ❏ bought the farm

DIFFERENCE Someone once said that the difference between men and boys is the price of the toys, which means the amount a male person spends on toys is indicative of whether he is a man or a boy. Since Texans think more

about girls than boys, a better version is the difference between women and girls is the price of the curls.

DIFFERENT As a wolf and a poodle dog ❏ as a hog and a herring ❏ now that's another box of worms altogether

DIFFICULT As teaching a mermaid to do the splits ❏ as eatin' Jello with chop sticks ❏ as putting up a tent in a windstorm ❏ as holding a handful of frogs ❏ as keeping mosquitoes out of a swamp ❏ as playing a harp with a claw hammer ❏ as blowing a smoke ring in a Dr Pepper bottle ❏ as roping (or riding) a lightning bolt ❏ as sneaking the crack of dawn past a veteran rooster ❏ as trying to burn wet snow ❏ as trying to hear a whisper in a whirlwind ❏ as chewing tobacco and whistling at the same time ❏ as hemming up hot gravy with half a biscuit ❏ as trying to blow out a gas lamp ❏ as trying to shovel sunshine ❏ as making butter out of skimmed milk ❏ as holding a wildcat under a number three washtub ❏ as plowing a wet field behind a drunk mule ❏ as shearing an elephant

DIFFICULT SITUATION The log is so crooked it won't lay

still in any position ❏ gonna
have to play the hand
blindfolded ❏ like trying to
sack up a den of rattlesnakes
(or a wildcat with a toothache)
❏ tough row to hoe ❏ we got a
lot of stumps in the field ❏
that'll separate the cowboys
from the greenhorns, which is
a Texas variation of separate
the men from the boys *See also
Hard To Do, Tough Job*

DIFFICULT TO ACCEPT
Hard (or bitter) pill to swallow

DIFFICULT TO HANDLE
He's hard to curry ❏ he's hard
to keep in a corral

DIG Gopher ❏ auger

DILEMMA Whether you're
hung as a lamb or a lion, you
will still be dancin' at the end
of a rope ❏ whether you die
from the chills or the fever,
you are still dead ❏ don't
know whether to wet or go
blind ❏ don't know whether to
go home or go crazy ❏ caught
between a rock and a hard
place ❏ caught between the
Devil and the deep blue sea

DILUTE Water it down

DISAGREE That log won't
float ❏ that dog won't hunt ❏
that rig won't drill ❏ that
dipper won't hold water

DISAGREEABLE He was
raised on sour milk and
paregoric

DISAPPEARED Couldn't find
hide nor hair of him ❏ like he
fell into a varmint hole and
pulled the opening in after
him

DISAPPOINTED As a bride
left at the altar ❏ as a coyote
with a rubber chicken

DISASTER A real train wreck
❏ the bottom fell out of the
milk bucket (or churn) ❏ the
roof caved in on the hen house
❏ all hell come undone

DISCOURAGED His tail is
dragging the ground ❏ his
dauber is down ❏ he's down in
the mouth ❏ he's run out of
heart ❏ his face is long
enough to eat oats out of a butter
churn

DISCOVERED Stumbled onto
❏ fell into

DISCUSSION Holding herd,
which is derived from cowboys
getting together to hold herd
and decide what must be done
with the livestock.

DISGRACED He sold his
saddle, which was about the
most disgraceful thing a
cowboy could do.

DISGRACED THE FAMILY
He up and registered
Republican, which is a
reference to Texas long being
a democratic stronghold. If
you insist, Democrat can be
substituted.

DISGUISED Gunny-sacked,
which refers to the practice of
old cowboys wearing gunny
sacks over their heads when
attacking sheep herders

DISHONEST *See Crooked*

DISHWASHER Pearl diver

DISLIKE Don't cotton to ❏
can't sit still for ❏ don't sit
right with me ❏ hate that
worse than the devil does holy
water ❏ don't hold with

DISLIKE, A LOT Wouldn't
wet on him if he was on fire

DISORGANIZED As a wild
hog drive ❏ he wakes up in a
different world every
morning ❏ he's running
around like a chicken with his
head cut off

DISORIENTED Walking
around in a fog

DISPOSE OF Rid yourself of
❏ get shed of

DISPOSITION, SOUR Raised
on pickle juice and vinegar

DISREGARD Don't put any
stock in ❏ pay it no never
mind

DISRESPECTFUL Offers no
more respect than a coyote does
to a jack rabbit

DISTANCE, EXACT House to
house. It might be 200 miles
between Dallas and Austin but
if you live in far North Dallas
and you're visiting someone
in South Austin, the true
distance -- the house to house
distance -- might be 250 miles.

DISTANCE, LONG A fur
piece, such as "It's a fur piece
from Dalhart to Brownsville"
❏ farther than the nekkid eye
can see ❏ long as a country
mile

DISTANCE, SMALL No piece
atall ❏ just a hoot and a holler
away ❏ just over yonder

DISTRACTED Forget the
mules, load the wagon

DISTRESSED *See In Trouble*

DISTURBANCE Somebody
hauled hell out of it's shuck
❏the peace has come undone
See also Commotion

DIVED Like a frog into a stock tank

DIVERSION Kill a skunk ❑ set fire to the barn (or town). The famous western gunfighter Doc Holiday killed his first man in a town called The Flats, Texas which was near Fort Griffin. As legend has it, his girlfriend, Big Nose Kate, became concerned the good dentist was going to be hung, so she set fire to the town as a diversion and helped Doc escape. The pair left Texas for good and headed for Tombstone, Arizona.

DIVIDE Cut it up like a boardinghouse pie, which refers to the fact that in an old boardinghouse there was generally only one pie to go around, no matter how many guests there were. Thus, the more the boarders, the smaller the piece of pie each received.

DIVIDE AND CONQUER A log is a log before you split it, but split it and it is no longer a log. Sam Houston once used this analogy when talking about a split in the democratic party.

DIVORCE Split the blanket ❑ show your mate to the gate ❑ deringed himself

DIVORCEE A grass widow ❑ half her double bed is going to waste ❑ she drinks doubles but sleeps single

DO GOOD Plow straight rows

DO GOODER Keeps his halo polished ❑ keeps the shiny side up

DO IT RIGHT Don't go off half cocked, go off full cocked ❑ if it's worth doin', it's worth doin' right

DO IT YOURSELF Roll your own ❑ paddle your own canoe ❑ saddle your own horse ❑ hitch your own team ❑ you gotta milk your own duck ❑ if you're looking for a good hand, try the end of your arm ❑ There is an old country saying for do-it-yourselfers. If you cut your own firewood, it will warm you twice. Lyndon Johnson once said, "The best fertilizer for a piece of ground is the boot prints of the owner," which roughly means the land that produces the best crops is the land that an owner works for himself.

DO-IT-YOURSELFER Any do-it-yourselfer should be proficient in stobery. A stob is a sort of makeshift wooden stopper or stake, usually made from the branch of a handy tree, that is one of the most versatile items known to mankind. It could be a plug for an oil pan, a bathtub stopper, or a plug for a broken water line, garden hose, or water cooler. A really big stob could be used as an emergency radiator cap if you didn't have too far to go. Anything repaired using a stob has received a stobectomy.

After stobs, the most important do-it-yourself tools are spit and baling wire. In Texas, it has been said if you have enough spit and baling wire, even Humpty Dumpty could be put back together again.

DOCTOR Pill roller ❏ medicine man ❏ saw bones ❏ pill wrangler ❏ cut-'em-up

DOG Hound ❏ skillet licker or pot licker, which refers to the practice of letting hound dogs lick cooking utensils clean after use, which saved a lot of washing.

DOG, GOOD A hard dog to keep under the porch (or wagon) which refers to the fact that the best dogs were not the ones that spent their time resting under the porch. The phrase is also used to describe a good person.

DOG, HARMLESS Wouldn't bite a biscuit or chase a cat ❏ wouldn't scratch fleas for fear they'd get hurt if they fell off

DOG, UGLY Someone ought to shave his rear end and make him walk backwards

DOING WELL Cooking on the front burner ❏ steppin' in high cotton ❏ living high off the hog

DON'T LOOK FOR TROUBLE Let sleeping dogs lie ❏ don't kick the cat ❏ if you pull a bull's tail you can expect to see horns

DON'T SURRENDER Never say die, say damn, which was a favorite saying of Jim Ferguson, the only Texas governor, to date, to be impeached ❏ As William B. Travis said from the Alamo, "I shall never surrender or retreat."

DON'T UNDERSTAND I hear you clucking but I can't find the nest ❏ I can see the fire but I can't find the camp ❏ I can smell the bacon but I can't find the breakfast table

DOUBLE TALKER Squawks out of both sides of his beak at the same time ❏ talks like he's got two mouths

DOUBTFUL Pigs'll fly before that happens ❏ it'll be a cold day in hell before that happens ❏ as much chance as a snowball in hell ❏ a jury wouldn't believe that if three preachers and the governor of Texas gave sworn testimony ❏ got about as much chance as a steer does of surviving a trip to a packing plant ❏ that'll be the day, which was John Wayne's favorite line when he played a grizzled old Texas cowboy in *The Searchers*. A young man in Lubbock, Texas saw the movie and became so infatuated with the line he used it as the title for a classic rock and roll hit song. His name was Buddy Holly. *See also Chance, Slim*

DRAGON FLY Mosquito hawk ❏ snake doctor

DREAD I'd rather have a wisdom tooth pulled than do that ❏ I'd rather have triplets than do that ❏ I'd rather get a poke in the eye with a sharp stick

DRESSED UP Like a mail order catalog on the hoof ❏ like a Dallas lawyer ❏ sporting a fancy riggin' ❏ looks like a bob war salesman, which refers to the fact that old-time barbed wire salesmen were often seen dressed well ❏ wearing his rodeo parade outfit ❏ looks like some deck of cards is missing a face card ❏ wearing go-to-meeting clothes ❏ wearing courting clothes ❏ wearing more stars than a clear night in July. Stars refer to silver ornaments worn on hat bands, belts, vests, etc., by old-time Texas cowboys. In *The Cowman Says it Salty,* Ramon F. Adams said there was an old Texas saying that, "for a Texas puncher not to be totin' stars on his duds is most as bad as votin'. the Republican ticket."

DRESSES POORLY The only time you see him dressed up is when he has to enter a plea in court. ❏ When she's dressed up she looks like a sow with side pockets

DRINK Hist one ❏ bend an elbow ❏ settle (or cut) the dust ❏ wet a beak ❏ paint your tonsils ❏ take on a talking load ❏ wet your whistle ❏ wear a blister on your elbow ❏ dip your bill

DRINK A LOT Drinks enough to float the battleship Texas, a bass boat, a house boat, a John Deere tractor, or all the logs in East Texas ❏ drinks enough to flood an armadillo hole ❏ drinks like

61

a poisoned pup ❑ he only drinks on the days of the week that end in y ❑ he's a cork (or cap) collector, which implies that once he starts drinking he finishes the bottle so there is no longer any need for the closure, be it cap or cork. In the old days someone who drank a lot was said to "throw the cork away" so it couldn't possibly be used again. *See also Drunk*

DRINK CHASER (WATER) Fire extinguisher

DRINK, MIXED Drown some bourbon (or another type of liquor), which is derived from mixing liquor and water

DRINK, STRAIGHT The gulp and shudder method

DRINK, STRONG After one drink of that, you'll be irresistible; after two drinks, you'll be indispensable; after three drinks, you'll be invisible; and after the fourth, you're bulletproof.

DRIVE-IN MOVIE Passion pit

DROPPED Like a hot horseshoe or rock

DROUGHT So dry the Baptists are sprinkling, the Methodists are using wash cloths, and the Catholics are giving rain

checks. In normal conditions, Baptists dunk and Methodists sprinkle ❑ the catfish are carrying canteens ❑ the trees are bribing the dogs ❑ In a bad drought, Texas cowboys often said they could see the cattle getting thinner. *See also Dry, Dry Land, Arid*

DRUNK (NOUN) Laps up liquor like a fired cow hand ❑ he wasn't born, just squeezed out of a bartender's rag ❑ his idea of a seven-course meal is a six pack and a toothpick ❑ a snorter and a snoozer ❑ still chaser ❑ he was still born ❑ on a worm diet, which refers to one who drinks Mexican tequila and eats the worm in the bottom of the bottle ❑ he's afraid to die because he don't think they serve anything stronger than seltzer water in heaven

DRUNK (VERB) Commode-hugging, hymn-singing drunk ❑ if he was shot through the head he'd have to sober up to die ❑ had too many dippers full ❑ couldn't pour whiskey in a barrel with the head out ❑ three sheets and a pillowcase to the wind ❑ got a terminal case of navelites, which is a disease cased by an almost constant pressure of the navel on the edge of a bar. Generally affects only professional drunks and jilted cowboys. *See also Intoxicated*

DRUNK AS A skunk, pig, or waltzing pissant ❑ as a hoedown fiddler, which refers to the days when cash was short and the fiddlers at a dance were often paid in whiskey, which meant they were usually drunk by the time the dance ended. Some old-timers claim the more the fiddler drank, the faster he played which may explain the term "frisky fiddler."

DRUNK DRIVER An autopsy looking for a place to happen ❑ motorized murderer ❑ he always wants to drive 'cause he's too drunk to sing

DRUNK, REFORMED Gave up the bottle to see what a snake really looks like or to see if elephants come in anything but pink ❑ decided to prove that a silk purse could be made out of a sow's ear

DRY As a frog under a cabbage leaf ❑ as the heart of a haystack ❑ as dust in a mummy's pocket ❑ as a blue tick hound dog under a wagon ❑ as popped corn *See also Arid, Drought*

DRY HOLE A duster ❑ didn't produce nothing but suitcase

sand, which means the oil well produced only sand so it's time to pack the suitcase and go home

DRY LAND Even the catfish have ticks (or flea collars) ❑ my three-year-old duck don't know how to swim ❑ the trees (or bushes) are chasing the dogs ❑ the land wouldn't support a horned toad family ❑ we only got a quarter of an inch of rain during Noah's flood ❑ I was ten years old before I saw a fat cow ❑ ain't enough grass to slip between the ribs of a mosquito ❑ the lizards are carrying army canteens *See also Barren*

DRY OFF Shake yourself

DRY WIT Rosin jawed

DUDE Rexall Ranger, which is the modern equivalent of "drug store cowboy" ❑ only horse he ever had was a charlie horse ❑ city slicker ❑ a New York cowboy ❑ wouldn't know how to mount a stick horse

DULL AS A week-old soda pop with the top off ❑ as last week's news

DULL EDGE Dull as a widow woman's ax. In the old days, when a woman lost her husband, a lot of her chores went unattended to unless she was still attractive (See Tall) ❏ wouldn't cut warm butter ❏ wouldn't cut ice cream after it sat out of the freezer all night ❏ wouldn't cut the heart of a watermelon, much less the rind.

DULL PERSON No speed and no sparkle ❏ his idea of excitement is spending a couple of hours in a Christian Science Reading Room ❏ if he was a light bulb, he wouldn't have more than five watts ❏ if he was bacon, he wouldn't sizzle when cooked

DUMB Don't have the sense to spit downwind ❏ enough to be twins ❏ he'd have to study up to be a half wit ❏ he thinks the Mexican border ought to pay rent ❏ has the IQ of a cantaloup ❏ never got past the third page of a first grade reader ❏ don't know come on from sick 'em ❏ one half as smart as a wooden Indian ❏ could screw up a two-car funeral ❏ he's like a catfish, all mouth and no brains ❏ don't have sense enough to pour rain water out of a boot *See also Ignorant, Stupid, Uneducated*

DUMB AS A stump ❏ as a snubbin' post ❏ as a

wagonload (or sled load) of rocks ❏ as a computer with the plug out ❏ as an armadillo. Although an official mascot of the state of Texas, the armadillo is still considered by many to be one of God's dumbest critters.

DURABLE As iron underwear ❏ as half-inch thick rawhide

DUST STORM Panhandle (or high plains) rain ❏ the dogs (or rabbits) are diggin' holes six feet up in the air ❏ blowing worse than Black Easter. On a Sunday morning in April, 1935 the worst sand storm in history struck most of the Texas panhandle as well as parts of several other states. The sun was blacked out and millions of acres of valuable top soil were lost. The day has come to be called Black Easter although it actually happened on Palm Sunday.

DUSTY Blowing so hard you couldn't find the beer cooler on the front seat of your pickup if you were driving it

EXASPERATED — she's dancin' in the hog trough

EARLY RISER Dew chaser ❑ races the crack of dawn to work ❑ gets up with the chickens ❑ has to pry up the sun with a crow bar ❑ he almost gets up early enough to meet himself going to bed

EARN A LIVING Bring home the bacon

EARS, LARGE Texan Howard Hughes said it best when he observed, "Clark Gable's ears make him look like a taxicab with the doors open."

EASE UP Cut me some slack ❑ lay back on my reins ❑ don't dance me so hard ❑ let the hammer down easy

EAST TEXAS The pine curtain

EASY No hill for a stepper ❑ no mountain for a climber ❑ piece of cake ❑ no chore for a doer

EASY AS Shooting ducks on a pond ❑ as cutting warm butter with a hot knife ❑ as shooting fish in a barrel (or dry creek bed) ❑ as catching fish with dynamite. When a dynamite charge is exploded under water, all the fish in the surrounding area are killed by the concussion. When the

dead fish float to the top they can be plucked out of the water, making this the easiest, though not the most sportsmanlike method of fishing.

EASY PART'S OVER All the white meat is gone and there is nothing left on the platter but necks, which refers to the fact that white meat is usually eaten first just as the easy part of a job is often done first.

EASY TO FIX It's a spit and baling wire job ❑ all it needs is a stobectomy *See Do-it-Yourself*

EASY TO USE As a rocking chair ❑ as a light switch ❑ as a fork

EAT Table grazing ❑ bite a biscuit ❑ line your flue ❑ put on the feed bag ❑ pad your belly ❑ put on a moral bag, which is the bag that is hung on a horse's head to allow for easy feeding

EAT A LOT He's eating like the Russian army was crossing the Rio Grande.

EAT ALL YOU WANT Pitch till you win

EAT ANYTHING He eats anything that don't eat him first ❑ He'll eat any critter as long as it has stopped wiggling, implying he will eat anything that has died.

EDUCATED Book learned and hog smart (horse can be used in place of hog)

EFFECTIVENESS The more straws in the broom, the more dirt you can sweep ❑ the longer the rope, the bigger the loop you can build, the reference being the bigger the loop, the more your can rope ❑ the softer the leather, the better the feel

EFFORT If it's worth doing, it's worth doing well. Texan Mildred "Babe" Didrickson Zaharris, the greatest woman athlete ever born, said, "If a game is worth playing, it's worth playing to win."

EFFORT, LARGE It took all the hands and the cook ❑ would have taken God eight days to get it done

EFFORT, WASTED Winking at a pretty girl in a dark room ❑ panning for fool's gold ❑ you closed the barn door after all the horses were out ❑ you built the windmill after the well went dry ❑ you're buying oats for (or whipping) a dead horse ❑ you're trying to train an old

dog ❑ you can't move a plow by tickling it with a feather ❑ you're banging your head against the outhouse wall *See also Wasting Time*

EGGS Hen fruit ❑ hen apples

EGGS, LARGE It only takes eight of them to make a dozen

EGO He's a legend in his own mind ❑ could strut sitting down ❑ considers himself the whole railroad including tracks, trains, and right of way ❑ too big for cowboy britches

EGO, DEFLATED Fell off his high horse ❑ his high horse came up lame ❑ someone knocked half the rungs out of his ladder ❑ someone pulled the rug out from under him ❑ somebody wet in his well

EGO, LARGE Thinks he's the only show pig in the pen ❑ if his head got any bigger, he wouldn't fit through the outhouse door ❑ thinks he's the only rooster in the barnyard ❑ wish I could buy him for what he's really worth and sell him for what he thinks he's worth *See also Aloof, Arrogant*

EIGHT (PLAYING CARD) Eighter from Decatur (Decatur, Texas, that is)

ELATED Homesteading cloud nine ❑ walking around three feet off the ground

ELDERLY Ready for a warm corner ❑ he was around when the Dead sea was only sick ❑ blooming for the pasture, which refers to his (or her) hair getting gray *See also Aging, Old*

ELUSIVE As a greased pig in a sauna bath (or steam room) ❑ he rarely comes out of the same hole he climbed into ❑ got more moves than a Rolex watch ❑ as a hide-behind bird, which is a rare bird that will sneak up and hide behind you. They are so quick that when you turn around for a look, they'll be gone and only tracks remain. It's been rumored that some tourists have gone home believing there actually is such a critter.

EMBARRASSED As an old maid baby-sitting a sea captain's parrot ❑ as a preacher with a broken zipper ❑ he's looking for a hole to hide in ❑ blushed to the roots (of her hair) ❑ got caught with his pants down and his boots off ❑ his suspenders snapped ❑ her garter snapped

EMBARRASSING A fine how do you do ❑ a fine howdy do

EMBEZZLE Figures don't lie but liars figure ❑ the books are half a bubble out of square ❑ someone balanced the books with a level that was out of plumb

EMERGENCY Hell's bells are ringing ❑ the finger is out of the dyke ❑ we've got an ox in the ditch ❑ the barn's on fire ❑ the electric fence shorted out, which is a real emergency since electric fences are often just a single strand of wire that would be no chore to break if the power failed

EMOTIONLESS Poker faced ❑ stone faced ❑ if he ever smiled, his face would crack open like a dropped watermelon

EMPLOYED Riding for a brand. Ranches are referred to by their brand, such as the XIT, 6666, or Pitch Fork. Thus when a cowpoke hired on regular with a ranch, he was "riding for the brand."

EMPLOYED, TEMPORARILY Roundup hand, which refers to ranches taking on extra help during roundup time ❑ working for day wages, which is what cowboys did when they didn't have a regular job.

EMPLOYEE Just gave you a job, didn't take you to raise □ hired hand □ hired gun □ field hand □ hireling

EMPLOYEE, WORTHLESS He either don't do what he's told or he don't do anything except what he's told. Bum Phillips once used such an expression to describe the two kinds of football players that are worthless. □ There is an old saying in Texas that the most worthless employee is the one who wears a hat, rolls his own smokes, and wears shoes that have to be tied. Such a person will spend so much time chasing his hat when it blows off, fiddling with his makings (the stuff used to hand-roll cigarettes), and retying his shoes that he won't have any time left to work.

EMPTY As a banker's heart □ as a dry hole □ as a brassiere (or girdle) hanging on a clothesline □ as last year's bird nest □ as last night's beer bottle □ as an ex-wife's (or ex-husband's) head □ as an old maid's dreams □ as a horse corral with an open gate

ENCOURAGE Light a fire in his tail (or overalls) □ push on the reins □ set him down on a branding fire □ jerk his

chain □ pull his string □ the sun don't shine on the same dog's rear end every day

END (NOUN) Tailgate □ hind end □ south end of a north-bound mule □ caboose

END (VERB) Close the range □ wet on the fire and call the dogs □ snuff out the lamp

ENDED Played out □ knocked down on (from auctions) □ fizzled out □ petered out □ all over but the shouting □ nothing left to do but kiss the bride, which implies that someone you cared for ended the relationship by marrying another

ENDING You can put that in your pipe and smoke it □ you can put that in your pan and bake it □ you can put your saddle on that and ride it home

ENDLESS There's always another calf to brand □ always another horse to break □ always another fence to mend □ always another squeaking windmill to grease □ always another gate off the hinge □ always another rat (or snake) to kill

ENDURANCE Bottom

ENGAGED She's been ringed

ENTERED *See Joined*

ENTHUSIASTIC He's got a Chamber of Commerce spirit ❑ bright eyed and bushy tailed ❑ a frisky fiddler

ENVIOUS If you got a heart transplant, she'd have to have one ❑ if your house had ants, she'd want termites

EPISODE Go round. Each day's events in a rodeo are referred to as a go round.

EQUALITY On a mule team, the scenery is the same for all the mules except the leader, which could be a Texan's version of Rank Has Its Privileges ❑ what's good for the gander is good for the goose ❑ stands neck and neck with ❑ six of one, half a dozen of the other ❑ When it rains, it rains on both sides of the fence. (In football, that would be both sides of the line of scrimmage) ❑ it's a hoss and a hoss, which is how Darrell Royal described two equally matched football teams.

EQUIPPED Armed to the teeth ❑ loaded for bear ❑ fitted out

EQUIPPED, POORLY You can't sell from an empty wagon ❑ you can't hunt with an empty gun ❑ you can dance

with a straw broom but it's better to use a girl

ERASE Blot the brand ❑ blotch it out ❑ wipe the slate clean ❑ dust the board

ERRAND BOY A go-fer ❑ a shagger, which is someone who shags fly balls ❑ a spear carrier

ERROR Hung the wrong horse thief ❑ sat down in your own coyote trap ❑ got caught in his own loop ❑ ripped his drawers (or britches) ❑ pulled your trigger without taking aim ❑ laid her egg in the wrong nest ❑ put your boot on the wrong foot ❑ that deer you shot turned out to be the neighbor's milk cow. Lead goat, bell goat, bell mare can be substituted for milk cow *See also Made a Mistake, Mistaken, Screwed Up*

ESCAPE Head for higher ground ❑ jump bail

ESCAPED Slipped the hobbles ❑ broke jail ❑ sawed off the handcuffs ❑ slipped (or spit out) the hook

ESSENTIAL INFORMATION The bare bones ❑ the meat without the fat

EULOGY A funeralization

EVACUATED Like red ants pouring out of a burning stump (or log)

EVALUATE Size 'em up ❑ see what they're made of ❑ you can't judge corn unless you look inside the shuck ❑ don't call him a cowboy till he does some riding and roping ❑ don't call it a cutting horse till it gets a calf out of the herd

EVASIVE When he ain't hemming, he's hawing ❑ he's beat around every bush in the county

EVENTS Goings on

EVERYBODY The whole outfit ❑ all the hands ❑ all the cowhands and the cook ❑ the whole outfit including cook, go-fer, and big auger

EVERYTHING Guts, feathers, beak, and all ❑ the whole kit and caboodle ❑ hook, line, and sinker ❑ the whole she-bang ❑ the whole shootin' match ❑ the whole enchilada ❑ the whole hog ❑ the whole load of watermelons, cantaloups, turnips, strawberries, or manure *See also Complete*

EVERYWHERE All over hell and half of Texas ❑ all over the entire pasture

EVIL CITY A letter addressed to hell would go there, such as "If you address a letter to hell it would be delivered to New York City." Although New York would be a popular choice for many Texans, any city outside of Texas could be substituted.

EVIL PERSON Wrath finder ❑ you might paint him into a corner but it won't be the amen corner ❑ would steal a widow women's only milk cow ❑ he'll never die in bed ❑ butter wouldn't melt in her mouth ❑ don't believe in taking prisoners ❑ keeps the ball of sin rolling ❑ in cahoots with the devil ❑ his reservation in hell was made the day he was born ❑ someday he'll be stringing barbed wire in hell ❑his life is a measuring stick for sin ❑ if you addressed a letter to the devil, the postman would put it in his box ❑ he's one of John the Baptist's snakes in the grass (Mathew 37, Luke 37) *See also Bad Person, Wicked*

EXAGGERATE Stretch the blanket ❑ stretch the facts ❑ his facts are elastic

EXAGGERATION Chamber of Commerce statistics

EXASPERATED As a settin' hen trying to lay a square egg ❑ as a snake without a pit to hiss in ❑ as a short tailed bull in fly time ❑ at the end of his rope (or tether) ❑ she's dancing in the hog trough, which is said of girls whose younger sister marries before them ❑ as a bridegroom at a shotgun wedding

EXCELLENT Dead solid perfect ❑ larrupin good ❑ the cat's meow

EXCEPTIONAL Would like to be gathering eggs and find that in my nest ❑ been to county fairs, goat ropings and world championship rodeos and I ain't never seen anything like it ❑ best I ever laid eyes on

EXCITED He's got biting ants in his britches ❑ her bobbin is wound tight ❑ all fired up like a steam locomotive ❑ running around like a chicken with his head cut off ❑ he swallowed his head and chinned the moon, which is a reference to the action of a bucking horse ❑ soaring with the eagles ❑ as a lizard on a hot griddle ❑ she was bawlin' and squallin'

and slinging snot every which way

EXCITING That'll get the dogs out from under the porch (or wagon) ❑ that'll pop the wax out of your ears ❑ that'd set the woods on fire ❑ a real stem winder ❑ that'd put lead in your pencil ❑ that'll melt your butter ❑ that'll put folks to talking ❑ that'll put the boys up on the top rail, which refers to rodeo cowboys seeking the safety of the top rail of a fence when a mad bull gets after them *See also Amazing*

EXCITING AS A wind-fanned West Texas grass fire ❑ as a circus fire ❑ as a fire at the IRS office

EXCLAMATION Well I declare ❑ I'll be switched (or jiggered)

EXHAUSTED Plum tuckered, tuckered out ❑ played out ❑ my get up and go got up and went ❑ plum tared (tired) *See also Tired, Weary*

EXPECT 'Spect ❑ I look for that to happen ❑ I'm betting on it

EXPECTANT As a bird watching a worm hole ❑ as a woman ten months pregnant

❑ as a buzzard circling a dying mule

EXPENSIVE You'd have to hock the family jewels to afford the down payment ❑ costs an arm and a leg ❑ cost three prices ❑ as popcorn at a picture show ❑ wallet buster ❑ unthrifty ❑ would make Neiman Marcus look like a discount store ❑ costs a pretty penny ❑ high as a cat's back

EXPERIENCED If he crows, the sun is up ❑ been down the road a piece in all kinds of weather ❑ he's been at the dance quite a spell ❑ sits deep in the saddle ❑ he's a horse wrangler from way back ❑ a master hand ❑ he can plow a long row in a short time ❑ he was already ten years old and half a cowboy when he was born. Texas golfer Lee Trevino claims he was already nine years old when he was born.

EXPERT Nobody could give him lessons ❑ could rope a jackrabbit with a grapevine ❑ a good judge of horse flesh ❑ ain't ever been bested in a horse trade ❑ could break the orneriest mustang without a bridle

EXPERTISE Strong suit ❑ money crop ❑ strong hold ❑ trump suit

EXPIRED *See Died*

EXPLAIN Tell them how the cow ate the cabbage ❑ burn that brand a little deeper *See also Clarify*

EXPLAIN FULLY Put all the cards on the table.

EXPLORE Plow new ground ❑ blaze a new trail

EXPOUND ON Fill it out with meat ❑ put some clothes on the skeleton ❑ color the picture

EXTRA Boot, as in "I'll give you $50.00 for the horse if you'll throw in a saddle to boot." ❑ excess baggage ❑ rumble seat rider ❑ the eighth man. In poker, some games use seven cards per hand, so eight people can't play since a deck has only 52 cards.

EXTRA MONEY Rat hole money ❑ cotton picking money ❑ wild hare stake ❑ scalp money ❑ egg money

EXTREMELY All get out, as in "He's happy as all get out." ❑ plumb, as in "I'm plumb tired."

EYES, LARGE Doe eyes ❑
bug-eyed ❑ calf eyes

EYES, RED as two cherries in
an Amarillo snow bank ❑
looks like a gas company road
map ❑ looks like a red spider
built a web in his sockets ❑
looks like two strawberries in
a snow drift ❑ looks like some
sack of Bull Durham is missing its string. Bull Durham
tobacco is packaged in a small
cloth bag with a red string that
is used to draw it closed.

EYES, SMALL BB eyes

EYES, SUNKEN Look like two
cigarette burns in a saddle
blanket

EYESIGHT, POOR Couldn't
read the big line on an eye
chart if you spotted him half
the letters ❑ it don't take him
long to read a newspaper
'cause all he can make out are
the headlines ❑ he's taking
braille by correspondence
course *See also Sight,
Impaired*

F

FITS — like a sock on a ducks beak

FACADE All vine, no watermelon ❑ all hat and no cattle, which means he dresses like a rancher but he don't own any cows

FACE CARDS (PLAYING CARDS) Paint cards ❑ court cards, royalty

FACT That's how the cow ate the cabbage ❑ if it ain't true, God's a possum ❑ if it ain't true, you can wet in my hat ❑ if it ain't true, there ain't a cow (or oil well) in Texas ❑ if it ain't true, may a wild steer hook my gizzard ❑ you can take that to the bank and borrow money on it ❑ you can bet the farm on that ❑ that's the name of that tune *See also Believe Me, Certain, Guaranteed, Reliable*

FAILURE He set out to be a swashbuckler but he buckled before he swashed ❑ didn't pan out ❑ didn't make the grade ❑ he blames everything on the weather or his raising ❑ fell off cloud nine into a thunderstorm ❑ got caught in his own loop ❑ when he made it into the fast lane he shifted into reverse ❑ He put his bucket down the well of financial security but the rope broke.

FAIR Middling good

FAITHFUL Dance with who brung ya. This is an old country saying which is derived from the fact that country girls would dance only with the boy that brought them to the dance. Darrell Royal, former coach of the Texas Longhorns, made the saying famous in 1965 after his 'Horns, previously ranked No. 1 in the nation, had lost three games. When asked if he would change his offense, Royal replied, "We're going to stick with what we've been doing. There's an old saying, 'You dance with who brung ya.'" Of all the quotes Royal gave us, this is the one most often repeated. *See also Loyalty*

FAKE A sheep in wolves clothes ❑ big barker, little biter ❑ as a tin quarter

FALFURRIAS, TEXAS Pronounced Fal-fur-us, a small town in far South Texas.

FALSE As election returns in Jim Wells county. In 1948, 202 votes mysteriously appeared in Jim Wells county to give Lyndon Johnson a victory, by 87 votes, in the race for U.S. Senator. No one ever explained how 202 people managed to vote alphabetically. ❏ Lessspecifically, False would be as election returns in a Republican (or Democratic) precinct ❏ as Chamber of Commerce Statistics

FALSE TEETH Store bought molars ❏ synthetic molars ❏ store teeth ❏ like stars, they come out at night ❏ Roebucks, which refers to the days when false teeth were ordered by mail from Sears.

FAMILIAR WITH See *Acquainted*

FAMISHED See *Hungry*

FANCY Cotton to, as in "She really cottons to big diamonds and little bathing suits."

FAR AWAY Right smart piece as in "It's a right smart piece from El Paso to Texarkana" ❏ so far you'd have to ride a pregnant mule to get there so you'd have a way back ❏ you'd have to pack a lunch to get there ❏ it'd take fourteen dollars in postage to get them a letter ❏ so far away overnight mail from the post office takes a week to be delivered *See also Rural*

FARMER Plowboy ❏ sod buster ❏ tractor wrangler ❏ plow wrangler ❏ plow chaser ❏ butter and egg man ❏ pumpkin roller ❏ clod hopper ❏ mule man, mule trailer, mule follower, all of which refers to the days when farmers plowed behind a mule instead with a tractor.

FARMER, UNLUCKY The only time he gets rain is when the crops are ready to harvest, which is about the only time a farmer doesn't want rain.

FASHION CONSCIOUS If she was a hen she'd lay pastel colored eggs

FAST Double quick ❏ in the wink of an eye ❏ in a heartbeat, as in "He can pick your pocket in a heartbeat" ❏ going hell bent for leather ❏ passed me like I was up on jacks in the garage ❏ burning rocket fuel ❏ he could outrun the beaters on an electric mixer *See also Quick*

FAST AS Greased, chain, or double geared lightning ❏ as a duck on a June bug ❏ as a cat with his tail on fire ❏ as bad news traveling at a church social ❏ as small town gossip, which is how Darrell Royal once described Longhorn back James Saxton ❏ as a shooting star ❏ as a tomcat shot with a boot jack ❏ as a turpentined cat ❏ as a hoop snake, which is a large reptile that curls himself into a loop, bites his own tail for balance, and rolls quickly out of harm's way. They are so fast no one has actually ever seen one. *See also Quick As*

FAST HORSE He can run from sun up to sun down in about half an hour

FAST PERSON He can blow out the lamp and get into bed before it gets dark ❑ he can beat a bull to a hole in the fence ❑ takes him fifteen minutes to draw to a halt ❑ can stay neck n' neck with a West Texas jackrabbit ❑ he gets there in one half less than no time ❑ he can gather up over yonder before you can bat an eyelash ❑ he could out run a six-legged bobcat ❑ he even sleeps fast. As Bobby Layne, the legendary quarterback from the University of Texas once said, "You don't need much sleep if you sleep fast."

FAST START Quick out of the gate (or chute) ❑ quick off the blocks

FASTER THAN A prairie fire with a tail wind ❑ a whirlwind can snuff a match ❑ a six-legged jack rabbit ❑ a minnow can swim a dipper

FAT AS A boardinghouse cat ❑ as a killing hog ❑ as a poisoned pup ❑ as a grub line coyote

FAT MAN Never seen anything that big without John Deere stamped on it ❑ looks like he ate his brother ❑ he don't care what you call him as long as you call him at meal time ❑ he has to sit down in shifts ❑ a walkin,' talkin' tub a lard ❑ a cellulite silo ❑ he's got enough tallow for two head of cattle *See also Obese, Rear End, Large*

FAT WOMAN Warm in winter, shade in the summer ❑ she puts her panty hose on with a crow bar ❑ split her dress up the side and you could make a tent for an entire Bohemian family ❑ she don't wear nothin' but Mother Hubbards, which are dresses that cover everything but touch nothing but the shoulders. *See also Rear End, Large*

FAVORITISM Plays brother-in-law

FEARLESS He'd walk through the valley of the shadow of death blindfolded, barefooted with one arm tied behind his back ❑ Old-time Texas Ranger, Bill McDonald, was said to be so fearless that, "he'd charge hell with a bucket of water." It's been said the only two things a cowboy was afraid of were a righteous woman and being afoot. *See also Brave, Courageous*

FEET The spur end, referring to the fact that spurs are always worn on the feet ❏ the forked end, referring to legs resembling a very large two-pronged fork

FEET, LARGE He has to put his britches on over his head ❏ he has a large understanding ❏ he has to buy two pair of shoes at a time because he throws away the shoes and wears the boxes

FELL Got his spurs tangled ❏ ate some gravel (or asphalt) ❏ joined his shadow in the dirt ❏ like he'd been hit between the eyes with the butt end of quirt (or scatter gun) ❏ like a wormed apple in a whirlwind

FEMALE Ol' slick legs ❏ belle ❏ gal ❏ darlin' ❏ little lady ❏ sweet thing ❏ filly ❏ heifer ❏ sage hen ❏ skirt ❏ honky tonk angel ❏ pullet, which can be used for any female, regardless of age, although it is generally used for younger ladies *See also Girl*

FEMALE, CONNIVING When she takes you by the hand she's tugging on your heart strings ❏ she didn't learn to cook because she was hungry ❏ she's always dragging her rope trollin' for some poor ol' cowboy that don't know no better ❏ she always wears a hat in case she runs onto a cowboy willin' to marry at the drop of one *See also Looking for a Husband*

FEMALE, DANGEROUS She plays with fire. When a woman plays with fire, it's a man that usually gets burned.

FEMALE, DESIRABLE She can ride any horse in my string ❏ she can eat crackers in my bed ❏ she can put her shoes under my bed ❏ she can squeeze my toothpaste anywhere she wants ❏ she'd make a man plow through a stump

FEMALE, EASY They call her "radio station" because anyone can pick her up, especially at night.

FEMALE, GATHERING Hen party ❏ quilting bee ❏ shower practice, referring to women holding showers for friends who are getting married

FEMALE, MEAN Her emery board is a whetstone, which is something men use to sharpen knives, so the implication is she sharpens her nails rather than manicures them. ❑ Some people use whampus cat (or kitty) for "mean female" although no one seems to know exactly what it means. The Itasca, Texas high school uses Whampus Cat as its team mascot and Bill McMurray, in his book *Texas High School Football* explains, "It's said this nickname came from a fan of an opposing team when he referred to Itasca playing like whampus cats." A good guess is whampus is derived from whomp us, and any woman that'll whomp you is certainly mean. Don Biggers, a newspaper man from out Rotan way, once did a series of whampus cat articles claiming the critters were part wildcat, part badger with a little wolf thrown in for good measure. Only tourists and the very young believed him.

FEMALE, RESTLESS A hard old gal to keep down on the farm

FEMALE, SHAPELY Built like a brick outhouse ❑ classy chassis ❑ more curves than a barrel of snakes ❑ walks with more motion than an ocean ❑

coke bottle figure (Classic Coke, that is) ❑ she'd take first place in the halter class ❑ her figure would raise steam from an icy heart ❑ her shape would make a freight train take a dirt road

FEMALE SUPERIORITY Houston's Liz Carpenter said it best, in a speech supporting Texas State Treasurer Ann Richards, with, "Roosters crow, hens deliver."

FEMALE, TOUGH She shaves her legs with 80-grit sandpaper ❑ she shaves her legs with a chainsaw

FEMALE, UNDERAGE Jail bait ❑ forbidden fruit ❑ Huntsville honey. Hunstville is where the main unit of the Texas Prison system is located.

FEMALE, UNMARRIED Bell chaser, as in wedding bell ❑ home wrecker ❑ keeps her hair combed and her purr tuned ❑ senorita, in Spanish

FENCE, GOOD A wire fence strung tight enough to pick a tune on.

FEW Pickin's are powerful slim

83

FIGHT A blood letting, a two-man square dance ❑ a Pecos promenade, which refers to the old days when fighting was not uncommon out west of the Pecos. If it hadn't been for a fella named Judge Roy Bean, things might have got plumb out of hand.

FIGHTER If you're gonna beat him, it will be after the fight ❑ if you wanna fight him, bring your lunch 'cause it will take all day ❑ he'll kick your backside till your nose bleeds ❑ he could whip his weight in wolves or bobcats ❑ he would fight a buzz saw and give it three turns head start ❑ he'll fight at the drop of a hat, any hat ❑ he'll whip you or get whipped trying ❑ if you take him on, you'll think you've been in a sack with a wildcat

FIGHTER, POOR Couldn't fight his way out of a paper sack ❑ he couldn't whip a crippled kitten ❑ couldn't beat his way out of a spider's web

FIGHTING They raised more dust in five minutes than Noah's flood could have settled ❑ only the absence of shooting irons prevented a killing ❑ they go at it buck tooth and hang nail, which is the Texas version of "fought tooth and nail" ❑ locking horns ❑ the fur (or feathers) was flying in all direction ❑ crossed sabres

FINALIZE Tie up the loose ends ❑ round up the strays ❑ dot the i's, cross the t's and run it by a lawyer

FINANCIAL CONDITION *See Bankrupt, Rich, Went Broke*

FIND Smoke 'em out ❑ flush 'em out ❑ hunt 'em up if you have to turn over every cow patty (or rock) in Texas, which is the Texas version of "leave no stone unturned"

FINE As frog hair split three ways ❑ as dollar cotton

FINGER, INDEX Trigger finger ❑ pointer

FINGERNAIL Claws for a male, love hooks for a female ❑ hammer magnet, which refers to people often striking their finger while hammering even though their target was a nail

FINGERNAIL POLISH Claw paint ❑ finger paint

FINISHED The prom, rodeo, dance, or hoedown is over ❑ that's the old ball game ❑ turn out the lights, the party's over, which is the title to a Willie Nelson song that was made famous by Dandy Don Meredith, the former Dallas Cowboy, during his broadcast days on Monday Night Football.

FIRM As bedsprings in a $100 mattress

FIRST First rattle out of the box, which refers to rolling dice out of a box.

FISH (NOUN) *See Catfish*

FISH (VERB) Gonna drown some worms, minnows, or crickets ❏ wet a hook ❏ bait a line

FISH, FIGHTING He jerked so hard on the line he pulled down my drawers (or britches), ladies can use dress or garter belt

FISH, LARGE Measured 14 inches between the eyes. Any number between 10 and 20 can be used since anything under 10 would be too small and no one would believe anything over 20.

FISH, OLD When we cut him open we found the Mayflower anchor

FISHERMAN A jerk on one end of a line waiting for a jerk on the other end ❏ bait killer, line runner, which refers to fishermen who prefer to use a trot line ❏ bass buster. Any other kind of fish can be substituted, such as crappie buster or catfish buster. Younger fishermen are junior bass busters and really young children are sunfish busters ❏ living liar. Everybody knows all fishermen except me and you are liars.

FISHERMAN, INEPT The biggest thing he ever hooked was the back of his lap ❏ he couldn't drown a plastic worm ❏ he don't know his bass from a hole in the ground ❏ he knows the two days fish are always biting, yesterday and tomorrow

FISHERMAN, LUCKY He fishes with a silver hook ❏ he could catch his limit in the Dead sea ❏ if he ran out of hooks, he could tie his line into a loop and lasso more fish than most people could catch ❏ he uses a magnetic hook

FIST The five of clubs

FIT As a fiddle

FIT, GOOD Fits like scales on a fish ❏ like bark on a tree ❏

like ugly on an ape ❑ like sardines in a can ❑ like hide on a horse ❑ like feathers on a duck

FIT, POOR Fits like a sock on a duck's beak ❑ fits like a boot on a bull ❑ fits like panty hose on a pig ❑ like a house coat on a hog ❑ like a bikini on a mermaid

FIT, TIGHT *See Tight*

FIVE (PLAYING CARD) Nickel, or buffalo nickel

FLAT AS A panhandle prairie ❑ the deck of an aircraft carrier ❑ a pancake ❑ a mashed cat (or snake) ❑ as an ironing board ❑ as a red wagon run over by a Peterbuilt

FLAT ROCK *See Rock, Flat*

FLEE High tail it ❑ skeedaddle out of here ❑ cut a hole in the wind

FLEXIBLE If he was hired as a geography teacher, he could teach that the world was flat or round, depending on school board preference.

FLIMSY As a three-dollar suitcase ❑ as a house of cards ❑ as a Kleenex shirt

FLOOD Water was hub deep to a Ferris wheel ❑ we had enough water to make Noah's flood look like a baby's bath water ❑ there was enough water to float the rock of ages ❑ there was so much water we had to use a skin diver to grease the windmill

FLOWED Like the Brazos river at flood stage ❑ like the water from a flash flood over a low water crossing ❑ like beer at a bachelor party

FLUSH (POKER HAND) All blue, which is used even if the cards are red or black ❑ caught five from the spade litter. Naturally, clubs, diamonds, or hearts can be substituted depending on your hand.

FLUSTERED In a lather ❑ walleyed ❑ foaming at the mouth

FOLLOW Ride in his dust ❑ run in his ruts ❑ tail 'em like a coyote after a lost calf ❑ eat some of his dust ❑ bird dog 'em

FOOD Vittles ❑ grub ❑ chuck, which refers to food from a chuck wagon on a trail drive

FOOD, POOR Ain't fit for nothing but a slop bucket or a

garbage disposal ❏ don't feed that to the hogs unless you want dead hogs

FOOLISH Only a fool would pick a fight with a skunk or a porcupine ❏ he'd buy hay for a nightmare ❏ he'd buy a square hula hoop ❏ if he was a mouse, he'd build his nest in a cat's box ❏ he could get held up through the mail

FOOT Wheel ❏ hoof

FOR A LONG TIME Till all the cows in Texas have been BBQ'd ❏ till the cows come home ❏ till hell freezes over thick enough to skate on

FORCE Put (or hold) his feet to the fire ❏ give him a dose of convincing

FOREMAN Segundo ❏ bull whacker, which was an old-time ox driver ❏ bell goat *See also Boss, Leader*

FOREVER As long as ducks (or geese) go barefooted ❏ till somebody slides home from first ❏ for good, as in "I'm yours for good, unless I get a better offer."

FOREST A big thicket

FORGOT It slipped through the cracks, which is a saying

that may have been derived from the days when wood planks were used as flooring. Anything that slipped through the cracks in the planks was generally forgotten until new flooring was installed.

FORT WORTH, TEXAS Pronounced Foat Worth ❏ also called Cow town ❏ Panther city ❏ Foat Worth is said to be where the West begins because Dallas is where the East peters out ❏ Folks in that town have been known to claim "You can't be a cowboy unless you were born in Fort Worth."

FORTUNATE They tried to hang him but the rope broke, or they would have hung him but nobody had a rope ❏ good fortune follows him around looking for a place to happen ❏ he fell into the outhouse and discovered a gold mine *See also Lucky*

FOUGHT Locked horns ❏ went at each other tooth and nail

FOUR (PLAYING CARD) Henry Ford or simply Ford

FRACTIOUS Gravel in his gizzard ❏ gravel in his craw

87

FRECKLES She looks like she swallowed a quarter and broke out in pennies

FREDERICKSBURG, TEXAS Pronounced Fred-ricks-berg, a small town in the Texas hill country not far from Luckenback.

FREE He ain't got nothing left to lose, which infers that a man who has lost everything is free from worrying about losing anything.

FRIEND Pardner ❑ sidekick ❑ shotgun rider ❑ running buddy ❑ compadre ❑ kemosabe, which is how Tonto referred to his Texas friend the Lone Ranger ❑ he chews tobacco off my plug anytime ❑ amigo ❑ "long as I got a biscuit, you got half" is a sign someone is a sure 'nuff friend ❑ we stick together through thick and thin, lose or win. The word Texas comes from the Indian word tejas (pronounced tay-hoss, never te-jays) which means friend or ally.

FRIENDLY Neighborly ❑ as a pink-eyed rabbit ❑ as a pup in a box ❑ he'd go to the end of the trail with you ❑ his porch light is always burning ❑ his welcome mat is always out ❑ keeps the latch string on the outside, which is a reference to the days before doorknobs when a string attached to a latch was used to open doors. The friendliest people always keep their latch string on the outside so anyone could open the door.

FRIENDSHIP Is like a cow's milk, you can't take it, it's got to be given. In *He Ain't No Bum* by O. A. "Bum" Phillips and Ray Buck, Phillips, former coach of the Houston Oilers, explained, " When you walk up to a cow, you can't milk her. A cow has got to let her milk down. She's gotta give it to you: you can't take it away from one, you ain't strong enough." Lyndon Johnson said, of friendship, "Never overlook an opportunity to do an honest favor for an honorable friend."

FRIGHTENED Scared stiff as a (See Stiff As) *See also Scared and Scary*

FRIGHTENING Would stand up the hair on a mink coat, stuffed animal, bearskin rug, or buffalo lap robe ❑ it'll make you ruin your shorts ❑ hair raisin' ❑ would scare you out of ten years' growth *See also Scary*

FRIONA, TEXAS Pronounced Free-on-a, a small town in West Texas

FRISKY Feeling his oats ❑ got steam in his boiler (or locomotive)

FRISKY AS A cutting horse ❑ as a pig in a new pen ❑ as a fresh born colt ❑ As an unsaddled horse, which, according to Darrell Royal, is how football players feel when they cross the fifty-yard line.

FRUGAL He crawls under the gate to save the hinges ❑ he won't take cold showers because goose pimples use up more soap ❑ he has short arms and deep pockets ❑ tight as a tick ❑ chews close and spits tight ❑ her pancakes are so thin they only have one side, implying she is stingy with her batter ❑ closed fisted ❑ a cardboard walker, which means he fills holes in the bottom of his boots with cardboard rather than spending money for new soles *See also Cheapskate, Miser, Stingy*

FRUSTRATED As a woodpecker in a petrified forest ❑ as a hog at a crowded trough ❑ as a gelding in a mare corral ❑ as a de-clawed cat trying to climb a shade tree ❑ as a

chicken drinking out of a pie pan

FULL As a tick on a dog's rear (or ear) ❑ stuffed to the gills ❑ chock full ❑ brim full ❑ to the limits of my springs ❑ gorged to the eyelashes ❑ two notches full, which means he had to loosen his belt two full notches

FULL HOUSE (POKER HAND) Full boat or the boat is floating

FULL MOON Full-grown moon ❑ Indian moon, which is derived from the fact that Indians often attacked during periods of full moon

FUN As feeding monkeys at the zoo ❑ as chasing armadillos

FUNERAL Buryin' ❑ plantin'

FUNNY A heap of hilarity ❑ knee slapper ❑ as a three-legged mule tryin' to pull a buggy

FUTILE *See Wasting Time, Useless*

GOOD — he sits tall in the saddle

GADGET Dohicky ❑ thingamabob ❑ whangdoodle ❑ dodad ❑ whatchamacallit

GAIN WEIGHT Put on tallow, which was a cowboy's word for fat. Tallow is the solid rendered fat of cattle and sheep that is used in the manufacture of soap candles and lubricants. Also bottoming out, which means, in this instance, his (or her) rear end is growing.

GALVESTON, TEXAS When you visit this city on the Texas coast, you might say you're going to visit a "gal with a vest on" which is the romantic notion for how the town was named. A less romantic notion is that the town was named for a Viceroy of Mexico named Galvez.

GAMBLE Buck the tiger. According to Ramon F. Adams, this term was derived from old-time traveling faro dealers who carried their gambling paraphernalia in a box with a tiger painted on the side.

GAMBLER Risk taker ❑ crap shooter ❑ wildcatter ❑ he'd bet on the sun coming up if the odds were right ❑ second cousin to Amarillo Slim, who is a noted Texas gambler ❑ if you cut him open, he'd bleed green felt, which means he spends his time leaning on the felt of a crap table ❑ the ice in his dice is never cold

GAMBLER, HONEST You could shoot dice with him over the phone

GAMBLERS ADVICE Never bet the farm if you can't afford to lose it ❑ a full house divided wins no pots ❑ a faint heart never filled a flush (or an inside straight)

GATHER Bale 'em up ❑ rustle 'em up ❑ round 'em up ❑ wrangle 'em up ❑ put a loop on 'em

GAVE UP The old dog is done hunting ❑ threw in the towel ❑ cashed in his chips ❑ sold his horse, which refers to an old-time cowboy selling his horse and giving up the good life of the open range ❑ she let her milk down, which refers to a milk cow giving up and letting you take her milk ❑ hollered calf rope ❑ unhooked the horses ❑ pulled on the whoa reins ❑ quit on account of my health, I wanted to keep it

GENTLE As a horse on a merry-go-round ❑ as a fawn, lamb, kitten, or ladies horse ❑

93

wouldn't harm a hair on a dog's head ❑ as a mother nursing a baby

GENTLY Treat it with kid gloves ❑ if you pull the reins too tight, the horse will buck

GENUINE Gen-u-ine ❑ real McCoy ❑ pure-d ❑ dyed in the wool ❑ sure 'nuff, as in "He's a sure 'nuff cowpuncher."

GET Fetch, as in "Will you fetch the beer."

GET ATTENTION Hit 'em between the eyes with a 2x4 ❑ knock him over the head with a singletree, which is what you use to hook a horse to a wagon ❑ put a shotgun in his ear

GET BUSY Shake a hoof ❑ get on with the dancing, branding, plowing, or rat killing

GET CONTROL Curry the kinks out of that bronc

GET DOWN TO BUSINESS Money talks, BS walks ❑ talk is cheap but whiskey costs money ❑ get down to the brass tacks

GET EVEN Turn about is fair play ❑ whatever goes around, comes around

GET GOING Giddyup ❑ kick some manure off your boots ❑ move your shadow

GET HELP Call in the cavalry (or Marines) ❑ organize a posse ❑ rustle up a thrashin' crew, which refers to the practice of neighbors pitching in to help one another thrash their crops.

GET OUT Adios the joint ❑ put some distance between you and here ❑ gather up your shadow and haul it out of here

GET READY Rosin up the bow, which refers to using rosin on the bow of a fiddle before playing ❑ fix bayonets ❑ comb your fur and tune your purr ❑ cock your pistol ❑ soap your saddle ❑ cinch the riggin' ❑ sharpen your hoe, which refers to the fact that you can chop more cotton with a sharp hoe ❑ grease your holster and file your sights, which refers to gunslingers getting ready for a shootout ❑ build a fire in the branding pen ❑ mount up

GET RID OF Get shed of ❑ shuck it

GET SERIOUS Get down to the nut cuttin', which is a reference to castrating bulls or pigs ❑ get down to cases

GET STARTED Get to plowing, hoeing, the branding, or the roping ❑ pull the trigger ❑ open the gate ❑ pull the string ❑ pop the cork

GET TO THE POINT Shell down to the corn ❑ sand through the veneer ❑ split open the watermelon ❑ skin down to the bone ❑ cut to the quick

GET TO WORK Quite spittin on the handle ❑ get some manure on your boots

GETTING BEHIND They're catching them faster than I can string 'em ❑ they're roping them faster than I can brand 'em

GETTING WORSE Going to hell in a hand basket. John Connally once said he decided to run for governor because he was concerned Texas was "going to hell in a hand basket" after a Republican, John Tower, got elected to the senate.

GIRL Filly ❑ sweet thang ❑ little darlin' ❑ little dumplin ❑ little lady ❑ muchacha *See also Female*

GIVE BIRTH Domino ❑ put another cowboy on the range

GIVE IT A TRY Cut your wolf loose ❑ When it comes to going into business for yourself, if you don't give it a try, you'll always work for the man that did.

GIVE ORDERS Scatter the riders (or hands)

GO AHEAD Let her rip ❑ turn it lose ❑ plow straight and don't look back ❑ open the gate

GO FOR IT Kick for the moon whether you hit the mark or not. During the Texas revolution, Colonel James Walker Fannin, Jr. used this phrase but he never got much of a chance to make the kicks. On Palm Sunday, 1836, Walker and more than 400 of his men were shot down in cold blood by Mexican soldiers, after having surrendered a week earlier. Also shoot the moon, which is a reference to the domino game called "moon."

GO WITH GOD Vaya con dios

GOAL LINE Alumni line, according to Darrell Royal

GOING WELL Going great guns ❑ the cotton's high ❑ runnin' with the big dogs

GOLIAD, TEXAS Pronounced go lee add, this town in South

95

Texas is referred to as Fort Defiance by some old-timers. During the Texas revolution, Colonel James Walker Fannin, Jr. christened the Goliad mission Fort Defiance. His defiance didn't last long since Fannin and more than 400 of his men were captured and executed.

GOD Sky King ❑ Foreman of the Grandest Jury ❑ the Judge

GOOD If it was any better, I couldn't stand it and the sheriff wouldn't allow it ❑ anything that good ought to be against the law ❑ crackerjack ❑ bueno ❑ couldn't beat it with a stick ❑ top drawer ❑ esta bien *See also Delicious*

GOOD-BYE Adios ❑ so long, Red Ryder

GOOD DAY A nekkid-on-the-back-porch sort of day. There is an old saying in Texas that goes, "As long as there's a God in heaven, a Democrat in the Governor's mansion and a pulse in my arm, it's a good day." The saying was most popular in the days when the democratic party had a choke hold on Texas.

GOOD ENOUGH *See Acceptable, Adequate*

GOOD GRIEF Good honk

GOOD LOSER You can be a good loser but you should bleed a little, which was a favorite saying of former TCU Coach Dutch Meyer.

GOOD LUCK Hope all your kids are born nekkid ❑ keep your wagon between the ditches ❑ may all your cattle be fat, your wife skinny, and your kids obedient ❑ draw a good bull, referring to rodeo cowboys drawing for which bull they will ride. The better the bull the better the chance to make a good ride.

GOOD MORNING Buenas dias (also used for good day)

GOOD NIGHT Buenas noches

GOOD PERSON He'll stand without hitching. Texan John Nance Garner once said to the Reverend Billy Graham, "I hear you will stand without hitching. I am glad of that. Out in my country a cow horse wasn't worth a damn unless he would do that. Most of the time there wasn't anything to hitch him to." Garner's country was South Texas, in and around Uvalde. ❑ pick of the litter ❑ he don't have any faults God would pay attention to or the Devil would be interested in ❏ if he was a dog, someone would a stole him when he was a pup ❏ he sits tall in the saddle ❏ he can march in my parade ❏ he's the best that ever drew a breath ❏ he's an uncommon common man *See also One of a Kind, Trustworthy, Dog, Good*

GOOD SHOT Could shoot the eyes out of a mosquito at 250 yards. Almost any small critter could be substituted for mosquito. Also, the distance can be raised or lowered depending on your mood. *See also Aim, Good*

GOSSIP Moccasin talk ❏ horseback opinion ❏ scandalization ❏ fence talk, referring to neighbors gossiping about other neighbors over the back fence

GOSSIPY Loose tongued ❏ leaky mouthed ❏ she'll peel your eye and bend your ear back ❏ like two geese on a new feed ground

GOT AWAY Slipped the bridle or noose

GOVERNMENT Pronounced gover-mint ❏ the public teat, which implies it is there to nurse everyone ❏ John Nance Garner said, "That govern-ment governs best which governs least."

GOVERNMENT EMPLOYEE He nurses on the public teat ❏ he dips his finger in the public lard bucket ❏ he cooks with public grease

GRANDE SALINE, TEXAS This small town in Van Zandt county is often referred to as Salt City because a considerable portion of America's salt supplies are produced in the area.

GRATEFUL Much obliged ❏ you've got a good turn coming whenever you need it

GRAVE Cold storage

GRAVY Texas butter, which is gravy made by throwing some flour into steak grease and letting it brown. When it begins to bubble you add some water and stir till thick and delicious.

GRAVY, POOR You couldn't cut it with a Bowie knife

GRAY HEADED Blooming for the retirement pasture

GREEN As fresh grass ❏ as mint money

GRIN, WIDE As wide as the wave in a slop bucket

GRINNING Like a possum eating persimmons (or yellow jackets) ❏ like a mule eating prickly pear cactus ❏ like a small dog with a big bone

GRIP Like vice grip pliers ❏ like a snappin' turtle

GROUND BALL Worm killer

GROWING Beginning to feather out ❏ gettin' some size to him ❏ blossoming out

GRUENE, TEXAS Pronounced Green, a small town Northeast of New Braunfels. The local honky tonk, Gruene Hall, bills itself as the oldest in Texas.

GUARANTEED You can bet your bottom dollar ❏ lead pipe cinch ❏ you can bet the ranch and all the cattle (mineral rights) on it *See also Certain, Reliable, Trustworthy*

GUITAR Texans pronounce it get-tar ❏ getfiddle ❏ getbucket

GUITAR PLAYER Picker, picker and grinner ❏ Texan Waylon Jennings claims he plays a "stuttering guitar."

GUILTY As sin ❏ got caught with his paw in the cookie jar ❏ caught red handed

GULLIBLE Man is the only animal that can be skinned more than once ❏ she believes all of the people all of the time

GUN Equalizer. When Samuel Colt invented his famous Colt 45 shootin' iron it is said he made all men equal.

H

HAPPY — as a dog with two tails

HAIR CUT Roach your mane

HAIR, MESSY Looks like you combed your hair with a skillet

HAIRY Big crop of locks ❑ sportin' enough hair to braid a well rope

HAIRY CHEST Got plenty of man feathers ❑ got enough hair on his chest to weave a Comanche blanket

HAND Mitt ❑ paw ❑ lunch hook

HANDLE The business end ❑ blister end. You don't wear blisters on your hand holding a hammer by the head.

HANDLE CAREFULLY Like you were trying to wrap a Vinagaroon scorpion in tissue paper ❑ like you were trying to put braces on a rattlesnake's fangs ❑ like you were trying to tie a bow tie on a bear ❑ like you were carrying an egg in a teaspoon

HANDWRITING, ILLEGIBLE Chicken (or hen) scratching

HANDY As a braille bible to a blind preacher ❑ as a pocket on a shirt ❑ as a heart transplant ❑ as sliced bread ❑ as electricity ❑ as a milkin' machine ❑ as a remote control on a television ❑ as a zipper on your jeans ❑ as the top rail on a fence ❑ as a ladder on a windmill ❑ as a cattle guard, which was an opening in a gate protected by a series of pipes spaced far enough apart to prevent livestock from crossing. You save a lot of time not having to open and close gates so they are very handy.

HANG ON Like a scared kid to a mother's skirt tail ❑ like an Indian to a red-eye jug ❑ like a tick to a dog's ear ❑ like a snappin' turtle, which, if legend is correct, means you'll hang on till it thunders. *See also Tight Grip*

HAPPY Tickled half to death ❑ content with all creation ❑ absolutely edified ❑chock full of glee ❑ doing double back flips ❑ swelled up with elation *See also Elated*

HAPPY AS A kid on Santa's lap ❑ as a kid pullin' a pup's ears ❑ as a pig (or hog) in slop ❑ as an armadillo digging grub worms ❑ as a hound in a tannery ❑ a horned frog on a red ant hill ❑ as a kid in a candy store ❑ as a pig in a peach orchard ❑ as a pup with two tails

101

HARD AS The hubs of hell ❑ as a frozen turtle shell ❑ as nails ❑ as a frozen worm ❑ as bois d' arc wood ❑ as an iron horseshoe ❑ as bricks ❑ as a rock

HARD SURFACE So hard a cat couldn't scratch it, which is based on the general belief that a cat can scratch almost anything, except a diamond ring

HARD TO DO As eating red beans with a pitch fork ❑ as wearing out a crow bar (or ax) ❑ as scratching your ear with your elbow ❑ as putting spilled toothpaste back into the tube ❑ as pushing a wheelbarrow with rope handles ❑ as getting all the coons in the county up one tree ❑ as threading a needle in the dark ❑ as putting boots on over wet socks ❑ as puttin' a nylon sock on a wet foot ❑ as catching a sand bass in a sock ❑ as cutting a hog with a dull knife ❑ as dodging rice at a wedding ❑ as flying with water wings ❑ as scratching a porcupine's back ❑ In his diary entry for August 19th, 1935 Hondo Crouch, former owner of Luckenback, Texas said, "The world's greatest thing is to be simple but it is so hard to be simple." *See also Difficult, Tough Job*

HARD TO FIND As a snake's (or worm's) shadow ❑ as a water lily in a desert ❑ as an elephant in El Paso

HARD WORKER Works as hard as a cold nosed bird dog ❑ he's hell on boot leather and cheap saddles ❑ works from can't see to can't see, which refers to the farmer or rancher who begins work before sunup and works till after sundown. The farmer who oversleeps and doesn't get to work until after dawn works from can see till can't see.

HARMLESS Toothless ❑ his horns have been sawed off ❑ his bark is worse than his bite ❑ wouldn't harm a sand flea ❑ he's gum mouthed, which implies he has lost all his teeth and thus his bite wouldn't hurt ❑ it's no skin off your moccasins (or boots)

HARMLESS AS A bowl of oatmeal ❑ as a shadow ❑ as an empty paper bag

HASTE *See Hurry*

HAT Stetson or John B, which are references to John B. Stetson who is credited with inventing the western-style cowboy hat, even though he was a Yankee ❑ war bonnet ❑ sombrero ❑ portable feed bag, which refers to cowboys sometimes using their hats to feed the horses

HAT, CROCKED Sloshed on

HAT, LARGE Big enough to shade you and your horse ❑ big enough to catch a bobcat under ❑ a ten-gallon hat. The term gallon is actually derived from the Spanish "galon" which were decorations Mexican vaquereos liked to wear on their hats and Texas cowboys followed suit. Some people credit Sam Houston with first using the phrase "hand me my ten-galon hat," which meant he had ten galons on his hat, not that it would hold ten gallons of liquid. If the truth were known, the biggest hat in Texas wouldn't hold much more than five gallons.

HAT, SMALL A stingy brim ❑ wouldn't shade half a head ❑ you couldn't use that to water a pissant, which refers to cowboys often using their hat to hold water for their horses

HAT, TIGHT You'll have to stick your head in a boot jack to get it off

HAUGHTY Too big for his britches ❑ never learned to swim cause he thinks he can walk on water if he ever falls in *See also Aloof*

HAZARDOUS As wading in quicksand over hell ❑ as grabbing a branding iron by the business end, which is the end that gets hot in the fire ❑ as a rattlesnake (or a bobcat) in your bedroll ❑ as a rattlesnake on your running board ❑ as stomping on a red ant hill ❑ as milking a wild longhorn cow ❑ as hollerin' "snake" at a quilting bee (or church revival) ❑ as kicking a loaded polecat ❑ as trying to separate two cats tied together by their tail ❑ as a tail hold on a grizzly bear, longhorn bull, wildcat, or polecat ❑ as trying to brand a mule's ear ❑ as trying to ride a cyclone with the bridle off *See also Dangerous*

HEADACHE Feel like an anvil was introduced to my noggin ❑ if a horse's head hurt this bad we'd have to shoot him ❑ I'd have to be dead three days before my head would stop hurting

HEADSTRONG Bull headed ❑ bull necked

HEALTH, GOOD Fit as a fiddle ❑ feeling frisky ❑ feel like I was raised in a hothouse (or incubator)

HEALTH, POOR Feel (or look) like death warmed over ❑ he'd have to get better to die *See also Ill, Gravely*

HEALTHY TOWN We had to hire a stranger to shoot himself so we could start a cemetery, which is a favorite saying of the folks in Van Horn, Texas

HEARING, IMPAIRED He's deaf in one ear and hard of hearing in the other ❑ he couldn't hear a gin whistle if he was sitting on it when it went off

HEART Ticker ❑ blood pump ❑ Cupid's target, which refers to Cupid shooting arrows into someone's heart

HEART BROKEN She threw a rock through the windowpane of my heart ❑ he threw a baseball through the window of my heart ❑ she broke my heart so bad it took two bottles of whiskey to splint it, implying someone went on a drunk after being jilted ❑ my heart was broken into more pieces than an empty milk bottle dropped on a concrete sidewalk ❑ my heart's so broken that all the spit and half the baling wire in Texas couldn't put it back together again

HEARTS (PLAYING CARD SUIT) Valentines

HEAVEN Texas. It has been said that when Texans get to heaven they have to be chained up to keep them from trying to go back home. Native daughter Tanya Tucker said it best in her song Texas When I die. She sang, "When I die I don't know if I'll go to heaven 'cause I don't know if they let cowboys in. If they don't just let me go to Texas 'cause it's as close as I've been." Other Texas phrases for heaven include the last roundup ❑ sweet by and by ❑ happy hunting grounds ❑ Sky Range ❑ Angeltown, Spiritville ❑ the Golden Range ❑ God's South Forty

HEAVY As a full-grown anvil ❑ as the anchor from the USS Texas ❑ as a frozen bear ❑ as the front end of a John Deer ❑ as a tow sack full of ball bearings ❑ enough to flatten wagon springs so much the running boards would be scraping ground ❑ as an elephant tusk with the elephant attached

HELL Fire and brimstone range ❑ the devil's playground ❑ Satan's suite

HELLO Texans say heidi or howdy, pardner

HELP Lend a hand ❑ take a turn ❑ turn a hand ❑ a lot of hands make work light ❑ catch my saddle, which was a phrase often used by a cowboy when he got thrown by an unruly horse and needed help in catching the horse so his saddle could be saved

HELP HER UP Tail her up, which is derived from grabbing the tail of an old cow and helping her to get to her feet

HELP, UNWANTED Too many cooks spoil the chili (or stew)

HELPLESS As a mute in handcuffs ❑ as a cow in quicksand ❑ as a cat up an East Texas pine tree ❑ as a grasshopper (or worm) on a red ant bed ❑ as a fox in a forest fire ❑ hog tied ❑ couldn't do nothing but let the mainspring run down, which means had to let events run their course

HENPECKED He jumps when she hollers frog ❑ steers clear of the henhouse so the roosters won't chase him ❑ his wife even complains when he makes too much noise in the kitchen

HICKEY Love bite ❑ monkey bite ❑ passion strawberry ❑ blood blister

HICO, TEXAS Pronounced Hi-co, never Hick-o, a small South Texas town.

HIDDEN A hawk couldn't find it on a clear day ❑ an airport security dog couldn't find it in a week

HIGH As the top of an East Texas pine tree ❑ enough to see the lights of Palestine (as in Palestine, Texas.)

HIGHWAY PATROLMAN Mustanger, which refers to Highway Patrolmen driving the new, very fast, Ford Mustangs so they can keep up with speeders.

HILLBILLY Hick ❑ hayseed ❑ cedar chopper ❑ yokel

HINDER Put a stob in his spokes ❑ chock his wheels ❑ loosen his cinch ❑ put a little sugar in his gas tank ❑ put a stob in his exhaust pipe

HIT Whallop ❑ whomp ❑ lambast ❑ crack his head ❑ give him a stinging lick ❑ rattle his teeth ❑ knock his gizzard loose ❑ tattoo him ❑ slap him a new hat size

HIT HARD It'll take two and a half days to get his breath back ❏ so hard he'll have to look out through an ear hole to see anything ❏ whallop him hard enough to knock his head down into his jeans so he'll have to open his zipper to peek out

HOE Cotton chopper ❏ weed killer

HOE USER Hoer, (think about it)

HOG Slop chaser ❏ rooter ❏ ham (or breakfast) on the hoof

HOLD ON *See Hang On*

HOLE IN A SOCK Grass hole, so a toe can come out for grass, don't you know

HOLLERED Like a stuck pig ❏ like a baby pig caught under a gate ❏ like a cat shot with a boot jack, which is rumored to be one of the leading causes of death among Texas house cats

HOMELESS As a poker chip.

HOMELY As a buck-toothed buzzard ❏ when she was a baby her daddy had to tie a T-bone steak around her neck to get the dogs to play with her ❏ hate to have a litter of 'em ❏ has to sneak up on a sink, a dipper, or a glass to get a drink of water ❏ has to sneak up on a mirror to fix her hair ❏ she ain't exactly a parlor orna-ment ❏ a hoss fly wouldn't look at her twice ❏ her hus-band would rather stay home than kiss her good-bye ❏ her face would look good in a bri-dle *See also Ugly*

HONEST As the day is long ❏ as a looking glass ❏ as a mirror image

HONEST PERSON As the horse between his legs ❏ square shooter ❏ straight shooter ❏ his word is as bind-ing as a hangman's knot ❏ you could shoot dice with him over the phone

HOPELESS Ain't got a prayer ❏ as whipping a dead horse ❏ following a cold trail ❏ you can't put out a barn fire with a dipper full of water ❏ buckin' a losing game ❏ as trying to fill up a bottomless pit ❏ as arguing with the angel of death

HORNED TOAD Horny toad ❏ horned frog. The truth is these little prehistoric-looking critters are not any kind of frog or toad, they are lizards.

HORSE, CUTTING *See Cutting Horse*

HORSE, GOOD BUCKER Gut twister ❑ bucks like he's a balloon with the plug out, which refers to the wild motion a balloon makes when the air is escaping ❑ could pitch off a plaster saddle

HORSE, MEAN He'll kick you into a funeral home ❑ he'll stick a hoof in your hip pocket ❑ he'll kick you high enough for St. Peter to brand your backside ❑ he'll pitch you so high an eagle will build a nest in your back pocket before you come down

HORSE, POOR Two-bit nag ❑ he don't do nothing but burn hay ❑ he'd rather eat a biscuit than run like Sea Biscuit

HORSE, REAR END Get up end, referring to the fact that a horse uses its rear legs to get himself up

HORSE, TAME Could stake him to a hairpin (or toothpick)

HORSE, UNBROKEN Bronc ❑ mustang

HOSPITAL Sick pen. On many ranches a separate pen was maintained where sick and diseased cattle were kept away from the healthy stock.

HOT The cows are shaded up ❑ he's spitting brown steam, which is a reference to tobacco juice spitters ❑ had to feed the chickens cracked ice to keep them from laying hard boiled eggs ❑ blisters are poppin' out on my boots ❑ the potatoes are baking in the ground ❑ the corn's poppin' on the stalk ❑ makes hell look like an ice plant

HOT AS A burning boot (or stump) ❑ as high school love ❑ as honeymoon sheets ❑ as a Cadillac bumper in July ❑ as a two-dollar pistol on Saturday night ❑ as a bed of mesquite coals in a BBQ joint ❑ as a fresh forged horseshoe ❑ as road tar in July ❑ as a Palacios parking lot ❑ as a fox in a forest fire ❑ as a cafe griddle ❑ as a depot stove ❑ as a June bride in a feather bed ❑ as hell's door handle, the hinges of hell, the hubs of hell, hell with the blower on, or the devil's roasting prong

HOT ENOUGH To boil mercury ❑ to roast marshmallows on the dash board of a pickup truck ❑ to boil spit on a sidewalk ❑ to melt the mercury in a thermometer ❑ to melt leather and it still on the cow ❑ to wither a fence post ❑ to sunburn a horned toad ❑ to buckle pavement on the interstate ❑ to hard boil an egg in a stock tank ❑ to fry an egg on the fender of your pickup

HOUSE Casa ❑ haciendo ❑ wickiup ❑ wigwam

HOUSTON Bagdad on the Bayou ❑ Bayou City ❑ Astrodome city ❑ Also the first word spoken from the surface of the moon. When the first spacecraft touched down, Neil Armstrong radioed, "Houston, Tranquility base here. The Eagle has landed."

HOW ARE YOU How ya' doing ❑ como esta

HUGE *See Large*

HUGGING They were so twisted up together you couldn't tell where the boy stopped off and the girl commenced

HUMBLE It's hard to be humble when you're from Texas.

HUMBLED He's got his hat in his hand ❑ he got knocked down a peg or two *See also Ego, Deflated*

HUMID I'm sweating setting ❑ humidity higher than an owl's IQ ❑ my upper lip is mildewing, which is a reference to people generally

sweating on their upper lip when it's very humid

HUNGRY Feeling gant ❑ my belly button is rubbing a blister on my backbone ❑ my stomach thinks my throat has been cut ❑ could eat the blades off a windmill ❑ could eat a handful of ball bearings ❑ could eat a saddle blanket after a day's riding ❑ just fry the skillet and throw away the handle *See also Starving*

HUNGRY AS a goat on a concrete pasture ❑ a coyote with a toothache ❑ as a woodpecker with a sore pecker or a headache ❑ as a wolf in a drought

HUNGRY ENOUGH TO Eat a chicken, feathers, beak, cluck, and all ❑ to eat a horned frog backwards. If you look at a horned frog, you 'll notice the horns point to the rear, so he would be hard to eat backwards unless you were very hungry ❑ to eat the skirts off a Mexican saddle ❑ to eat a longhorn steer, hide, horn, hooves, and beller

HURRY Spur the flanks ❑ get the lead out ❑ come a whipping ❑ fan the fat (use the spurs) ❑ jingle your spurs ❑ rattle your hocks ❑ ride like a deputy sheriff ❑ lay the quirt to 'em ❑

get into high gear ❏ like a
house afire ❏ don't spare the
horses ❏ use that rowel ❏
come at a double trot ❏ pop
some leather ❏ hurry 'cause
early don't last long ❏ don't
spare the horses ❏ flap your
chaps

HURTING Punishing, as in
"I wore my boots without socks
and the blisters that were
raised are sure punishing
me."

HUSBAND Running mate ❏
my bigger half ❏ the ball and
chain ❏ warden ❏ my kid's
daddy ❏ the old man ❏ honey
doer

HYPOCRITE Most of his
religion is in his wife's name

I

INDEPENDENT — as a dog on ice

I DECLARE I swan ❑ I'll be darn

IDEA A young impulse

IDEA, GOOD Neon light idea ❑ an idea that was cooked on the front burner

IDENTICAL Spittin' image of ❑ dead ringer for ❑ scissored from the same piece of cloth *See also Alike*

IDENTIFIED Read his iron ❑ checked his dog tags ❑ read his scars

IDIOT Chuckleheaded ❑ he couldn't get a prostitute a date on a troop train ❑ his IQ is equal to one-half his hat (or boot) size ❑ churnhead ❑ you could keep him busy for half a day by asking him to find the top of a ball bearing or the corner in a round room *See also Dumb, Ignorant, Stupid*

IDLE About one-half as busy as a ghost town undertaker or telephone operator ❑ got nothing to do but stand around and scratch his seat ❑ a man who ain't doin' nothing ain't making mistakes or learning ❑ just standing around with his teeth in his mouth ❑ as much to do as a hibernating bear

IF If a hog had wings he'd be an eagle ❑ if a pig had wings, he'd be a chicken hawk ❑ if a frog had wings he wouldn't bump his behind when he jumped ❑ if ifs and buts were candy and nuts what a merry Christmas we'd have, as Texan Don Meredith was fond of saying on Monday Night Football

IGNORANT He's got the IQ of hanging beef ❑ he's a might shy in schoolhouse learning ❑ don't know cream from cantaloup ❑ don't know his hiney from a gin whistle ❑ don't know rock salt from bee honey ❑ couldn't find an egg under a sitting hen ❑ couldn't dig fish bait in a worm farm ❑ don't have the sense God gave a screwdriver, goose, grasshopper, saddle horn, or sack of flour ❑ he'd play Russian roulette with a single-shot derringer ❑ his mind is always in a mist *See also Dumb, Idiot, Stupid*

IGNORE Like a bus driver does a hitchhiker ❑ pay him no never mind ❑ don't take any stock in that ❑ let a sleeping dog lie

ILL Took sick ❑ green around the gills ❑ riding the bed wagon, which refers to cowboys who became sick on a

113

trail drive and had to ride the bed wagon rather than their horse *See also Ill, Gravely , Look Sick, Sick*

ILL, GRAVELY You better warm up the hearse ❏ he's so far under the weather that the only way back is through heaven (or hell), which infers someone is going to die and the only way to return is to be reincarnated ❏ he paid the wrong preacher ❏ he's got one boot in a pine box ❏ his last hope is a faith healer *See also Health, Poor*

ILLEGAL On the hot side of the law ❏ ain't square (or plumb) with the statues

ILLEGITIMATE He's a descendent of a long line his mother heard in a honky tonk ❏ brush colt ❏ camp meeting baby ❏ woods colt ❏ oil field colt ❏ the baby didn't come early, the wedding came late ❏ the parents ate supper before they said grace ❏ the parents planted the corn before they built the fence

ILLITERATE He can't read writing or write reading ❏ if he knew two languages he'd be bi-illiterate ❏ if you write him a letter, write slow 'cause he can't read fast

IMAGINATIVE Imagineer, which is how Hondo Crouch described himself

IMITATING Walking in someone else's boots (or tracks)

IMMATURE Acts his hat size instead of his IQ ❏ half baked ❏ a fuzzy thinker ❏ happiest when he's playing with a string of spools. On the frontier, mothers tied empty thread spools together as a toy for the kids

IMMORAL Suffers from a lapse in the code of decency ❏ never could decipher the code of ethics ❏ got leaky morals ❏ got the morals of an alley cat

IMPATIENT Chomping at the bit ❏ fighting the bit. Generally speaking, a horse that is fighting the bit is either ready to run or ready for you to get off

IMPORTANT PERSON Big frog in the pond ❏ tall hog at the trough ❏ tush hog ❏ big buck at the lick ❏ when he does something, it sets folks' tongues to wagging, which is a reference to people talking about anything an important person happens to do ❏ his name spends as much time on the front page of the paper as

114

the name of the paper *See also Boss, Leader*

IMPOSSIBLE You can't sweep sunshine off the porch ❑ you can't hitch a horse with a coyote ❑ two pounds of manure won't fit in a one-pound sack ❑ can't make a silk purse out of a sow's ear ❑ can't drop a cat on his back ❑ can't dip well water with a tea strainer ❑ can't teach a longhorn steer to sing the Aggie war hymn ❑ can't pull a ten-horse load with four Shetland ponies ❑ can't put a duck egg in an eagle's nest and get an eagle ❑ can't scratch a wet match ❑ can't pole vault with a pitchfork ❑ crops don't grow by moonlight ❑ can't throw a big loop with a small rope ❑ as finding a horse thief in heaven ❑ even the smallest anvil won't float ❑ Texans usually take the attitude that nothing is impossible, but some things take a little longer than others to get done

IMPOTENT He's ain't got no lead in his pencil ❑ he ain't got no sting in his stinger

IMPRACTICAL As carrying a settin' hen to Sunday school

IMPROBABLE It would take a big woman to weigh a ton ❑ it

would take a big biscuit to weigh a pound

IMPULSIVE He jumps at the drop of a hat, anybody's hat

IN AGREEMENT We're singing off the same song sheet ❑ singing off the same page in the hymnal ❑ hitched to the same plow (or wagon)

IN CONTROL He's holding all the aces ❑ he's got the bull by the horns ❑ he's got the key to the gate ❑ he's got the cattle gathered and penned

IN DANGER You're flying with one wing ❑ you're dancing in a mine field ❑ you're dancing with the devil and they are playing his tune ❑ you're not only behind the eight ball, you're behind the whole rack ❑ you're juggling hand grenades and the pins are comin' loose ❑ you're walking a high wire and the net has a big hole in it ❑ you're tied to the tracks and the train is on time *See also Dangerous, In Trouble, Trouble*

IN LOVE Got her brand on my heart ❑ got Cupid's cramps ❑ wearing Cupid's hobbles ❑ got calico fever ❑ she's got my stake pin in her court ❑ his heart is connected to his hand, implying that he fell in love when they first held hands

IN POOR CONDITION It'll take a faith healer to repair it

IN THE REAR Eatin' drag dust, referring to riding drag on a trail drive

IN TROUBLE Your biscuits are burning ❏ staring down the barrel of a real dilemma ❏ you parachuted into a volcano ❏ holding a pair of threes against a full house ❏ in a wild bull's pasture without a tree ❏ up a creek without a paddle and the boat is leaking ❏ up the range without a horse ❏ bucking in the rodeo without a pickup man ❏ you've kicked over a hornet's nest ❏ the slop hit the fan, implying that slop would be spread everywhere ❏ in a pickle ❏ the deck's stacked against you ❏ the fat is in the fire ❏ church is out ❏ on the horns of a dilemma ❏ it's third and long ❏ dippin' snuff out of a can of rat poison ❏ in a hell of a fix. While serving as Secretary of War for the Republic of Texas, Thomas J. Rusk is credited with saying, "We are in a hell of a fix. Let's go to the saloon, have a drink, and fight our way out of it." *See also Trouble, In Danger*

INCENTIVE Added money. In a rodeo the purses are made up of contestant entry fees and "added money" contributed by the rodeo committee ❏ boot, as "I'll throw in a set of new tires to boot if you'll buy my old pickup."

INCLINED Got a mind to, as in "I'm got a mind to go along with you on that."

INCLINED, SOMEWHAT Got half a mind to, as in "I've got half a mind to paint the barn and surprise the missus."

INCLUDE Deal me in ❏ set another place at the dinner table

INCOMPATIBLE As a 45 shell in a shotgun ❏ as water and oil

INCOMPETENT He couldn't drive a nail into a snow bank with a sledge hammer ❏ couldn't ride a nightmare ❏ couldn't split enough firewood to fry an egg ❏ couldn't cut a lame cow from the shade of a mesquite tree

INCONSISTENT Runs hot and cold ❏ king of the crawfishers ❏ wishy washy

INCONSPICUOUS As a blanket Indian on a reservation ❏

as a tree in a forest, as a cow chip in a pasture ❑ as a peach (or pecan) on a tree

INCORRECT Barking up the wrong tree ❑ saddling the wrong horse ❑ hitching the team to the wrong wagon ❑ chopping on the wrong tree ❑ sawing the wrong limb ❑ cutting (or skinning) the wrong cat *See also Mistaken, Wrong*

INDEBTED TO Beholding to ❑ I'd rather owe it to you than to beat you out of it

INDECISIVE He's like a grasshopper, liable to jump one way as another ❑ he don't know whether to fish or cut bait ❑ don't know whether to ride or rope ❑ he don't know whether to brand or go bowling

INDELIBLE Tattooed on ❑ branded on

INDEPENDENT As a dog (or hog) on ice ❑ keeps his forked end down (stands on his own two feet) ❑ takes no sass but sassparilla ❑ saddles his own horse ❑ rides his own trail ❑ totes her own skillet ❑ paddles his own canoe or rows his own boat ❑ cooks his own beans (or chili) ❑ stews in his own broth ❑ rolls his own loop ❑ makes his own gravy

INDIAN Hair raiser ❑ whiskey warrior ❑ land moccasin, as opposed to a water moccasin, which is a snake ❑ buffalo hunter ❑ barebacker, referring to the fact that Indians didn't need saddles to be expert horsemen

INDICATIVE If it looks like manure, smells like manure, and tastes like manure, it's probably manure ❑ where there's smoke there's fire ❑ where there's cows there's cow chips ❑ the tongue always seeks the tooth that hurts ❑ if the saddle squeaks, it ain't paid for, which refers to cowboys buying their saddles on time. The leather wouldn't be broken in fully and stop squeaking before the bill was paid off. ❑ In the oilpatch, indicative is "if it winks, it'll screw." Wink, in this case, is the very first little turn of a tight bolt. When you get that first little wink you know you can unscrew the entire bolt.

INDIFFERENT He don't give didly squat

INDISCREET He'll talk ropes in the house of a man who was hanged

INDOORS You can't get rained on indoors. Bum Phillips believed so strongly in that principal that he wouldn't wear his hat when the Oilers played at home inside the Astrodome.

INEBRIATED *See Intoxicated, Drunk*

INEPT He tried to drown himself in a shower ❏ he'd walk himself to death in a revolving door ❏ only opens his mouth to change feet ❏ couldn't swallow his own spit ❏ couldn't spit over his chin ❏ if he had to go into a battle of wits, he'd have to go unarmed ❏ he walks around with his zipper unbuttoned, which can be traced to Lyndon Johnson. He once said of his staff, "They aren't walking around with their zippers unbuttoned," but he didn't explain how you unbutton a zipper.

INEVITABLE The girls get better looking when it's almost closing time ❏ you give a dance you gotta pay the band ❏ you might as well take the bull by the tail and face the situation ❏ a fox will fool with chickens till he feels buckshot in his behind ❏ you got to play the hand you're dealt ❏ if he's a rooster, he'll crow ❏ if he's a dog he'll bark and bite ❏ every turkey has his Thanksgiving ❏ a horse's tail will catch cockleburs ❏ a

bird in the hand leads to messy fingers ❏ chickens will come home to roost sooner or later ❏ what goes around comes around

INEVITABLE, ALMOST Sunshine always follows a storm, unless the storm was at night

INEXPERIENCED Green broke filly ❏ still wet behind the ears ❏ bench warmer ❏ so green he could hide in a lettuce patch ❏ there are only three things he can do and all of them are nothing *See also Rookie, Tenderfoot*

INITIAL *See First*

INJURED Took hurt ❏ the doctor said not to lift anything heavier than a biscuit or a nightgown ❏ my gears are out of mesh ❏ my dauber's dented ❏ feel like I was booted over a seven-foot branding coral fence ❏ crippled up ❏ stove up ❏ got a broken spoke ❏ feel like I was eaten by a coyote and dumped over a cliff

INJURED, SLIGHTLY I'm cut up some but I ain't gushing blood ❏ hurtin' some but it's not as bad as rivet burns, which refers to the rivets on a pair of blue jeans. If you sit too close to a fire while wearing jeans, the rivets will get very hot. When you stand up you get burned in places that are hard to scratch when they start healing.

INNOCENT As a newborn colt, lamb, calf, or armadillo ❏ as little Red Riding Hood

INNOVATIVE "If you want to catch a mouse you got to make a noise like a cheese." So said Texan Charles Tandy, founder of Tandy Corporation.

INSANE Slipped a cog ❏ snapped a link in his trace chain ❏ touched in the head ❏ addled in his thought box ❏ a little shy in the hat size ❏ if you were going to drive him crazy, it would be a short trip ❏ he's cross threaded ❏ there's a bug in his program ❏ got a slip in his differential, one of his axles is bent *See also Crazy*

INSIGNIFICANT The small end of nothing whittled down to a point ❏ chicken feed ❏ small potatoes ❏ just one blade on the windmill ❏ don't amount to a hill of beans ❏ just a drop in the bucket (or Gulf of Mexico) ❏ as a minnow in a stock tank ❏ nothing to write home to mother about ❏ just one post in the XIT fence line. The three million acre

XIT ranch, once located in the Texas panhandle, had hundreds of miles of fence and thousands of fence posts which meant each one, in itself, was insignificant *See XIT*

INSIGNIFICANT PERSON Just a small spoke in a big wheel ❏ just one more hand on the range ❏ he don't drive the train or blow the whistle ❏ a little frog in a big pond

INSULT If you were mine, I'd trade you for a flea bitten old hound dog and then shoot the dog ❏ she don't sweat much for a fat woman ❏ Texan Hugh Roy Cullen said, "Don't give anyone reason to feel insulted, and don't never take an insult."

INTELLIGENCE Uses his brain to keep blisters off his feet ❏ got more facts than a mail order catalog ❏ if you don't know the difference, it don't make any difference ❏ knows better than to get off a swimming horse and grab him by the tail. In swimming a river with a horse, the intelligent rider will slid off to the side and hold on the saddle horn while helping the horse kick. This method allows the cowboy to easily swing back into the saddle when the river is crossed. On the other hand,

119

if you hold onto the horses tail and let him tow you across the river, he will probably run off when he gets to the other side, leaving you to shake yourself and walk home. *See also Smart*

INTELLIGENCE, AVERAGE He knows enough not to wet on an electric fence ❑ knows enough to come in out of the rain ❑ knows enough to pour rainwater out of a boot ❑ on a good day he can tell a mule from a racehorse

INTEND Aim to, as in "I aim to get the fence mended one of these days."

INTERCEPT Head 'em off at the pass

INTERFERING You're dipping your quill in my ink bottle ❑ you're branding my cows ❑ you're messing with what comes under the heading of my business ❑ you're hanging your wash on my line ❑ you're tryin' to put your leg in my shorts ❑ you're dippin' snuff out a my can

INTERMITTENT On and off like a firefly's light ❑ on and off like a refrigerator light

INTERRUPT Another county was heard from ❑ horn in

INTIMIDATE I'll kick your butt so high you'll have to unbutton your Levis to tell if it's day or night ❑ I'm gonna knock you so far into the ground you'll take root and sprout ❑ read him the riot act ❑ melt his backbone ❑ tie a knot in his pistol barrel

INTIMIDATED As an oilman in a banker's office ❑ as a hen in a coyote den ❑ Richard "Racehorse" Haynes, one of the most famous Texas lawyers of all time, once said, "..I have never been intimidated since I was a pimple-faced kid on Iwo Jima, and I don't intend to be intimidated again." A lot of Texans feel the same way.

INTOXICATED Knee-walking, snot slinging drunk ❑ he's floored and frenzied ❑ he couldn't see through a ladder with two tries ❑ couldn't hit the ground with his hat in four tries *See also Drunk*

INVESTIGATE Take a look see ❑ check his herd to see if your brand shows up

INVINCIBLE He's bulletproof ❑ he's armor plated ❑ he's wearin' a blacksmith suit, which is a suit of armor

INVOLVED In the hunt ❑ got his finger in the pie ❑ got his iron in the fire ❑ bogged in it all the way to his saddle skirts ❑ up to his eyeballs in it *See also Among*

INVOLVED DEEPLY He went whole hog

IRRATIONAL He took leave of what little sense he had

IRRESISTIBLE As jackrabbit liver is to a channel cat

IRRELEVANT Nothing but squaw chatter ❑ horse feathers

IRREVOCABLE As a flushed toilet ❑ as a burned out light bulb ❑ as a castrated bull ❑ as a death sentence half an hour after the hanging

IRRITATED My stinger's out ❑ my dauber's down ❑ got a thorn in my paw ❑ gettin' ready to come apart at the seams ❑ got a burr under my saddle ❑ got a thorn in my side ❑ got my tail feathers ruffled *See also Angry, Mad*

IRRITATING Grates on my nerves ❑ cocks my pistol ❑ primes my stinger ❑ gets my dander up ❑ chaps my butt ❑sticks like a thorn in my short ribs

IT'S OVER That's the opry ❑ that's the ball game ❑ you might as well call the dogs and pour the coffee on the fire

J

JUMP — into bed together

JACK (PLAYING CARD)
Hooker ❑ junior

JAIL Hoosegow ❑ booby hatch
❑ calaboose ❑ clink ❑ pokey
❑ can ❑ juzgado

JAWS, STRONG Like a bolt
cutter ❑ like the beak of a
snappin' turtle

JEANS, TIGHT Look like
they were tattooed on ❑ looks
like she was melted down and
poured in them ❑ looks like
they were painted on ❑ it took
two hours of wiggling to get
'em on ❑ she'll have to bend a
crow bar gettin' 'em off

JILTED Her bass spit out the
hook ❑ dropped him like a hot
horseshoe ❑ changed everything about her but her name ❑
she's haunting my pillow ❑
dodged the ball and chain ❑
got over her in less than one
half the time you can hold a hot
branding iron ❑ she quit him
like a dead horse does a wagon

JOIN Put my marbles in with
yours ❑ crawl into the bedroll
❑ jump into bed together, as in
"We jumped into bed together
and opened a cafe" ❑ throw in
with ❑ stick your oar in his
pond ❑ tie in with ❑ fall in
with ❑ wiggle on in ❑ pick a
spot on the company stringer
❑ take a hand ❑ drop your

rope in with ❑ take off your
boots and wade on in ❑ throw
your sombrero (or hat) into the
ring ❑ mosey on up to the
trough

JOINED Welded fast together
❑ handcuffed, hitched, sol-
dered, or married to ❑
galvanized together

JOKED Fed 'em a load of corn
❑ scalped his goat

JOKER (PLAYING CARD)
Bloke ❑ bluke ❑ bug ❑ court
jester

JUDGE Hizoner ❑ statue
wrangler

JUDGEMENT, POOR He's
selling his horses to buy horse
feed ❑ he's buying feed for a
mechanical bull

JUKEBOX Cowboy stereo ❑
honky tonk angel's best
friend

JUMPED Quit the earth like a
dynamited stump ❑ like he got
a cattle prod caught in his cov-
eralls ❑ like a bull out a chute
No. 2 ❑ like a fish on a hook ❑
like a frog trapped under a
bucket ❑ like a frog's leg in a
frying pan ❑ like he sat down
on a hot horseshoe ❑ swallowed his head or sunfished,
which are terms associated

125

with a pitchin' horse that
jumps and turns from side to
side

JUMPS Like a whang-doodle,
which is a Texas-sized kan-
garoo-like animal with a
large flat tail. Its habitat is the
Palo Duro canyon area and its
tail allows the critter to jump
off the rim of the canyon and
make a nice soft landing
hundreds of feet below. The
whang-doodle is so rare, some
people consider it a mythical
critter.

JUMPY Fiddle footed ❑
horsey ❑ got a gut full of bed
springs ❑ dancin' like a bobber ❑ hearin' hoof beats ❑ as a
cat on ice ❑ got a frog in her
bra ❑ got a scorpion in his
shorts

JUNK Plunder

JUST ARRIVED Right fresh
from ❑ new to these parts ❑
just struck town

K

KEEPING BAD COMPANY — if you sleep with a dog you'll wake up with fleas

KEEP BUSY Hold your nose on the grindstone ❑ tend to your knitting

KEEP TRYING Church ain't over till the choir sings amen ❑ keep plugging ❑ keep shooting, you'll eventually hit something ❑ pitch till you win ❑ keep going till the cows come home (or till hell freezes over) ❑ keep plowin' till the mule dies or the ground freezes ❑ keep dealing ❑ even if you're down, you can still swing from the floor ❑ saddle sores eventually heal and only your best girlfriend will ever see the scars, which implies you should keep riding despite the pain of saddle sores *See also Persevere*

KEEPING BAD COMPANY If you bed down with hound dogs, you'll wake up with fleas ❑ if you make friends with the devil, you'll wind up on his prong

KID *See Child*

KIDDING Your shucking me ❑ pullin' my leg ❑ hoorahing me ❑ they're wetting in my boots and telling me it's raining ❑ rawhidding ❑ hurrahin' *See also Joked*

KILL Dry gulch ❑ blow out his lamp ❑ snuff out his candle ❑

rid the ground of his shadow ❑ shoot daylight into him, which means shoot a hole into him so daylight can get through ❑ pull him up by the roots ❑ give him a ticket for the hereafter then punch his ticket ❑ dispatch him to hell

KILLER Widow maker ❑ orphan maker ❑ home wrecker ❑ everything he touches turns to rigor mortis ❑ he didn't cut those notches in his gun for whittling practice

KIND Got a heart as big as all of Texas, Dallas, all outdoors, a watermelon, or a saddle blanket ❑ wouldn't hurt a flea (or chigger) ❑ got kindness enough to kill a cat

KIND OF Kind a like

KING (PLAYING CARD) Cowboy ❑ killer ❑ big bull

KNEES Prayer bones

KNIFE Pig sticker ❑ cowboy (or Texas) toothpick ❑ two blader, Bowie ❑ lock blade ❑ case knife ❑ pocket skewer

KNIFE, DULL You could ride all the way to town on the sharp side of the blade without a saddle or even a blanket

KNIFE, WITH ILLEGAL BLADE Dallas special ❑ Texas special

KNOCKED DOWN Dusted his pants

KNOCKED OUT Laid out cold as a wedge ❑ he dropped like an anvil fell on his head. Windmill wrench, cotton bale, tractor or most anything heavy can be substituted for anvil

KNOWLEDGEABLE Plenty savvy ❑ he didn't just come in on a load of firewood (wintertime) or cantaloups (summertime) ❑ knows how to stake a horse ❑ knows how to bait a hook ❑ knows more about it than a jackrabbit knows about running ❑ knows more about it than a whiteface calf knows about sucking ❑ what he don't know ain't worth learning. It was said of J. Frank Dobie that what he didn't know about longhorn cattle wasn't worth learning *See also Smart, Intelligence*

L

LEADER — tall dog in the pack

LACKING A bit shy ❏ on the stingy side

LADIES MAN Woman or skirt chaser ❏ could charm the pants off the Mona Lisa *See also Womanizer*

LAME Sorefooted ❏ short booted, which implies he's wearing boots that are too small which certainly causes sore feet

LAND A piece of ground ❏ a spread ❏ an acre accumulation

LAND, FERTILE You can plant a horseshoe nail and grow a horseshoe ❏ you could plant a penny and grow a copper tea kettle ❏ you could plant a nail and grow a crow bar ❏ you could plant some wind and grow a windmill ❏ you could plant a toothpick and grow a railroad tie

LAND, POOR God forsaken country ❏ you can't grow anything but broken dreams ❏ tumble weed territory ❏ can't grow anything but Johnson grass and jimson weed *See also Arid, Barren*

LAND, RICH As rich as the dirt in an old abandoned cow pen (or feed lot)

LANDSCAPING The bush bidness

LARGE A picture of that would weigh five pounds ❏ enough to store hay in ❏ enough to burn diesel, which refers to the days when anything that burned diesel was large, such as a truck or a tractor *See also Big*

LARGE AMOUNT A whole pocket full, a barrel full ❏ a wagon load ❏ right smart of, as in "He got a right smart of trouble from his mother-in-law" ❏ got more of those than hell has sinners or heaven has angels ❏ got more of those than there are liars in Texas

LARGE PERSON She fell down and rocked herself to sleep trying to get up ❏ she shakes instead of rattles ❏ if he was cooked properly, he'd feed the Argentine Army ❏ his shadow would weigh ten pounds ❏ it takes a big loop to rope him ❏ he blazes a wide trail ❏ fills up a huddle ❏ takes a big stick to knock him down ❏ looks grained up and ready to ship to market ❏ ought to bed down with the night herd ❏ for size and weight, he'd match a champion bull at the State Fair *See also Big Person, Fat*

LAS VEGAS Lost Wages, Nevada. There's the old story about the Texan who went to Las Vegas in a $25,000 Cadillac and came home in a $250,000 bus, as in Greyhound

LAST The tail end ❏ the end of the trail ❏ the tailgate

LAST CHANCE You're loading your last bullet ❏ if you know any good prayers, now is the time

LATE NIGHT Just this side of bedtime

LAUGH, HEARTY Like a double-jawed hyena ❏ shake your belly

LAWBREAKER Careless with the statues ❏ even ignores the law of gravity

LAWMAN Law bringer ❏ badge toter ❏ star strutter *See also Highway Patrol, Police*

LAWYER Law wrangler ❏ statute wrangler (also used for judge) ❏ legal eagle ❏ legalized con man ❏ ambulance chaser ❏ (See Wasteful for description of waste involving lawyers.) Lyndon Johnson once said, "In Texas there is a saying that a town which can't support one lawyer can always support two." It is a well known fact that a lawyer is the only natural enemy to an insurance company.

LAWYER, GOOD A real ground hound, which means he can have you back on the ground or street quickly after an arrest

LAY DOWN Sun your heels, which implies that the only time your heels see the sun is when you are laying down

LAY DOWN THE LAW Read 'em the scriptures (or statues)

LAZY He's like a blister, never shows up till the work is done ❏ old never-sweats ❏ he'll starve to death someday 'cause he won't work and he's too lazy to steal ❏ he has to prop himself up to spit ❏ he'll never drown in his own sweat ❏ he ain't afraid of hard work 'cause he can lay down beside it and sleep like a pup ❏ a saw rider, which refers to one man not pulling his weight while on one end of a two-man crosscut saw ❏ won't even swat flies ❏ riding the single tree (letting another horse do the work) ❏ spends most of his time on the loafer's log (or bench) ❏ spends his time looking for sundown, shade and payday ❏ too light for heavy work and too heavy for light work ❏ if he was a dog he wouldn't wag his own tail ❏ a hand sitter, which is a derivative of sitting on his hands ❏ he claims he was wounded in the war but no one has ever seen a scar *See also Loafer*

LEAD Shepherd 'em ❏ blaze the trail ❏ take the bull by the tail

LEADER Bell cow, bell mare, or bell wearer ❏ ringleader ❏ rules the roost ❏ chief cook and bottle washer ❏ big buck at the lick ❏ tall dog in the pack ❏ stud buzzard ❏ the head eagle. When former Governor Jim Ferguson arrived at a meeting, one of his aides remarked, "All you owls hunt your holes, the eagle is here," the obvious reference being that an owl is no match for an eagle *See also Boss, Important Person*

LEAKY So full of holes it wouldn't hold hay ❏ sieve bottomed

LEARN Wise up on ❏ study up ❏ practice up ❏ get the hang of ❏ get posted on

LEARNED OF Got wind of

LEARNING Beginning to make a hand

LEAVE Make some boot tracks ❏ drag your carcass out of here ❏ head 'em up and move 'em out ❏ pull your picket pin and drift ❏ hit the trail ❏ cut a trail ❏ put the wind to your back and ride ❏ pull up stakes, which is a reference to the stakes used to keep horse in place ❏ move it on down the line ❏ skeedadle out of here ❏ get along on ❏ hit the breeze ❏ strike camp ❏ put wheels on the whore house and haul butt ❏ gather up some over yonder ❏ fade into the sunset ❏ promenade for home ❏ vamoose ❏ get while the gettin' is good

LEAVE IT ALONE Let it be ❏ let sleeping dogs lie ❏ let him play his own hand

LEAVE FAST Drag your navel in the sand or fill you vest pockets with dirt, both of which imply you should run close to the ground ❏ jump the dust ❏ hightail it ❏ light a shuck, which is a reference to dry corn shucks burning very quickly ❏ get the hell out of Dodge ❏ tear out like a ruptured duck ❏ tuck your tail and lite out ❏ pop some mesquite ❏ like a glory-bound bat or a bat out a hell

LEAVING I'm goin to the house ❏ feeling mighty temporary ❏ not long for this place ❏ feel the get up and gos coming on ❏ he bought a trunk and packed it ❏ pulled his freight and left

LEERY This old crow has eaten enough field corn to know scarecrows sometimes carry shotguns ❏ this old fox has raided enough chicken coops to know there ain't no free lunch ❏ I've robbed enough nests to know you can't enjoy eggs if you're picking buckshot out of your behind ❏ I've caught too many coyotes to put my foot in a trap ❏ got a twitch in my jaundice eye

LEFT Struck the trail ❏ took to the tall timber ❏ took out ❏ lit out ❏ got off toward ❏ left out ❏ cut a trail ❏ withered from ❏ split the breeze ❏ he's a long time gone ❏ made for, as in "He made for the hills when he heard the sheriff was looking for him."

LEFT IN A HURRY Vamoosed ❏ raised more dust than Noah's flood could settle ❏ raised enough dust to choke a buffalo herd ❏ took off in such a hurry he didn't have time to take his real name

LEFT EARLY Jumped the gun ❏ jumped the traces ❏ beat the

bell ❏ beat the clock or gun ❏ broke the barrier

LEFT SIDE Haw, which was the old mule driver's word for left

LEGS Wheels

LEGS, LONG High rumped ❏ mighty leggy ❏ grand daddy long legs ❏ lanky legged ❏ stilt legged

LEGS, THIN Spider legs ❏ chicadee legs ❏ banty rooster legs

LESSON, FOR CHILDREN Bringing up lecture

LET GO Turn a loose ❏ give him his head, which refers to giving a horse his head by releasing a tight hold on the reins so he can run better

LET ME DO IT Let me rock the baby

LET THEM GO Set 'em free ❏ set 'em loose ❏ let her rip ❏ open the shoot ❏ open the cage

LET'S DO IT Let's do some dancin' ❏ let's get at it ❏ let's rodeo

LIAR Him and the truth ain't going steady (or related) ❏ truth stretcher ❏ don't dance

with the facts ❏ his story don't
track with the facts ❏ got his
facts tangled ❏ he couldn't get
a notary to certify he was alive
❏ talks through his hat ❏ fork
tongued, which comes from the
forked tongue of a snake ❏
he's lying through his teeth

LICE Walking dandruff

LIE (NOUN) Windy ❏
whizzer ❏ yarn ❏ ain't
square with all the facts ❏ tall
tale ❏ cock and bull tale ❏ as
shy of the truth as a pig (or turtle) is of feathers ❏ corral dust

LIE (VERB) Pull a sandy ❏
tell a windy ❏ spin a yarn (or
tall tale) ❏ can tell a yarn as
long as a rustler's dream

LIE, BIG A boldface lie

LIED TO Sold me a bill a
goods

LIFE, SIMPLE A five and
dime existence, which implies
someone lives such a simple
life he can purchase anything
he wants at a five and dime
store

LIFELESS *See Dead*

LIFETIME From crawling to
crutch ❏ from womb to tomb ❏
all my born days, as in "I've
been a Democrat (or

Republican) all my born
days"

LIFT Hist ❏ hoist ❏ histed

LIGHT As a sparrow feather
❏ as an empty egg shell ❏ as a
hummingbird's feather ❏ as
an ant's eyelash

LIGHT A MATCH Scratch a
match ❏ scratch a boot

LIGHTEN THE LOAD Bury
the whiskey and draw a map,
which is a reference to the old
days when a loaded wagon
had trouble making it over
rough terrain. It such a case,
any spare whiskey was often
buried so it could be retrieved
later.

LIKE Mighty fond of ❏ right
fond of ❏ cotton to ❏ took a
fancy to

LIKEABLE When he cashes
in his chip, the funeral will be
standing room only

LIMP As a dish rag ❏ as an
empty glove ❏ as a bar-
tender's rag ❏ as a cup towel

LIQUOR Likker ❏ firewater
❏ whusky ❏ red eye ❏ rot gut
❏ joy juice ❏ nose paint ❏
tarantula juice ❏ conversation juice, which refers to the
fact that many people get

talkative when they drink ❑ coffin paint ❑ snakebite medicine, which refers to the old practice of pouring liquor on a snakebite ❑ mountain lion milk ❑ crazy water ❑ panther piss ❑ tiger milk ❑ antifreeze ❑ hooch ❑ wild mare milk ❑ joy water ❑ snake venom ❑ giggle water ❑ witch's piss ❑ squaw piss ❑ tonsil paint ❑ whoopee water ❑ embalming fluid ❑ courage water ❑ stagger juice *See also Whiskey, Champagne*

LIQUOR, SMOOTH Sipping whusky

LIQUOR, STRONG Bumble bee whisky ❑ gator sweat ❑ will jump your IQ fifty points per swallow ❑ will make you act single, see double, and pay triple ❑ would melt your tonsils ❑ enamel solvent, which implies it will melt your teeth ❑ would make a jackrabbit spit in a coyote's eye ❑ brave maker *See also Drink, Strong & Whiskey, Strong*

LITTLE Puny ❑ runtified ❑ stingy sized ❑ half pint ❑ thimble sized ❑ thumb sized ❑ poco

LIVING DANGEROUSLY Messin' with your heartbeat ❑ wading in a pool of quicksand over hell

LIVING GOOD Riding a gravy train with biscuit wheels

LIVING ROOM Parlor ❑ sitting room ❑ front room

LOADING CHUTE Where the cows go out and the money comes in, as Lyndon Johnson explained to reporters touring his hill country ranch

LOAFER Charter member of the spit and whittle club, which refers to men who frequent courthouse benches and pass the time spitting tobacco juice and whittling twigs ❑ you'll never see manure on his boots ❑ calfin' around ❑ coffee cooler ❑ porch sitter ❑ red flagger, which refers to the person on the road construction gang who does nothing but use a red flag to control traffic ❑ spends his time looking for sundown and payday ❑ thumb twiddler ❑ porch preacher *See also Lazy*

LOAFING Wasting daylight ❑ pirooting, which is a cowboy term for fooling around doing nothing ❑ foot dragger ❑ spending his days in the porch (or wagon) shade ❑ chasing butterflies

LOCATED NEAR In this neck of the woods

LOITERED Dallied around town

LONER Lone wolf ❏ rides his own range ❏ chews his own cud

LONESOME As a preacher on payday, referring to the fact that preachers are not always well paid ❏ as a windmill on a still day ❏ as an orphan calf ❏ as a lighthouse keeper ❏ as an umbrella salesman in a drought

LONG As a country mile ❏ as a rainy Sunday afternoon ❏ all drawn out ❏ as a wagon track ❏ as a West Texas well rope ❏ as a stake rope ❏ as plow lines ❏ reins on a forty-mule team ❏ as an old maid's dream

LONG AGO When the Dead sea was only sick ❏ before women got the vote ❏ when the devil was a pup ❏ before the frost melted off hell ❏ when snakes walked (or had legs) ❏ when Moby Dick was just a minnow,

LONG DISTANCE Fer piece ❏ a good piece ❏ quite a ways ❏ from here to hell and gone ❏ as far as an outhouse on a cold morning ❏ long as the Texas Oklahoma border, which is the longest border between any

two states, measuring over 900 miles.

LONG LASTING It'll outlast the Alamo ❏ as a pair of steel handled post hole diggers ❏ as a crow bar

LONG TIME Coon's age ❏ a month a Sundays, which is about seven months in duration ❏ quite a spell ❏ a long spell ❏ since God knows when, as in "I ain't seen him since God knows when" ❏ a right smart spell ❏ till hell freezes over ❏ till the cows come home ❏ till a snapping turtle turns loose

LOOK Eyeball ❏ look see ❏ look-a-here

LOOK ALIKE Dead ringer ❏ spittin' image

LOOK EVERYWHERE Search high and low ❏ turn over every rock, cow chip and rotten log in Texas ❏ beat all the bushes

LOOK FOR *See Search*

LOOKING FOR A HUSBAND Draggin' her stake rope ❏ trolling for a breadwinner and using a short skirt for bait *See also Female, Conniving*

139

LOOKING FOR A JOB *See Unemployed*

LOOKING FOR TROUBLE Walking around half cocked ❑ pawin' the dirt ❑ hornin' the bush ❑ scratchin' around in the turmoil pen

LOOKS, BAD Like he was run over by a switch engine ❑ like he hard wintered ❑ looks like he was pulled through a bob war fence backwards by a bobcat *See also Appearance, Bad*

LOOKS, DECEIVING Powder and paint will make a woman look like something she ain't ❑ just cause a chicken has wings don't mean it can fly ❑ a wagging tail has no control over a dog's mouth, which means even a dog that looks friendly can bite you ❑ just 'cause the water is still don't mean it ain't deep ❑ any cat would kill you if it was big enough ❑ ugly icing don't mean the cake will taste bad *See also Appearance, Deceiving*

LOOKS, GOOD All combed and curried

LOOKS GOOD IN ACTION Show bucker, which refers to a horse that bucks best in a rodeo

LOOKS LIKE Favors ❑ such as "He favors his father."

LOOKS SICK Peaked lookin' ❑ he's green around the gills *See also Ill*

LOOP *See Rope Loop*

LOOSE Uncinched ❑ the bridle's off ❑ the gate's open ❑ limbered up ❑ as a goose, which refers to the loose bowls of your average goose

LOOSENED UP Her personality began to purr and hum ❑ his personality erupted like a baby volcano

LOSER Hitched his wagon to a falling star ❑ a clinker ❑ couldn't beat a drum ❑ don't go home with his tail up ❑ should a called a cab instead of the bet ❑ Darrell Royal said, "There is no laughter in losing." Blaine Nye of the Dallas Cowboys said, "It doesn't matter whether you win or lose but who gets the blame."

LOSING Paying the wrong preacher ❑ suckin' hind teat ❑ playing second fiddle ❑ fightin' a non-payin' proposition ❑ betting on a lame horse

LOSING MONEY Your wettin' in the cash box, implying

the money is wet and thus ruined and lost ❑ got a hole in the profit sack ❑ our bottom line is shrinking faster than a grape in a blast furnace or an ice cube in an oven

LOST Brought in a dry hole ❑ finished out of the money ❑ a day late and a dollar short ❑ took it on the chin ❑ got caught nappin' ❑ every turkey has his Thanksgiving ❑ came up on the short end of the stick ❑ got a chamber pot instead of a jackpot ❑ couldn't find hide nor hair of it

LOST AN ARGUMENT His thinking packed more weight than mine

LOST APPETITE He's off his feed

LOST BABY TEETH Shed his colt teeth

LOST CONTROL Come undone ❑ come apart at the seems ❑ went to pieces

LOST EVERYTHING Got plucked cleaner than a Thanksgiving turkey or a Sunday chicken ❑ she lost everything but the rustle in her dress and the snap in her garters

LOST PERSON Had to run an ad in the paper for someone to come and get me ❑ couldn't find him if you combed all of Texas with a fine tooth comb ❑ even his own bloodhound couldn't find him in a week of good weather ❑ don't know where I am and got no mother to guide me home *See also Missing*

LOT Heap of, as in "He's in a heap of trouble" ❑ a sight of, as in "I got a sight of work to do" ❑ a posse of ❑ beaucoup ❑ a whole passel ❑ big batch ❑ whole slew ❑ big litter ❑ many a, as in "He's had many a girlfriend" ❑ a bushel basket, a gunny sack or a peck sack full, any of which would be a lot if you were talking about diamonds ❑ a big chunk of ❑ a plenty as in "She scared me a plenty" ❑ a good many ❑ great mess of, as in "He caught a great mess of fish" ❑ a full wagonload

LOUD Enough to rattle the rafters ❑ to wake the dead ❑ as a hungry calf ❑ as boot heels on a bare floor ❑ as fresh shod horses on a concrete sidewalk ❑ enough to be heard in the next county ❑ to wake the dead ❑ as thunder ❑ outroar a buffalo ❑ hear him a mile against the breeze ❑ enough to scare bulls off the

141

bed ground ❑ enough to jar pecans off the tree *See also Noisy*

LOUD MOUTH His bark is enough, he don't need a bite

LOUISIANA NATIVE Coonass, which is not considered derogatory. *See also New Orleans*

LOVE May not make the world go round but it sure makes the trip more pleasant

LOVER Got Romeo blood in his veins *See also Ladies Man*

LOW A scared rabbit couldn't go under it ❑ a snake couldn't get under if he'd been run over by a truck

LOYALTY Be true to your own heart ❑ stand by your man *See also Faithful*

LUCK Better to have a little luck than a lot of learning. Sid Richardson, famous Texas oilman, once said, "I'd rather be lucky than smart cause a lot of smart people ain't eatin' regular." H.L. Hunt, once the worlds richest man, said, "You have to be lucky." One of H. L.'s sons, Ray Hunt said, "Given the choice between luck and intelligence, always take luck." *See also Plan Ahead*

LUCKY If he bought a cemetery, he'd strike oil digging the first grave ❑ if he fell into an outhouse, he'd come out smelling like a Tyler rose. Tyler, Texas bills itself as the rose capital of the world ❑ could draw a pat hand from a stacked deck ❑ as a car-chasin' dog ❑ lady luck stays camped on his shirttail ❑ he'd get American change if he spent a confederate dollar ❑ he could pitch pennies down the neck of a swinging beer bottle ❑ always draws the best bull, which is a reference to rodeo cowboys drawing for the bulls they will have to ride. The best bull is the one that will buck wildly so the rider can earn more points *See also Fortunate*

LUKEWARM Cowboy cool ❑ touchin' hot

LUNCH Dinner to a Texan

LYNCH Cow pasture justice ❑ somebody get a rope ❑ string 'em up ❑ turn an oak into a court room ❑ give a little necktie party ❑ stretch some hemp ❑ extra-legal hanging

M

MEAN — as a bulldog on a gunpowder diet

MAD On the prod, the peck, or the warpath ❑ plum riled ❑ got his dauber down ❑ got his stinger out ❑ lathered up ❑ got a craw full of sand and fightin' tallow ❑ her fangs and fingernails are flashing ❑ he's spittin' spite ❑ he's all horns and rattles (horns from a bull, rattles from a rattlesnake) ❑ boiling over with prejudice ❑ walled his eyes and bowed his neck ❑ got his dander up ❑ got a burr under his saddle (or in his boot) ❑ eating fire and spitting smoke *See also Angry*

MAD AS A fighting cock ❑ as a rained on rooster or a wet hen ❑ as a bullfrog in a thumb tack factory ❑ as a bull in a red dye factory ❑ as a rattler in a roadrunner's sights, which refers to the fact that roadrunners will actually stalk, kill, and eat rattlesnakes ❑ a red-eyed cow ❑ a bear with two cubs and one sore teat ❑ as a teased snake ❑ a wet hornet ❑ as fogged fire ants

MAD ENOUGH TO Eat bees ❑ chomp a big chunk out of the head of an ax ❑ to put something on you Ajax won't take off ❑ to spit nails ❑ to kick a hog barefooted ❑ to eat the devil with the horns on ❑ to bite the head off a hammer ❑ to bite a bullet plumb in two

MAD RUSH Wild stampede

MADE A MISTAKE Misfired ❑ wet in your own well ❑ two-stepped to a waltz, which is a big mistake in Texas ❑ zigged when you should have zagged *See also Error, Screwed Up*

MAIL ORDER CATALOG Wish book ❑ sheep herder's bible ❑ outhouse bible

MAIN STREET Main drag

MAINTAIN CONTROL Keep the gate closed because a loose mare is always lookin' for a new pasture ❑ hold the fort ❑ keep the fence up ❑ As Texan Lee Trevino said, "We all leak a little oil, but the good ones control the flow."

MAKE A CHOICE Cut one out of the herd ❑ pick one out of the litter ❑ name your poison, which means make a choice of drinks ❑ pick your pasture ❑ draw a bead on one ❑ choose your weapon ❑ in a race, everybody has to pick his own horse

MAKE IT SHORT Cut a few corners off ❑ trim the fat ❑

knock some links out of the chain

MAKE LOVE Make whoopee

MAKE PEACE Bury the hatchet ❑ smoke the peace pipe ❑ sign a treaty ❑ let bygones be bygones

MAKEUP War (or love) paint

MAKING PROGRESS Getting the corn ground ❑ getting the fields plowed ❑ getting the calves branded

MAN Hombre ❑ good old boy ❑ redneck ❑ ol' hairy legs ❑ hombre

MAN, GOOD *See Good Person*

MAN, OLD Codger ❑ old-timer ❑ geezer ❑ antique ya-hoo *See also Elderly, Old*

MANAGEABLE It's been whittled down to size

MANAGEMENT, POOR Selling his hogs to buy hog feed

MANNERS Eatin' regulations

MANNERS, POOR He'll wait on you like one hog waits on another ❑ he invented the boardinghouse reach, which is

the practice of just reaching for what you want rather than having it passed to you ❑ he'd sop biscuits and slurp coffee out of a saucer at a White House breakfast

MANY More than Carter had oats (or liver pills) ❑ thick as fiddlers in hell ❑ thick as ticks on a hound dog ❑ thick as flies in a garbage dump *See also Lot*

MARKED Branded ❑ ear marked

MARKED CARDS Doped cards ❑ branded cards ❑ cards that can be read from either side

MARKSMAN A meat gitter ❑ could shoot a yellowjacket off a cactus at 500 yards ❑ could shoot the eye out of a gnat at 100 paces *See also Aim, Good*

MARKSMAN, POOR Couldn't hit the side of a barn from inside the barn. Outhouse can be substituted for barn.

MARRIAGE Men are born free so if they marry it's their own fault

MARRIED Got hitched ❑ trot-tin' in a double harness ❑ welded into a neck harness ❑

necked in harness ❑ com-
mitted matrimony with ❑
double hitched ❑ hitched to run
in a double harness ❑ yoked
up with ❑ lassoed ❑ holy bed-
lock

MARRIED FOOLISHLY He
picked his wife by the glow of a
neon light, which means he
was drunk at the time

MARRIED MAN Private in
the honey do army, which
means his wife is always
saying honey do this or honey
do that ❑ carryin' her brand ❑
roped to a heifer ❑ he's broke
for domestic work ❑ he baled
the mare ❑ he dropped a rope
on her

MARRIED WOMAN She's
double ringed, meaning she
has an engagement ring and
a wedding ring ❑ she's
carrying his brand ❑ finally
got him in her web ❑ she
chased him till he caught her

MARRIED UP IN CLASS
Outmarried himself

MASSIVE *See Large*

MEAN A bucker and a
snorter, referring to a mean
rodeo bucking horse ❑ a bad
Indian ❑ an ornery old cuss ❑
a scalp hunter ❑ two shades
meaner than the devil hisself

❑ a good man not to mess with
❑ a fire eater, good reputation
for cussidness ❑ a bad hombre
❑ keeps his stinger out all the
way ❑ cut his teeth on a gun
barrel ❑ he don't wear a belt
gun for ballast ❑ if he says
giddyup, you better go ❑ he's
proof there are more horse's
butts than there are horses ❑
he'll get on you like ugly on
an ape ❑ his mother had to
feed him with a slingshot *See
also Evil Person, Vicious,
Wicked*

MEAN AND CUNNING He's
mean enough to suck eggs out
of a widow woman's basket
and cunning enough to hide
the shells on a neighbor's
porch

MEAN AS A bulldog on a
gunpowder diet ❑ as a curly
wolf ❑ as an old range cow ❑
as hell with the hide off ❑ as a
cornered cottonmouth ❑ as a
caged cougar ❑ as a rodeo bull
❑ as a pit bull dog ❑ as eight
acres of snakes ❑ as mule on
a sawdust diet

MEANNESS Cussidness ❑
orneryness ❑ double
cussidness

MEAN WOMAN She's an expert at chunkin' firewood (or
skillets) ❑ keeps hot water on

147

tap to scald neighborhood dogs with

MEANINGLESS Hog wash ❏ buffalo chips ❏ horse (or frog) feathers ❏ a mare's nest

MEANINGLESS AS Earrings on a sow ❏ as eye shadow on an eagle ❏ as perfume on a pig ❏ as a silk nightgown on a scarecrow ❏ as socks (or tennis shoes) to a grub worm ❏ as panty hose to a pig

MEASUREMENT, APPROXIMATE Use an appropriate number of ax handles as in "He's two ax handles wide" or "He stands four ax handles high" ❏ or "He's no taller than half an ax handle" ❏ As a rule of thumb an ax handle measures about thirty inches.

MEET A CHALLENGE Take the bull by the tail and face the situation

MEETING Pow wow ❏ prayer session ❏ get together

MEETING OVER Court's adjourned ❏ that's the rodeo (or ball game)

MEMORY, POOR For the life of me, I can't recall it ❏ his recall needs an overhaul

MEN Menfolk

MERINGUE Calf slobber

MESS Fine kettle of fish ❏ the works are balled up ❏ a real sow's nest

MESSED UP Boogered up

MESQUITE Pronounced mess-skeet

MEXIA, TEXAS Pronounced Ma-hay-ya, a small town in central Texas which was made famous by the old joke about the two traveling salesmen who were agruing over how to pronounce the name of the town. They decided to settle the argument by asking a local citizen so they stopped at the first place they came to and went inside. A young lady approached and asked if she could help. "Can you tell how to pronounce the name of this place?" asked one of the men. Sure," she replied, "it's Daree Queen."

MEXICO Old Mexico ❏ land of manana

MIDDLE Smack dab in the heart ❏ down the chute ❏ the heart

MIDDLE OF THE ROAD Gunfighter's sidewalk. It's

been said gunfighters walked the center of the street so they could watch both sides of town easier.

MIGHT Libel to, such as "I'm libel to do just that."

MILK Udder delight

MILK A COW Pump a cow ❑ shake hands with some teats

MILK, CURDLED Clabber

MILK, TURNING Blinky

MIND Thinker ❑ head filler

MIND YOUR OWN BUSINESS Tend to your own knitting ❑ saddle your own horse ❑ mend your own windmill ❑ use your eyes to look and your sense not to see ❑ every man has to skin his own skunk ❑ cut your own firewood ❑ mend your own fences ❑ chew your own tobacco ❑ hoe your own weeds ❑ stay on your own range

MIRACLE Water-walking act

MIRROR Looking glass

MISCHIEVOUS PERSON Rounder ❑ maverick

MISER Wouldn't loan you a nickle unless the Lord and all

the disciples countersigned the note ❑ the way to his heart is through your pocketbook ❑ so tight he squeaks when he walks ❑ still got half of his third grade allowance ❑ got four cents out of every nickel he ever made ❑ skinflint ❑ tightwad ❑ wouldn't pay a nickle to see a pissant eat a bale of hay ❑ he'll squeeze a dollar until the eagle screams ❑ he'll choke a dollar until George Washington turns blue *See also Cheapskate, Frugal, Miser, Stingy*

MISERABLE Got misery up to my armpits (or eyeballs)

MISFORTUNE He messed in his mess kit

MISLED He wet in my boots and swore it was raining ❑ he lead me down a cold trail

MISSED Off the mark ❑ by a country mile ❑ a miss by an inch is as good as a mile

MISSING He's off the home range ❑ he's off the reservation ❑ he came up absent ❑ can't find hide nor hair of him *See also Lost*

MISTAKEN You roped the wrong steer ❑ you hit on an empty chamber ❑ barking up the wrong tree ❑ roping the

149

wrong calf ❑ puttin' your saddle on the wrong horse ❑ pulled the wrong sow's ear ❑ milked the wrong cow ❑ got the wrong dog by the tail ❑ it's the stallion that picks the mare, not the other way around ❑ it's the bull that picks the heifer, not the other way around *See also Error*

MISTER Senor

MISUNDERSTOOD He's singing off the wrong song sheet

MOANS Like the enchanted rock. Between Fredericksburg and Llano there is a large boulder that moans whenever the weather changes, which has "enchanted" people for generations.

MONEY Wampum ❑ geetus ❑ chunk-a-change ❑ dinero ❑ H.L. Hunt said, "Money is nothing. It is just something to make bookkeeping more convenient." Clint Murchison, Jr. had a different view. He said, "Money is a lot like manure. If you pile it up in one place it stinks like hell. But if you spread it around it does some good."

MONEY, SMALL AMOUNT Chicken feed ❑ scalp money ❑ egg money

MONTAGUE, TEXAS Pronounced Mon-tage, a small town in North Texas not far from the Oklahoma border

MONTGOMERY WARD Monkey Ward

MOONSHINE Worm medicine

MORALS, POOR *See Immoral*

MORNING Sunup ❑ daybreak

MOSQUITO Skeeter ❑ nail ripper ❑ had a mouth like an ice pick and could drill right through a boot

MOSQUITO, LARGE Could stand flat footed on the ground and kiss a rooster on the beak ❑ half a dozen of 'em could pull a man off a horse ❑ it's been speculated that some Texas mosquitoes get as big as a duck but most rarely get larger than a sparrow

MOST Lion's share

MOTEL Public bunkhouse

MOTHERLESS Dogie

MOTIONLESS Laid there like a sack of flour (or feed) ❑ sat still as a frozen anvil

MOTIVATE Spur the horse. A horse that has been spurred is motivated to run

MOTIVATIONAL SPEECH Chalk talk, which is derived from sports coaches using chalk and a blackboard to explain how plays are supposed to work

MOTORCYCLE Murdercycle ❑ suicycle

MOUNT UP Fork your pony ❑ strike leather ❑ warm you leather

MOUSE Cheese burner

MOUTH, DRY Feels like the Russian army marched through my mouth in their sock feet ❑ dry as a mummy's pocket ❑ couldn't raise enough spit to repair anything, which is a reference to making repairs with spit and baling wire

MOUTH, LARGE Bucket mouth ❑ gopher trap ❑ big enough to hold an andiron

MOUTHFUL Beak full ❑ double cheek full ❑ looks like he swallowed a pair of love birds ❑ looks like he threw up his heart

MOVE Change range (or pastures, camps) ❑ got a new bedground

MOVE IT Get it out from under foot

MOVES A LOT Got tumbleweed blood in his veins

MOVES CRAZY Like a full balloon with the air running out ❑ like a knuckleball ❑ like a straw in a whirlwind ❑ like a loco'd calf ❑ like a pup looking for a place to lay down (or squat)

MOVIE Picture show, movin' pictures

MOVIE, WESTERN Horse opera

MRS Missus ❑ ma'm ❑ senora, in Spanish

MUCH A heap sight

MUDDY ENOUGH To bog a bird's shadow ❑ to bog a horse all the way to the rider's hat

MUDDY ROAD Heavy road

MUSIC, LIVELY Foot stompin' music ❑ music that is connected to your boots

MUSICIAN, GOOD He can hit every note except the ones in

the bank ❏ he picks on golden
strings ❏ he can make a
washtub and a dinner bell
sound like a symphony
orchestra

MUSICIAN, POOR He can't
take notes, much less play
them ❏ he better practice
dodging beer bottles before he
tries to play in a Texas honky
tonk

MY TURN They're playin'
my tune ❏ they dialed my
number ❏ it's my turn in the
barrel

N

NAKED — in Texas is nekkid

NAKED Nekkid. No one in Texas is naked or nude, they are nekkid. Also runnin' around in the altogether ❑ polishing (or sunnin') his birthday suit ❑ didn't have on enough clothes to pad a crutch ❑ ain't got on so much as a stitch ❑ without a shuck on ❑ buck nekkid ❑ got nothing on but the radio (or television) ❑ bare behinded ❑ he's stitchless

NAKED AS A scalded hog, which refers to the process of slaughtering hogs where they are boiled, then all the hair is scraped off ❑ as a plucked chicken ❑ as a jaybird ❑ as a worm without an overcoat

NAKED WOMAN A doubt remover ❑ an imagination killer

NAME Handle

NAP Siesta ❑ checking my eyelids for leaks

NARROW As a branding chute (or loading chute)

NARROW ESCAPE By the skin of my teeth ❑ barely got out with my hide intact

NARROW MINDED Wears a blind bridle

NATURAL As a duck in water ❑ as a pig in slop ❑ as flies on a watermelon rind

NEAR *See Close*

NEAR MISS The bullet went by close enough to raise a blister ❑ the car went by so close I could smell the driver's breath

NECESSARY You don't get lard unless you boil the hog ❑ you can't be a cowboy if you can't ride a horse

NECHES Pronounced na ches, this Indian word for friend supplied the name for a river and a town in Texas.

NECK Gozzle

NECKTIE Choke strap ❑ feel like I was tied to a snubbin' post

NEED As much as a scalded dog needs a stock tank

NEEDLESS As perfume for a pig

NEGOTIATION Dickering ❑ horse trading

NEIMAN MARCUS Needless Markup, which is considered derogatory and makes fun of the traditional high prices in the store. There was a time when anybody who was anybody in Texas did their shopping at Neiman's. Weatherford native Mary Martin, the famous actress, once said she grew up like every other little girl in Texas, "dreaming of the day she got a dress from Neiman Marcus."

NERVE He's go the nerve of a 20-year veteran on the bomb squad ❑ he's got more nerve than a toothache in a molar

NERVOUS Shaking so much she could thread the needle on a sewing machine with it a running ❑ got an itchy trigger finger ❑ he's sweating bullets ❑ he's hearin' footsteps ❑ he's twitchin' and shaking like a wet dog ❑ his stomach is balled up in a knot ❑ as a grass widow at a camp meeting ❑ couldn't draw an easy breath ❑ chute crazy, which refers to cattle being nervous to enter a narrow branding or loading chute ❑ got a belly full of bedsprings ❑ got a crick in his neck from lookin' over his shoulder

NERVOUS AS A long tailed cat in a room full of rocking chairs ❑ as a frog in a frying pan ❑ as a pig in a packing house ❑ as a whore in church, a soiled dove in Sunday

school, or a painted lady at a prayer meeting ❑ as a settin' hen at a wolf (or coyote) convention

NERVY As a 350-pound cat burglar ❑ as a 250-pound ballet dancer

NEVER The flames of hell would be as cold as a strawberry popsickle before that would happen (any flavor can be substituted for strawberry) ❑ in a pig's eye

NEVER ENDING There is always another fence to mend, field to plow, or well to dig ❑ like wiping with a bicycle inner tube

NEW Fresh, as in "He got a fresh horse" ❑ young, as in "He just had a young idea" ❑ hot off the press (or fire)

NEW DEVELOPMENT New wrinkle in the old shirt

NEW INVENTION Newfangled contraption

NEW ORLEANS, LOUISIANA Pronounced New Are-learns. Also known as the coonass capital of the world. *See Louisiana Native*

NEW ORLEANS SUPERDOME To a Texan, it's the Coonasstrodome.

NEWCOMER Pilgrim ❑ nester ❑ a Johnny come lately

NEWLYWEDS Sleeping double in a single bed ❑ fresh married ❑ new to the halter ❑ green broke for matrimony. A "green broke" horse is one that has been broken to accept a rider but has not been trained to ride.

NEWSPAPER ARTICLE A piece in the paper

NIGHT Between suns ❑ prowling time ❑ coon time, which refers to hunting coons at night when they are out searching for food

NIGHT, DARK *See Dark Night*

NIGHTFALL Sundown. In the foreword for *Sure Enough, How Come* by F. W. Van Emden, J. Frank Dobie wrote, "One time I shot a young Doctor of Philosophy from Harvard for grading down a Texas freshman because he had used the word 'sundown' in a theme. The grand jury did not so much as investigate."

NIGHT SHIFT Night herding ❑ singing shift, which refers to cowboys singing to the cattle at night to keep them quiet

NIGHT WORK Working between suns

NINE (PLAYING CARD) Cat card, which refers to a cat having nine lives

NO No dice ❑ does a chicken have lips ❑ can a donkey fly ❑ can a rattlesnake whistle Dixie ❑ does dirt taste good ❑ does a windmill pump oil ❑ does a bull give milk

NO GOOD No account

NO HURRY Get it done by the second Wednesday of next week

NO MATTER WHAT Come hell or high water ❑ no matter how the cards fall

NO ONE Narry a soul

NO OPENING Full handed

NO OPTIONS We're string haltered

NO WAY In a pig's eye ❑ fat chance ❑ slim chance. As Houston Astro pitcher Larry Anderson pointed out, "How come fat chance and slim chance mean the same thing?"

NO WAY OUT We're in a box canyon ❑ we're in a swamp full of alligators and the drain is plugged ❑ there ain't no key for the gate and the fence is too high to climb

NOD Give 'em a tuck ❑ dip your hat

NOISY As a teaspoon in a garbage disposal ❑ as an old wagon on a frozen road ❑ as a slow moving windmill crying for oil ❑ pair of dancing jinglebobs ❑ as a calf crying for mamma ❑ as geese on a new feed ground ❑ as a pig eatin' charcoal *See also Loud, Sound*

NONCONFORMIST Maverick. The term originated before the Civil War when financier Sam Maverick took a herd of cattle in settlement of a debt. When his cows started having calves, they went unbranded and came to be called Mavericks. Today, anyone who doesn't conform to the norm is a maverick. ❑ he throws a different loop ❑ he two-steps to his own beat ❑ he uses German Shepards to hunt coons ❑ he wears straw hats in winter ❑ As J. Frank Dobie said, "Conform and be dull."

NONE Nary a one ❑ not a lick of ❑ not a blessed one

NONEXISTENT Rooster eggs ❑ donkey eggs ❑ bull's milk ❑ mare's eggs ❑ like being a little bit pregnant, there ain't no such thing

NON-PAYING Riding a free horse

NONSENSE Burro milk, horse feathers ❑ hog wash ❑ for the birds ❑ bull feathers ❑ hooey ❑ heifer dust ❑ cockamamie ❑ rigamarole ❑ don't make no never mind ❑ buffalo chips ❑ bally hoo ❑ bull oney ❑ a crock of cow confetti ❑ Mexican oats

NONSENSE, POLITICAL Gobblegook. The term was coined by Texan Maury Maverick, a descendent of Sam Maverick, while serving in Congress. He used the term, which he said was derived from watching turkeys gobble and gook, to refer to political statements that were ridiculous nonsense, as are most political statements.

NOON TO MIDNIGHT Evening

NOONTIME High noon ❑ dead center day ❑ lunch time

NORTH Yankeedom, which is roughly described as anywhere north of the Red River

NORTHER Came on so sudden the front half of the horse was frothy and the back half was frozen ❑ came on so sudden that boiling water froze so fast the ice was still warm ❑ came on so sudden the ducks froze to the stock tank before they could get airborne ❑ then there is the classic story of the farmer who was out plowing and one of his mules died from sunstroke. While he was off looking for a replacement, a norther struck and the other mule froze to death. (In Texas, a norther is a cold front that comes up quickly from the north and is usually associated with high winds and a quick, dramatic temperature drop.)

NOSEY Always hunting something to meddle in ❑ got her nose in everybody's business but her own

NOT COMMUNICATING You're preaching to the choir, which implies the preacher's message is not getting through to the entire congregation.

NOT INTERESTED Don't give a hoot or a holler ❑ wouldn't touch that with a ten-foot pole ❑ wouldn't touch that with your pole ❑ don't give a wrap or a hooey (wrap refers to tieing up a calf's legs and a hooey is a knot)

NOT INVOLVED Don't have a cock (or dog) in that fight ❑ don't have a bull in that rodeo ❑ he'll have no more to do with that than I will in admitting him to heaven ❑ not on my dance card

NOT MY FAULT I didn't string the bow ❑ I didn't light the fuse ❑ I don't drive the train or blow the whistle

NOT PRACTICAL You can shear a pig but you'll get a lot more noise than wool ❑ you can cut firewood with a pin knife but the first flames will be a long time coming ❑ a bucket under a bull will get full but it won't be with milk

NOTHING Nuthin' ❑ not a blooming thing ❑ neither hide, nor hair, nor horn ❑ just a load of post holes

NOTHING IS IMPOSSIBLE Cows eat salt blocks one lick at a time ❑ never has been a hoss that can't be rode or cowboy that can't be throwed ❑

This Dog'll Hunt

Texans generally take the attitude that the impossible just takes a little longer than usual to accomplish.

NUECES Pronounced new aces, this Spanish word for nuts is also the name of a Texas river which flows into the Gulf of Mexico at Corpus Christi.

NUDE *See Naked*

NUISANCE He's pain in the back of the lap

NUMEROUS As ants on a dead worm ❏ as oil wells in Texas ❏ as hailstones ❏ as many as carter has liver pills ❏ as hair on a dog's (or coyote's) back ❏ thick as fleas on a mongrel dog ❏ as foot-soldiers in the Chinese army ❏ as relatives at a rich uncle's funeral ❏ as cow chips on a cattle ranch ❏ so many you couldn't stir 'em with a stick

NUTTY As a Corsicana fruitcake ❏ as a box of soft-shell pecans ❏ as a bag of circus peanuts *See also Crazy*

O

OUT OF CONTROL — the tail is wagging the dog

OAF Empty skulled ❑ feather headed ❑ hollow headed ❑ leather brained ❑ sawdust brained ❑ mental mummy ❑ hamster brain ❑ bubble head ❑ yahoo ❑ rattle brain ❑ scatterbrained ❑ chucklehead ❑ bucket head ❑ clabber head ❑ mud head ❑ lumberhead ❑ churn head ❑ plumb weak north of the ears *See also Dumb, Ignorant, Stupid*

OATH I'll be giggered ❑ jumping jehoshaphat ❑ gee wilikers ❑ by cracky

OBEDIENT Stump broke ❑ as a trained pig. Darrell Royal once said, "Every coach likes those old trained pigs who'll grin and jump right in the slop for him." He was referring to football players.

OBESE Looks like he's perfected the boardinghouse reach ❑ beef plumb to the hocks ❑ heavy in the middle and poor on both ends ❑ 20 pounds (or a dozen biscuits) away from a sideshow in the circus ❑ the tongue and buckle of his belt are strangers *See also Fat, Rear End, Large*

OBLIGATED Obliged to ❑ if you're gonna rock, you gotta have a roll ❑ if you give a dance, you gotta pay the band (or at least the fiddler)

OBNOXIOUS Hell bent for trouble ❑ he believes the only business that happens is his business

OBSERVE Hide and watch ❑ keep your eyes peeled

OBSERVANT Quick eyed ❑ smart eyed ❑ eagle eyed

OBSOLETE As a buffalo hunt ❑ as a drive-in movie ❑ as an eight-track tape ❑ as a bois d'arc brick (see bois d'arc)

OBSTACLE A stump in the cotton patch ❑ a root in the sewer line ❑ tall hurdle to jump ❑ tall horse to saddle ❑ tall fence to climb

OBSTINATE Wouldn't move camp out of the way of a prairie fire ❑ ornery as a rat-tailed horse at fly time ❑ you couldn't melt him down and pour him into anyplace he didn't want to go

OBVIOUS Could read that with one eye tied behind my back ❑ plain as the nose on your face ❑ don't have to tell a cat what to do with a mouse ❑ the cards are all face up on the table ❑ if the windmill is running, the wind is blowing ❑ plain as rabbit pills in a sugar bowl. Since rabbit pills are black they would indeed be obvious in a bowl of white sugar ❑ goes without saying ❑ if it had been a snake it would a bit you sure

OCCASIONALLY Every now and again

ODD That's a horse of a different color

ODOR, BAD Smells like a bouquet of stinkweed ❑ like a burning hay field ❑ like a wet dog ❑ like fifty cents a gallon perfume ❑ like the business end of a polecat ❑ like a sewer main with the cork out

ODOR, GOOD Like a baby's breath ❑ like a perfumed cat (or poodle dog) ❑ as rain, which refers to the sweet, gentle odor often associated with a rainstorm ❑ sweet as fresh mowed grass

OFFICE JOB Sitting down job

OFFENSE The best offense is a good defense. Darrell royal once pointed out, "You don't lose a game if your opponent doesn't score."

OFTEN Oft times ❑ many a time ❑ more than a time or two

OIL Pronounced awl ❑ Black gold ❑ Texas tea

OIL FIELD Oil patch

OIL FIELD WORKER Roughneck

OIL FIELD WORKER, INEXPERIENCED A worm

OK Mighty fine ❑ that'll do nicely *See also Agreeable*

OLD As a rock ❑ about the same age as the Brazos River ❑ he could have been a waiter at the Last Supper ❑ as dirt ❑ as sin, implying something has been around since garden of Eden days ❑ she's as old as her tongue and older than her teeth *See also Aging, Elderly*

OLD DAYS Horse and buggy days ❑ back when granddaddy was a pup

OLD FASHION From the old school ❑ old-timey ❑ ol' time ❑ from the good old days

OLD PERSON The Dead sea wasn't even on the critical list when he was born ❑ got plenty of wrinkles on his horns ❑ he was born 10 years before Moses ❑ he's living on borrowed time and three payments are past due ❑ old-timer ❑ codger ❑ no spring chicken ❑ gummer ❑ geezer ❑ galoot ❑ buzzard ❑ aged out ❑ diehard ❑ old fogies *See also Elderly*

OLD WOMAN Battle ax

OLDEST The granddaddy of 'em all

OMINOUS As a skeleton dangling in an oak tree, which refers to the days when a horse thief was lynched and left hanging in the tree as a warning to other rustlers

ON TOP Atop, as in "We had to get the cat down from atop the tree."

ON CREDIT On tick ❏ it belongs to me and the bank, credit union, savings and loan, or mortgage company

ON FIRE A far. Texas youngsters who hear the story about the wise men coming from afar to see the baby Jesus assume they were fireman.

ON HIS OWN Paddling his own canoe ❏ on his own hook ❏ branding his own cows ❏ ridin' for his own brand

ON HIS SIDE I'm siding with him

ON TARGET Where the feathers fly is where the shot will lie ❏ you hit the can (or bottle) *See also Aim, Good*

ON THE MAKE On the prowl ❏ cattin' around ❏ pickin' up strays ❏ prowlin' the honky tonks

ON YOUR OWN It's root hog, or die, which means an old hog that won't root around for his own food will surely die

ONCE Wunst

ONCE OR TWICE A time or two

ONE HUNDRED A hunard

ONE TIME A flash in the pan

ONE OF A KIND PERSON Nobody can hold a candle to him ❏ when they made him they broke the mold ❏ cream of the crop ❏ if he's not alone in his class it wouldn't take long to call role, which is how Bum Phillips described Earl Campbell *See also Good Person*

ONIONS Skunk eggs

OPEN The gate's unlocked ❏ the latch string is on the outside ❏ the breech is open ❏ the fence is down ❏ the lid's off

OPEN A BUSINESS Set up shop

OPEN MINDED The only thing he sets in concrete are fence posts

OPERA Opry

OPINIONS Like noses (or other parts of the anatomy), everyone has one ❏ the difference between a rat and a rabbit depends on who is doing the eating ❏ Lyndon Johnson said, "We don't all see everything alike. If we did we'd all want the same wife."

OPINIONATED He ain't no fence rider or line walker, which means he always has an opinion one way or the other

OPPONENT, EASY A breather. Every football coach likes to have one or two breathers on his schedule.

OPPOSE I won't set still for that ❏ goes against my grain ❏ goes against my raising

OPTION Dealer's choice ❏ ladies' choice ❏ you can stand pat, draw, or get the sandwiches, referring to the options in a friendly poker game

ORATOR Speechist ❏ speechifier

ORDINARY Plain everyday bowlegged human ❏ just an old shoe ❏ everyday wash

ORNERY As a mule colt

ORPHAN Dogie, which is a motherless, and consequently, fatherless, calf

OTHER Tuther

OTHER SIDE Yonder side ❏ back side ❏ flip side ❏ under side

OUT Like Lottie's left eye (or just eye), refers to Lottie Deno, the famous female gambler in Texas during the days of the old west. Although unable to see out of her left eye, she still managed to win a pot or two. Doc Holiday and his girlfriend, Big Nose Kate, were friends of Lottie before Doc killed his first man near Fort Griffin and had to high tail it to Arizona. In 1933, famous Texas bank robber Clyde Barrow felt the law was closing in on him and Bonnie Parker when he said, "Sooner or later they'll catch us and we'll be out like Lottie's eye." He was correct.

OUT DO I'll do you one better ❏ put the big britches on him

OUT OF CONTROL The tail is wagging the dog ❏ the herd's stampeding ❏ the bridle's off ❏ he's a runaway freight train ❏ the well's gushing ❏ running wild ❏ the lid's off ❏ needs roping

OUT OF DANGER Out of the woods

OUT OF LINE Doing something they oughten

OUT OF PLACE A duck (or fish) out of water ❏ as a mule in a buggy harness ❏ as a crane in a goldfish pond ❏ as a sidewinder on a sidewalk ❏ in the wrong cage ❏ as heavy metal music in a honky tonk ❏ as a hiccup at a funeral or a prayer meeting ❏ as turtle eggs on an Interstate highway, which would be out of place since turtles usually lay their eggs in soft dirt, not on hard cement

OUT OF PRACTICE Plumb out of the habit of doing it ❏ rusty as a twenty-year-old windmill

OUT OF SHAPE Breathing from memory ❏ there ain't as much tone in his muscles as there is in a guitar without strings ❏ When Abe Lemons was head basketball coach at the University of Texas,

someone asked if he jogged. "Hell no," replied Lemons, "I want to be sick when I die."

OUT OF STOCK Fresh out of ❏ the wagon's empty ❏ the cupboard is bare

OUT OF TOWN Off the reservation

OUTDOOR TOILET Reading room ❏ throne room ❏ outhouse ❏ back house ❏ closet out back ❏ Sears order desk, which refers to the old practice of keeping the Sears mail order catalog in the outhouse

OUTMANEUVER Wheel 'em and deal 'em

OUTLAW Bandito ❏ horse thief ❏ long rider ❏ the moon is his sun *See also Crooked, Criminal, Thief*

OUTRUN THE LAW There's a saying in Texas that goes, "You might be able to outrun his old Chevrolet, but you can't outrun his old two way," which means even if you can outrun the lawman's car, you can't outrun his radio call for assistance. Since many highway patrolmen drive Ford Mustangs these days, a better version might be "You can outrun his old Ford, but you can't outrun his old finger," which means he can get his finger on the radio button before you can get away.

OUTSMART Out coyote 'em

OUTSTANDING Couldn't beat that with a claw hammer ❏ a good farmer is one that is out standing in his field

OVER THE HILL He's not only over the hill he's over the Guadalupe mountains ❏ being over the hill is better than being under it *See also Elderly, Old*

OVERANXIOUS He rared up to go but he couldn't go because he was rared up ❏ it was an early worm that was eaten by the early bird ❏ chomped at the bit so much he broke off a wisdom tooth at the roots

OVERATE Over grazed ❏ took on a nap load, which refers to the habit some have of taking a nap after a big meal

OVERBEARING Acts like he's got a bill of sale on the whole county

OVERCONFIDENT Acting a little big for his britches ❏ settin' himself for a long fall ❏ he thinks he's bulletproof or invisible

OVEREXERTED Split his britches ❏ popped her girdle

OVEREXTEND He's bit off more than he can chew (or swallow) ❏ got more on his plate than he can say grace over

OVERFLOWING Slopping over

OVERKILL Killed too dead to skin

OVERLOADED My cup runneth over with opportunity ❏ spread too thin ❏ carrying more than a pack horse ❏ got more than I can shake a stick at ❏ bogged to the saddle skirts ❏ my wagon springs are flattened to the axle ❏ got more ground cleared than I can plow ❏ got himself spread so thin you can see through him if the light's right

OVERREACT Don't build a bond fire to roast marshmallows

OWN It's carrying my brand ❏ it's mine, all bought and paid for ❏ it's all mine, lock, stock, and barrel

P

PICKUP — a cowboy Cadillac

PACKED Like hogs at a trough ❏ like sardines in a can ❏ like cows in a boxcar, which refers to shipping cattle by rail when you pack as many as you can into a boxcar

PAIR A cow and a calf ❏ a duet, as in "She has a duet of kids."

PAJAMAS Sleeping drawers

PALACIOS, TEXAS Pronounced Pa-lay-shush, a small town in South Texas where thermometers have been known to melt.

PALATIAL Makes a king's bedroom look like a ranch bunkhouse. On a ranch, the bunkhouse was not the most well appointed of rooms

PALESTINE, TEXAS Texas holy city. There is an old joke about the young Texan who was asked where Jesus was born. After guessing Athens and Carthage, the young man gave up and the Sunday School teacher said it was Palestine. The young Texan, replied, "I knew it was somewhere in East Texas."

PANCAKE Hen fruit stir

PANIC A stampede, which is a reference to cattle panicking and stampeding, a trail drivers nightmare

PANICKED He stampeded the herd ❏ he shot out the lights ❏ he tipped over the outhouse

PAN, LARGE Roundup pan, which refers to the fact that during a roundup there are generally lots of mouths to feed so the largest pans around were used for cooking

PANTING Like a lizard on a hot rock ❏ like a hound dog that run a coon two counties ❏ his tongue was out so far he was lapping up dirt

PANTS Britches ❏ breeches ❏ pantaloons ❏ Levis ❏ jeans

PANTS, SHORT High water britches, which is derived from the practice of rolling up your pant legs to wade through high water. For a Texan, any pants that don't reach almost all the way to the ground are high water britches

PANTS, TORN IN THE REAR Looks like he ate an alley cat, which implies the cat was clawing and scratching on the way out as well as on the way in

PARENTAL AUTHORITY Woodshed diplomacy ❏ a

mama hen has the right to peck her chicks on the head if they need it

PARENTS Folks

PARK BENCH Spit and whittle bench ❑ loafers log

PARKING TICKET Bill for landing

PART OF Part and parcel of

PARTICIPATE If you ain't branding, you can hold a rope ❑ if you ain't skinning, you can hold a leg

PARTICIPATED Had a hand in, such as "He had a hand in lynching the horse thief."

PARTICULAR PERSON He'd complain if they hung him with a new rope ❑ wouldn't steal a chicken if it wasn't a brown leghorn ❑ when she checked into heaven she insisted on seeing the upstairs

PARTNER In Texas, it's pardner

PARTNERSHIP Pardnership ❑ in bed together ❑ in cahoots

PARTIER Born under a honky tonk moon

PARTY (CELEBRATE) Staying out with the dry cattle. Refers to dry cows staying out in the pasture rather than coming in to be milked.

PARTY (NOUN) A bee, as in a quilting bee ❑ shootaree ❑ fiesta ❑ fandango

PARTY GOER Hell (or cane) raiser ❑ ring tailed tooter ❑ Saturday night sinner

PARTY TIME Let's rodeo ❑ wanna rodeo ❑ let's honky tonk ❑ the honky tonk moon is up

PAST, QUESTIONABLE Got blind spots in his back trail

PASSED AWAY *See Died*

PASSED GAS A roar in his rumble seat

PASSED ME Thundered by like we were set up on jack stands ❑ went by in a blur ❑ fogged right on by

PASSENGER Window watcher

PATH TO RIGHTEOUSNESS The good road is straight and narrow, which is why it's so darn hard to follow

PATIENCE Hot will cool if greedy will let it ❑ of an angel assigned to a Texan ❑ Texan Sam Rayburn said the three most important words in the English language are "just a minute."

PATIENT As a circling buzzard waiting for a sick mule to die

PATRIOTIC Flag waver ❑ anthem singer ❑ he even knows his school song

PATRONIZE Plays up to ❑ butters up ❑ kisses his foot (or other parts of the anatomy)

PAY ATTENTION Pay some mind to ❑ set your mind on it ❑ even a horse wearing blinders can see what's up ahead if he'll just look

PAY UP Pony up ❑ cough it up

PAY YOUR DUES Earn your spurs ❑ if you give a dance, you gotta pay the band (or the fiddler)

PEACE LOVING If God had intended me to fight like a dog, he'd have given me longer teeth and claws ❑ he's more of a lover than a wild bull rider

PEDERNALES Pronounced Purr-din-alice. A river in South Texas.

PEOPLE Folks ❑ common folks ❑ everyday folks

PEOPLE, GOOD My kind of folks

PERFECTIONIST Don Meredith said it best when he described Tom Landry as a perfectionist, "If he was married to Racquel Welch," Meredith said, "he'd expect her to cook." A perfectionist lady might be one who, if married to Burt Reynolds, would expect him to mow the lawn.

PERFORMANCE, POOR Gave it a lick and a promise

PERFUME Parfume ❑ liquid lure ❑ follow-me-boys ointment ❑ liquid fly paper, which refers to a woman dabbing on the perfume in the hopes of catching a man like fly paper does a fly ❑ phoo-phoo water ❑ holy water, which means when she puts it on she prays she will smell good enough to attract a man

PERMANENT Set in cement or concrete ❑ you can't blot a brand, which means once a brand has been burned into the hide of a steer, it's permanent. A brand can be changed by a rustler but it cannot be erased ❑ carved in stone ❑ dyed in the wool, which refers to the fact that once the dye is in the wool, it is there to stay

PERSEVERE Hard work keeps the fences up ❑ the best buck gets the doe ❑ if the steer wouldn't come to the branding fire, take the fire to the steer ❑ catch a fish, even if you have to dig a canal and drain the tank ❑ if steel won't cut it, diamond will, which is a reference to using diamond drill bits ❑ ride her out ❑ lick by lick, any old cow can polish off a grindstone ❑ if you mind your knitting, you'll eventually have a sweater that will fit someone ❑ Old-time Texas Ranger Bill McDonald said, "No man in the wrong can stand up against a man in the right who keeps a comin'." It could also be said that no man could stand up against a woman who keeps a coming. Hugh Roy Cullen said, "Anybody can swim into a whirlpool. It's coming out of it that counts."

PERSIST Stick to your guns ❑ the squeaking wheel gets the grease ❑ it's eight seconds to ride and a lifetime to think about it. This refers to a rodeo

cowboys having to ride bulls and bucking horses for eight seconds. Whether they make the ride or get thrown off, they get to think about it the rest of their lives. A variation of this is often used by a football coaches, whose team is behind at half time, when he says, "You have 30 minutes to play and a lifetime to think about it."

PERSON, SUPERFICIAL An empty bucket makes the most noise. The reference here is that an empty bucket will get dropped and kicked around, which makes a lot of noise, while a full bucket will be handled carefully. The inference is that a superficial person will make a lot of noise while a person full of character will not.

PERSON OF HIGH ESTEEM He's all beer and no foam

PERSON OF LOW ESTEEM He's all foam and no beer

PESTER Worry him a link or two ❑ get under his saddle like a cocklebur

PHYSICIAN *See Doctor*

PIANO PLAYER Ivory tickler, which refers to the days when the keys of a piano where made of ivory ❏ piano pounder, which is how Bob Wills described his piano player, Al Strickland

PIECE A chunk

PICK THE BEST Get the pick of the litter ❏ separate the wheat from the chaff. Chaff is the seed coverings and miscellaneous debris that is separated out in thrashing ❏ cull the lot. It's been said the man who culls the crop of girls, spends a lot of nights alone

PICKUP TRUCK Pickemup ❏ cowboy Cadillacs ❏ pickup. In Texas it isn't necessary to include "truck" since everybody knows a pickup is something you drive, not something you find in a honky tonk. It has been said you can't be a real Texan if you don't drive a pickup

PILOT Propeller boys ❏ fly boys ❏ jet wrangler

PILOT, POOR A hangar flyer, which implies he spends more time around the hangar talking about flying than he does in the air

PIOUS Preacherfied

PIOUS WOMAN Raised on prunes and proverbs

PISTOL Hog leg ❏ six shooter ❏ persuader ❏ peacemaker ❏ shootin' iron ❏ 45 ❏ pistole ❏ lead pusher ❏ lead chucker ❏ cutter ❏ belt gun ❏ Saturday night special *See also Gun*

PLAIN Unplowed ❏ unvarnished *See also Obvious*

PLAIN AS Fresh plowed ground, which infers that no crop is growing, thus the ground is plain ❏ as the nose on your face ❏ as the top line on an eye chart ❏ the ears on a mule

PLACE TO SET A spot to squat ❏ a hunker down spot

PLAGIARISM He'd publish the Ten Commandments (or bill of rights) under his name if he could get away with it

PLAN AHEAD Build the fence before you buy the cattle (or horses) ❏ build a coop before you buy the chickens ❏ drill the well before you build the windmill ❏ Noah built his ark before it started raining ❏ Hugh Roy Cullen said, "If you plan anything before you do it, you will usually come out all right. When you jump into anything without thinking about it ahead of time, you've got to trust luck." As the old saying goes, no amount of planning will replace blind luck.

PLAN TO STAY Aim to stick around a spell ❏ brought my toothbrush and a change of underwear

PLANO, TEXAS Pronounced Plain-oh, never Plan-oh, a mid-sized town just north of Dallas in Collin County, known for producing legendary high school football teams.

PLAY Horse around, which refers to the playfulness of an unbridled horse

PLAY BY THE RULES According to Hoyle. In gambling, especially poker, it could be "according to Doyle." This is a reference to Doyle "Texas Dolly" Brunson, considered by many to be the best high stakes poker player ever to lift a chip. *According to Doyle* was the title of a book published by Brunson in 1984.

PLAYER Shooter, which is derived from shooting dice in a crap game

PLAYFUL AS A calf in clover ❏ as an unbridled horse

PLEASING That's so good it would make childbirth a pleasure ❏ tickled my fancy ❏ it'll warm your gullet ❏ a sight for sore eyes ❏ it'll make your skin tight

PLEASED Tickled to death ❏ pleased as punch ❏ my toes are tingling

PLENTY Got it in carload lots ❏ in wholesale lots ❏ a whole deck of ❏ a whole herd of

PLOW Turn some clods ❏ go stare at the mule's rear, which refers to the days when farmers plowed behind mules so there wasn't too much scenery

PLUMBER Pipes doctor

POISON Pizzen

POKER GAME, SMALL Saddle blanket game. The cowpunchers on the trail never had a table to play cards on so they simply spread a saddle blanket on the ground.

POKER HAND, POOR Holding a paregoric

POLICE Po-leece ❏ do-right boys ❏ bear ❏ Federales ❏ rangers ❏ county Mountie ❏ badge toter ❏ arm of the law ❏ pavement pounder *See also*

Highway Patrolmen, Lawmen, Outrun the Law

POLITICS "The science of public service," according to former Texas Governor Pat Neff ❑ those that can, do, those that can't, run for office ❑ legalized larceny

POLITICAL A fool and your money are running for office

POLITICIAN Baby kisser ❑ spoiled by being given a pull on the public teat ❑ When flour salesman W. Lee "Pappy" O'Daniel ran for governor he couldn't vote for himself because he didn't pay his poll tax, claiming, "No politician in Texas is worth $1.75" He won anyway. O'Daniel is often credited with coining the phrase "Washington is the only lunatic asylum in the world run by its own inmates."

POLITICIAN, POOR He couldn't get elected if he ran unopposed ❑ he couldn't get elected fiddler general of Texas

POND, SMALL Tank ❑ stock tank ❑ dirt tank ❑ watering hole

POOR Couldn't buy hay for a nightmare ❑ as a lizard-eating cat ❑ ain't got a pot to pee in or a window to throw it out of ❑ had to wear a straw hat to Christmas. In Texas you wear straw hats in the summer and felt hats in the winter, thus anyone wearing straw at Christmas would be too poor to buy a felt hat ❑ my folks told me Santa got killed in the world war ❑ hogs wouldn't eat our slop ❑ so poor I had a tumbleweed as a pet ❑ boots so thin you could see the wrinkles in my socks ❑ didn't have enough clothes to dust a fiddle or pad a crutch *See also Bankrupt, Broke, Destitute, Poverty Stricken*

POOR, BUT PROUD Too poor to paint, too proud to whitewash

POOR QUALITY Crow bait ❑ cull ❑ ain't worth two bits ❑ put together with spit and baling wire ❑ plug ❑ ain't worth a hoot or a holler *See also Worthless*

POPPED Like a firecracker

POPPED OPEN Like a morning glory

POPPED OUT Like a spit watermelon seed

POPULAR As an oilman's (or banker's) daughter

This Dog'll Hunt

POPULARITY Bum Phillips said, "No matter how popular you are, the size of your funeral depends on the weather."

PORCH Gallery ❑ veranda

PORK SKINS Cracklin's

POSITIVE Right sure ❑ sure as hell's hot ❑ you can tattoo it on the wall (or your forearm) ❑ you can write it in ink *See also Certain, Fact, Guaranteed, Reliable*

POSSIBLE Even a blind hog finds an acorn now and then ❑ never been a horse that can't be rode or a cowboy that can't be throwed ❑ anything is possible if you have the know-how or the money

POSSESSIONS Belongings ❑ plunder

POTATO Tater

POTENT Can cure more than patent medicine ❑ as a broken bottle of French perfume in a boy's dorm ❑ as a mare's breath

POUTER Thumb sucker

POVERTY STRICKEN Poor as a lizard-eating cat ❑ poor as a church mouse ❑ poor as a

sawmill rat ❑ ate so many armadillos when I was young, I still roll up into a ball when I hear a dog bark ❑ we had to fertilize the sills before we could raise the windows, which is how poor Bum Phillips said his family was *See also Broke, Destitute & Poor*

POWERFUL PERSON If he crows it's daylight. It was said of Houston's Jesse Jones, "When that rooster crows, it's daylight in East Texas." Jones owned considerable land and lumber holdings in East Texas.

PRACTICAL JOKER His main crop is tom foolery ❑ he'd pull the leg of a wild bull for a laugh

PRACTICE Dry shooting (or frying). Dry shooting is learning all about shooting a gun without using any ammunition. Dry frying is learning how to cook without having any grease in the skillet

PRAYING Talking to headquarters

PRAYING MANTIS Devil's walking stick

PREACHER Bible thumper (or pounder) ❑ sin buster ❑ parson ❑ sky pilot ❑ padre ❑ gospel shooter ❑ bible banger ❑ gospel grinder ❑ devil chaser ❑ gospel wrangler ❑ hallelujah peddler ❑ pulpit pounder ❑ sin killer ❑ the Lord's deputy ❑ Heaven's posse foreman ❑ hell, fire, and brimstone man ❑ hell, fire, and damnation man

PREARRANGED It's already been cut and dried ❑ the wool is already dyed

PREDICAMENT A communist plot *See also In Danger, In Trouble*

PREFERENCE Druthers ❑ rather do that than dig for buried treasure ❑ beats a poke in the eye with a sharp stick ❑ whatever pops your cork, whatever blows your dress up ❑ whatever winds your clock ❑ as soon do that as eat a bug ❑ a wink is as good as a nod to a blind mule

PREGNANT Heiferized ❑ she's sitting on a nest ❑ she swallowed a pumpkin seed ❑ she's flying her flag at half mast ❑ a heavy springer ❑ her apron is riding high ❑ got one in the oven ❑ got one in the chute ❑ looks like she swallowed a watermelon seed

PREGNANT WITH 2ND CHILD She's got one bucking and one in the chute, which is a reference to loading rodeo chutes

PREPARED Done my homework ❑ primed and ready ❑ got the rifle sighted in ❑ running on a full tank ❑ ready for all comers ❑ hunkered down and raring to go

PRESUMPTUOUS Just because you donate an organ to the church, don't mean you call the tunes to be played

PRETEND Shooting at the hump. Anyone shooting at the hump of a buffalo, where there are no vital organs, was just pretending to hunt

PRETTY Purdy

PRETTY AS A field of bluebonnets ❑ as a picture ❑ as a fresh painted wagon ❑ as a speckled pup under a wagon

PRETTY GIRL Cheerleader material ❑ a real looker ❑ a real beaut ❑ eyeball pleaser (or soother) *See also Female*

PREVAIL *See Persist, Persevere*

PRIDE So thick a Bowie knife wouldn't cut it ❑ every old hen thinks her chicks are best

PRIORITIZE Don't chase grasshoppers when the hogs are eating the corn ❑ get your ducks in a row ❑ don't be baiting rat traps in the barn when coyotes are after the spring calves

PRISONER Penitentured

PRIVATE As underwear ❑ as your dirty wash

PROBABLE Likely as not ❑ in all likelihood, it'll happen

PROBLEM Grasshoppers in the axle grease ❑ a fly in the buttermilk ❑ we got a yellow jacket nest in the outhouse ❑ that's the thorn in my side ❑ a fly in the ointment ❑ a firefly in the milk churn ❑ a burr under his blanket *See also In Trouble, Trouble*

PROFESSION Stock in trade ❑ his main (or long) suit

PROFICIENT He's been doing that since before he could drool ❑ right handy with, as in "He's right handy with a fork" ❑ on a first name basis with, as in "He's on a first name basis with the business

end of a hoe." *See also Experienced*

PROGRESSING Made it to the fast lane but I'm still on a farm to market road

PROMISCUOUS Free for all

PROOF Got the deadwood on 'em ❑ the low down

PROSPEROUS Living high on the hog ❑ sitting (or living) in high cotton ❑ he sneezes through silk, a reference to someone well off enough to afford silk handkerchiefs *See also Rich*

PROSTITUTE A John's dear, which is a takeoff on John Deere tractors ❑ fallen angel ❑ soiled dove ❑ pavement princess ❑ painted lady ❑ trick wrangler ❑ flatbacker ❑ floozy ❑ hooker

PROTECT Guard that like a farmer does a watermelon patch ❑ scarecrow it ❑ bury that bone so no other dog'll get it ❑ look after it like a blue jay guarding her nest (or a she bear with cubs)

PROTECT YOURSELF Circle the wagons ❑ fort up

PROTECTED He's bulletproof, he's fired proof, which

means someone isn't likely to be fired from a job

PROTESTED Raised a bigger stink than a herd of polecats.

PROUD He's swelled up like a poisoned pup ❑ swelled up like a frog in a churn ❑ struttin' like a gobbler at layin' time

PROUD AS A peacock ❑ as a dog with two tails ❑ as a pup with a new collar

PROVIDER, POOR The bacon he brings home is just sow's belly ❑ he don't bring home enough bacon to fill a toy skillet

PROVOKED Egged me into it

PRUDE Old iron pants

PRUDENT Don't waste buck-shot on a sparrow, which basically means don't waste ammunition killing a sparrow since they are too small to eat and too hard to clean

PUNISH Take 'em to the woodshed ❑ fix (or clean) his clock ❑ clean his plow ❑ dust his feathers

PURE As driven snow

PURPLE As eggplant

PURSE Pocketbook

PUSH Mash. In Texas you don't push a doorbell, you mash it.

PUT IN WRITING Script it ❑ black and white it

PUT IT ON Like a mud plaster

PUZZLED Buffaloed ❑ the windshield of my mind is fogged over

QUICK — as a minnow can swim a dipper

QUALIFIED Earned his spurs ❑ made the grade

QUALITY, GOOD Blue ribbon fine ❑ cream rises to the top ❑ a State Fair winner, which refers to winning entries in the annual contests held at the State Fair in Dallas

QUALITY, POOR Don't make the grade ❑ alligator bait ❑ middlin' poor ❑ wouldn't even make honorable mention at the State Fair

QUANTITY A mess of ❑ a dose of ❑ a whole slew of ❑ a plenty ❑ right smart of ❑ more than you can shake a stick at *See also Lot, Many, Numerous*

QUARTER Two bits ❑ juke-box feed

QUEEN (PLAYING CARD) Mop squeezer ❑ washer woman

QUEER As a three-dollar bill ❑ as pink ink

QUICK Moves mighty sudden like ❑ went by so fast I thought I was backing up ❑ plenty pronto ❑ double fast ❑ could thread a needle mounted in a running sewing machine ❑ lickety split ❑ on the trigger or draw *See also Fast*

QUICK AS A minnow can swim a dipper, which Darrell Royal says is how fast a punt return can kill you in a football game ❑ as beaters on an electric mixer ❑ as the flames of hell can scorch a tail feather ❑ as the snap of a bull whip ❑ as a hiccup ❑ as a New York minute ❑ as a heart beat❑ as heaven's gate slams shut on a horse thief ❑ as a settin' hen on a June bug ❑ as you can bat an eye ❑ as a winter wind can lift a dead leaf ❑ a roadrunner on a rattler ❑ as a hair trigger will get you shot in the foot ❑ as a hot iron can scorch a cotton dress *See also Fast As*

QUICK ACTING Goes through you like bunkhouse (or mess hall) chili ❑ goes through you like corn through a goose ❑ like a dose of Epsom through a widow woman

QUICK TEMPERED Has a fuse shorter than an ant's eyebrow ❑ hair trigger temper ❑ he's prone to flying plumb off the handle ❑ evil tempered ❑ he shoots first and doesn't even bother to ask questions later

QUIET You could hear hair grow ❑ you could hear the break of day ❑ as a nightgown dropped on a plush carpet ❑ the silence was deafening ❑

you could smell the odor of
dead silence ❏ you can hear a
hummingbird's heart beat ❏
well muzzled ❏ prayer time ❏
library time ❏ talks one half
as much as an oyster with his
shell shut ❏ you could hear a
pin drop on a cotton bloom in
the next county ❏ he never
mixes breath and tongue oil ❏
you could hear a field mouse
wetting on a cotton boll

QUIET AS A snowflake on a
feather ❏ as a thief in the dark
❏ as a deaf mute's shadow ❏
as a grave at night ❏ as a
church mouse ❏ as a well
greased wagon in sand ❏ as
the rustle of a cotton dress

QUILTS Soogans ❏ Baptist
pallet

QUIT Pulled my lariat ❏
cashed in ❏ threw my spurs
away ❏ sold my horse and
sacked my saddle ❏ called it a
day ❏ threw in (or folded) my
hand

QUIT DRINKING Weaned
myself off the bottle

R

RUNNIN' — around like a chicken with his head cut off

RACE Running match

RAIN, HARD A frog (or toad) strangler ❑ a goose drowner ❑ a gully washer ❑ like a cow peeing on a flat rock ❑ like somebody knocked over the water tank ❑ a dam duster ❑ a chunk, stump, cob, or clod floater ❑ duck drencher ❑ raining cats and dogs ❑ pouring bull frogs and heifer yearlings ❑ rained like God pulled the cork or opened the drain

RAIN, INTERMITTENT My double barreled shotgun only got wet in one barrel ❑ you could count the drops

RAIN, SOFT Lasted about as long as an old woman's dance ❑ just enough to run off the roof

RAINY Duck weather

RAMBUNCTIOUS Hell raiser ❑ feeling his oats

RAN Like a jackrabbit feeling a coyote's breath on his back side *See also Runs*

RANCH, SMALL An oleo ranch, which means it is a cheap spread ❑ a tumbleweed outfit ❑ a cocklebur outfit ❑ don't have enough beef to hold a BBQ

RANCH, LARGE Measured by MPG, which is miles per gate.

RANCHER Fluent in hoss talk (or chatter) ❑ speaks cow like a steer ❑ what he don't know about cattle don't need to be known

RAPID *See Quick, Fast*

RARE As bluebonnets in October ❑ as an old maid's wedding anniversary ❑ ain't seen one of those in a coon's age ❑ as a white blackbird ❑ as a round trip ticket to heaven ❑ as a one-legged hurdler ❑ as a tear at a boot hill burying. In the days of the old west, it was generally the bad men and outlaws who were buried in boot hill so there weren't a lot of tears shed over them ❑ as a jackelope, which is a Texas jack rabbit that has spiked horns like an antelope. These critters are the result of Texas jackrabbits being so big that male antelopes often mistake them for female antelopes during mating season. Fortunately for the jackrabbits, they can usually outrun the antelope so the offspring that would have been produced - the jackelope - are extremely rare. *See also Scarce*

RARE MEAT The brand is still smoking ❑ seen a cow cut worse than this get well ❑ just thrown across the fire ❑ if I got caught eating this in someone else's pasture, I'd go to jail for rustling ❑ all they did was knock the horns off ❑ get me a Band-Aid and I can save the steer

RASCAL Yahoo ❑ ring tailed tooter ❑ rounder ❑ maverick ❑ pistol ❑ wild turkey ❑ wild and wooly ❑ corker ❑ scoundrel

RATHER Druther

RATTLE Like BBs in a box car ❑ like marbles in a washtub

RATTLESNAKE Bell tailed snake ❑ buzzer tailed snake

REACTED QUICKLY It don't take him long to look at a hot horse shoe. This saying is derived from the joke about a know-it-all who visited a blacksmith shop. Although warned not to, he picked up a red hot horseshoe and naturally dropped it very quickly. When asked if it was too hot to handle, he replied, "Naw, it just don't take me long to look at a hot horseshoe."

READY Got his holster tied down ❑ she's all brushed and curried ❑ he's got the hammer cocked ❑ she's combed her fur and tuned her purr ❑ he's all saddled up ❑ he's screwed down and sitting deep in the saddle, which means he's ready to ride

READY, ALWAYS You'll never find him sitting on his gun hand

REAL Sure enough genuine ❑ sure 'nuff ❑ natural born, as in "He's a natural born cowboy"

REAL COUNTY There is a real Texas county named Real but it is pronounced ra al, which is Spanish for royal.

REAL MAN Got hair on his belly and gravel in his guts

REAPPEARED Bobbed up again, which is a reference to fishing with a bobber

REAR END Patoot ❑ back of the lap ❑ part of the chicken that went over the fence last ❑ south end of a north bound mule (or horse) ❑ bohunkus ❑ rump ❑ south pasture ❑ hindquarters ❑ hind tail (or end) ❑ tailgate ❑ sitter downer ❑ differential ❑ beehind

REAR END, LARGE She looks like two hogs are living in the back of her jeans ❑ heavy bottomed ❑ he measures two ax handles wide between the hip pockets ❑ her jeans are living proof that 50 pounds will fit in a 25-pound sack ❑ if you tell him to haul butt, it would take two trips, minimum ❑ he's got the old office job spread, implying that those who sit all day will have a larger rear end than those who are on their feet most of the time.

REAR END, SMALL Looks like some witch doctor shrunk his hiney instead of his head ❑ skinny hipped ❑ runt butt ❑ a hummingbird hiney ❑ if he ain't careful, he'd fall plumb through an outhouse hole

REBEL Maverick *See also Nonconformist*

RECALL I'm minded of ❑ that minds me of ❑ that brings to mind

RECKLESS As a calf kicking yellow jackets ❑ he filed the half cock off his gun, which means the gun wouldn't have a safety

RECONCILE Never let the sun set on a problem

RECORD Put it in the tally book. A tally book is where the ranch recorded its cattle holdings

RECOVER Don't cry over spilt milk ❑ pull yourself up by the boot straps ❑ pick yourself up and dust off the dirt ❑ you never fall so far that you can't climb back up

RECOVERED Gave his pall bearers the slip ❑ got the swagger back in his walk and the valor back in his backbone.

REDUCE Whittle it down to middlin size

REFORMED HIPPIE Born again redneck

REFORMED SINNER He got painted into an amen corner

REFUGIO, TEXAS Pronounced Re-fury-oh, a small town in deep South Texas.

REGULAR As clockwork ❑ as a duck goes barefooted

RESEMBLES Favors ❑ takes after

RELATED Off the same coil ❑ out of the same case ❑ cut from the same bolt ❑ they climb the same family tree

RELATIVES Kin ❑ kinfolk ❑ blood kin ❑ kissin' kin ❑ blood relations ❑ the folks ❑ suitcase company, which implies they stay longer than just plain friends

RELATIVES, DISTANT We're last cousins

RELAX Breathe easy ❑ rest your mind ❑ sit a spell ❑ barn your brain, which is a reference to putting horses in the barn after a ride ❑ no one ever got bit by a dog's shadow ❑ it'll all come out in the wash

RELEASE Cut 'em loose ❑ let loose all holts (holds) ❑ open the cage or cell door ❑ jerk off the bridle and turn a loose ❑ cut the reins ❑ saw off the handcuffs

RELENTLESS Don't believe in breathing spells

RELIABLE If he says a pissant can pull a boxcar, you can hook 'em up ❑ you can hang your hat on it *See also Certain, Fact*

RELIGIOUS PERSON Everything he says is fodder for a sermon ❑ cut his teeth on a collection plate ❑ camps out

in the amen corner ❑ a branded and earmarked Christian ❑ runs under the cross brand *See also Reformed Sinner*

REMEMBER Keep green the memory of ❑ get your recollections started ❑ jump start your memory

REMINDS ME Puts me in the mind of ❑ calls to mind

REMODEL Fresh paint covers a lot of dirt

REMOTE Clear to the back side of nowhere *See also Rural*

RENT A CAR Hire a rig

REPAIR Put the pieces back together ❑ spit and baling wire it, give it a stobectomy (See Do-it-yourself)

REPAIR, TEMPORARY Clodhopper or sharecropper repairs, which is mending a fence by using baling wire to connect rusty barbed wire to a rotten fence post.

REPEAT Ride over that trail again ❑ run that horse by me one more time

REPEATEDLY Time and time again

REPEATING You've already whipped that old dog ❑ you've already run that horse into the ground

REPENT You better apply to St. Peter for a passport

REPRIMAND Read 'em the riot act ❑ read 'em the ranch (or boardinghouse) rules

REQUIREMENT If you give a dance in Texas, you better hire a band with a fiddle player

RESCUE Save the bacon ❑ pull the fat out of the fire ❑ snatch victory from the jaws of defeat ❑ save his hide

RESEMBLES Favors

RESERVE Ace in the hole (or up the sleeve)

RESIST She got up on her hind legs like a frightened mare ❑ buck, as in "He'll buck any attempt to close the saloon."

RESPECT, EARNED *See Friendship*

RESOLVED It all came out in the wash

REST Cool your heels ❑ rest your saddle ❑ shade up ❑ sit a spell ❑ take a breather ❑ if you rest you rust

RESTLESS Chomping at the bit ❑ as a kid in church ❑ as a hen on a hot griddle

RESTRAIN Keep the lid screwed on ❑ keep 'em on the reservation ❑ lock 'em up and swallow the key ❑ use piggin' string if you can't find hand-cuffs. Piggin' string is the short rope a cowboy uses to tie up the legs of a calf in a rodeo.

RESTRAINED Bridled ❑ clipped my wings ❑ hogtied ❑ hamstrung

RESTROOM Necessary room ❑ inside outhouse

RETALIATE Fix his wagon ❑ wind his clock ❑ what goes around comes around ❑ give him a dose of his own medicine ❑ give him back his hard times

RETREAT Drop back a notch or two ❑ come down a rung or two ❑ fire and fall back

RETIRE, EARLY Go to bed with the chickens

RETIRED Pasturized ❑ out to pasture ❑ joined the spit and whittle club ❑ traded his gold watch for a rockin' chair ❑ moth balls have replaced his ball bearings ❑ the wife's gettin half the money and twice the husband

RETRACTION He's eating crow, feathers, beak and all

RETRIBUTION Whatever fits around the devil's neck will also fit around his waist, which is an old East Texas saying that roughly means anyone who treats you bad will get a dose of their own medicine.

RETURN SECRETLY Circle back

RETURN TO WORK Get back to your rat killing, rodeoing, or branding

REVENGE Put a stinging lizard (scorpion) in his pocket and ask for a match

REVERSED It's bassackwards

RICE Swamp seed

RICH Got enough money to burn a wet elephant (or mule) ❏ got enough to pay the Bill of Rights ❏ eats high on the hog ❏ could hunt with the Hunts ❏ he owns controlling interest in half of all creation ❏ richer than the dirt in an old cow pen ❏ he could air condition hell ❏ carries a wad big enough to choke a horse ❏ got more money than God ❏ in the lap of luxury

RICH BUT INEPT Born with a silver foot in his mouth. This phrase was immortalized by Texas State Treasurer Ann Richards in her keynote address at the 1988 Democratic National Convention. She made the remark with reference to George Bush. Also, he puts his handmade boots on the wrong feet

RIDE A HORSE Flap you chaps ❏ work your spurs

RIDICULOUS Horse feathers ❏ as trying to catch rain water in a dip net ❏ as asking John Wesley Hardin to guard the jail *See also Irrelevant*

RIFLE Smoke stick ❏ meat gitter

RIFLE, POWERFUL Kicks hard enough to get meat at both ends, implying it will kill game with a bullet fired from one end and scrape the hide off your shoulder with the kick from the other end

RIGHT SIDE Gee, which is an old-time mule skinner's word for right

RIGID As a crow bar ❑ as a windmill wrench ❑ as a frozen rope *See also Stiff*

RIO GRANDE RIVER Texans drop both the "e" and the River for simply the Rio Grand. Translated it means grand river.

RISES, FAST As fertilized weeds ❑ as oil from a gusher ❑ as gasoline prices in an oil shortage

RISES, SLOW As biscuits in a cold oven ❑ as a hot air balloon in hell ❑ as smoke off a fresh cow patty

RISK, SMALL Gambling with someone else's chips ❑ playin' with someone else's money

RISK TAKER A riverboat gambler ❑ wildcatter ❑ blazes his own trail ❑ plays dominos with his eyes closed ❑ shoots dice over the phone

RISKY As sitting on a powder keg and smoking a four-bit cigar ❑ riding for a fall ❑ you're playing cards with the devil and there ain't no limit ❑ you're dancing with the devil's girlfriend ❑ you're wading in quicksand ❑ you're climbing a lightning rod in a thunderstorm ❑

you're out on a limb that is being sawed off behind you ❑ Lyndon Johnson said, "When you crawl out on a limb, you might have to find another one to crawl back on."

RIVER, FALLING The river shallowed down

ROADRUNNER Paisano (pi zah no) ❑ chaparral bird. These fast, elusive birds, which are occasionally seen running across roads in South and West Texas, are one of the few natural enemies of the deadly rattlesnake.

ROBBED Picked clean as a dog's bone ❑ stole blind ❑ they took everything but the air in my lungs *See also Lost Everything*

ROCK, BIG Enough to use as an anchor on the battleship Texas ❑ big enough to hold down a wagon in a whirlwind ❑ would make the rock of Gibraltar look like a kid's skipping stone ❑ weighs more than the rock of ages ❑ if it was steel it could be an anvil

ROCK, BIG AND FLAT If a cow wet on that she could water half an acre. For the uneducated, a cow wetting on a flat rock produces a splatter that gets everything wet for at least half an acre.

ROCK, FLAT Skipping stone, which refers to flat rocks being the easiest to skip across a stock tank when you don't have anything else to do

RODEO A real Texan will always say row-dee-o, never, ever row-day-oh.

ROLEX WATCH In good times, it was a Texas Timex. These days a lot of folks are tryin' to tell time on a pawn ticket.

ROLL IT UP Spool it

ROLLING Like a horse taking a dirt bath ❏ like a wallowing buffalo

ROMANTIC As a river walk, especially a San Antonio river walk ❏ as the Texas moon. Although it has never been proven to be fact, many Texans believe the moon that shines over Texas is a little bigger and a little brighter that anywhere else.

ROOKIE Still wet behind the ears ❏ greener ❏ greenhorn ❏ so green he could hide in a lettuce patch ❏ green as two-week-old corn ❏ short horn *See also Tenderfoot*

ROOM, COLD Cold enough to hang meat in ❏ a shiver shack ❏ would make a deep freeze look like a steam room

ROOMY Got enough room to cuss the cat without getting a mouthful of fur

ROPE String ❏ silk manila, which, for a cowboy, is the standard of perfection as far as ropes are concerned ❏ portable cow catcher. To a cowpoke, a rope was the most versatile of tools. It doesn't rust, need grease, oil, or paint ❏ has no moving parts to break down and won't boil over in summer or freeze up in winter.

ROPE CONTEST A ropin'

ROPE, LONG Brag rope, which implies someone is skilful enough to make and control a very large loop, something to brag about, indeed.

ROPE, SHORT Piggin' string, which is the short rope rodeo cowboys use to tie the feet of calves in the calf roping event

ROPE LOOP, LARGE A prairie or West Texas loop. The larger the loop, the easier it is to rope something. In

West Texas there aren't a lot of brush and trees to get in the way so you can build a bigger loop.

ROPE LOOP, SMALL A South Texas loop, with reference to the above entry, in South Texas there are a lot of brush and mesquite trees which can make using a large loop difficult. The smaller the loop the harder the roping is to get done.

ROPER, GOOD A small-loop man ❑ he could put a loop over a tick on a mule's back with a barbed wire rope ❑ a one-loop man, which means he'll rope his target with only one loop ❑ he could rope an eagle if they weren't so hard to slip up on

ROPER, POOR A three-loop roper, which means it takes him at least three loops to catch his target ❑ couldn't get a rope on a steer if he sent the loop registered mail ❑ a big-loop roper

ROUGH AS A stucco bathtub ❑ as a petrified corn cob ❑ a wood rasp ❑ as tree bark ❑ burlap underwear ❑ as a woman's leg that ain't seen a razor in three weeks ❑ as barbed wire dental floss

ROUGH LOOKING Grizzled

ROUNDED As a dry land terrapin shell ❑ as the top of a ball bearing

ROUNDUP Cow hunt

ROUTINE Just another day at the ranch ❑ another day another dollar

RUDE Evil mannered ❑ suffers from hoof in mouth disease ❑ she'll even interrupt you when you talk in your sleep

RUIN, EMINENT The weevils are in the cornmeal

RUINED Ruint ❑ shot to hell ❑ messed with the playhouse ❑ gone to the dogs

RUN Shake a hoof ❑ fog it ❑ smoke your boots ❑ burn some boot leather ❑ scorch the pavement ❑ melt your tennis shoes

RUNAROUND Gave me a song and dance ❑ crawfished me

RUNS FAST As a scorched cat ❑ like a rabbit in a tunnel ❑ runs like Satan's breath was singeing his neck hair ❑ when he stops, it takes his shadow half an hour to catch up ❑ as a buck shot coyote ❑ as a rat up a rafter ❑ ran so fast the heat in his boots cauterized the blisters on his feet ❑ he's fleet a foot ❑ a real road eater ❑ he splits the wind and skins the ground ❑ moves fast enough to catch yesterday *See also Fast, Quick*

RUNNING AROUND Like a chicken with his head cut off

RURAL We lived so far out in West Texas the sun knocked a brick out of the fireplace every time it went down ❑ we lived so far out in the country that sunshine had to be piped (or trucked) in ❑ we live so far out in the country, we have to grease the wheel bearings three times just to make it to the main road ❑ we lived so far out in the country that my grandfather started to town to vote for Teddy Roosevelt and got there in time to vote for Franklin ❑ so far out into the country we didn't get the Grand Ol' Opry until Tuesday night, which is a reference to Saturday night radio broadcasts of the Grand Ol' Opry from Nashville, Tennessee. A more modern equivalent would be so far out in the country we don't get Monday Night Football till Wednesday morning

RUSTLER He raises cattle faster than anyone in Texas ❑

his calves don't suck the right cows ❑ packs a long rope, which refers to rustlers throwing big loops made from long ropes so they could catch cattle easier

RUTHLESS He doesn't have the conscience of a smuggler ❑ don't belive in taking prisoners ❑ he shoots first and forgets the questions ❑ his blood runs colder than freon in an air conditioner ❑ he'd dip an old maid in honey and stake her to an ant hill ❑ a bigger blood sucker than count Dracula hisself ❑ he shoots anything that moves *See also Mean, Vicious*

RUTHLESS WOMAN She's got the heart of a black widow spider. The black widow spider, common in Texas, is known for eating its mate. That's ruthless.

S

SAD — a., a d g whose family moved off an' left him

SACRIFICE Throw the rabbit to the coyotes ❑ waste a virgin ❑ throw your doll in the fire. This is a reference to the Indian version of the origin of the bluebonnet flower. As the story goes, an Indian tribe was suffering through a severe drought and their medicine man said the only way to bring rain was for someone to offer his most prized possession as a sacrifice to the gods. None of the adults would comply so finally a little girl threw her rawhide doll into a fire and it was destroyed. Before the flames had died down, it started to rain and the first bluebonnet sprang up in the ashes of the fire.

SAD Eye watering ❑ would jerk tears from a glass eye ❑ would produce enough tears to float an anvil ❑ would water the eyes of a veteran angel

SAD AS A hound dog whose family moved off and left him ❑ as a henpecked husband with a harem

SAD PERSON He's so down in the mouth he could eat oats out of a churn ❑ got an overdose of woe ❑ sad enough to cry a waterfall ❑ it would take a river of whiskey to drown my blues ❑ the bottom dropped out of his harmony

SADDLE UP Throw some leather on a horse

SADDLE SORES Saddle roses ❑ saddle strawberries

SADDLE, TEXAS STYLE Double fired or double barrelled saddle. Traditionally, Texas cowpokes used a heavy stock saddle with high cantel, large pommel, square skirt and two cinches.

SAFE As the inside of a snuff box in grannie's apron ❑ as a church meeting ❑ as being in God's back pocket ❑ as a squirrel up a tree ❑ as a field mouse in a haystack ❑ as a worm in a hole

SALAD BAR Garden corral

SALESMAN Drummer ❑ peddler

SALESMAN, GOOD Could sell a double bed to the Pope ❑ could sell ice cubes to Eskimos ❑ could sell snow shoes in San Antonio ❑ could sell sheep shears to a cattleman ❑ he sells the sizzle, not just the bacon ❑ could sell a furnace to the devil

SALESMAN, POOR Couldn't sell Popsicles in hell ❑ couldn't sell the devil an air conditioner ❑ he couldn't sell

201

tickets to the ark if it had been raining for two weeks

SALOON Beer joint ❑ honky tonk ❑ cantina ❑ watering hole ❑ road house ❑ cow country oasis ❑ hot joint that serves up cold beer ❑ liquor locker

SAN ANTONIO Pronounced San-Ann-tone by real Texans ❑ Also, Santone ❑ Alamo City ❑ the county seat of Bear (Bexar) county. If you spend any time in San Antonio, you will notice the streets seem to be laid out strangely. Popular legend has it that a blind Spaniard on a drunk mule laid out the city.

SANDSTORM Duster ❑ black duster ❑ black blizzard *See also Dust Storm*

SANK Like a rock with a hole in it ❑ like an anvil in a stock tank. An anvil is very heavy and would sink quickly in any body of water ❑ did a Titanic imitation

SATISFIED As a dead pig in the afternoon sunshine

SATISFYING Hits the spot ❑ fills the bill

SATURDAY Bath day

SAVE Salt some away, which is a reference to using salt to preserve meat

SAW (NOUN) Sawdust maker

SAW (VERB) Seen, as in "I seen who robbed the gas station." ❑ spied, as in "I spied a new pickup I'd like to have." ❑ laid eye's on, as in "It's the best I ever laid eyes on"

SAW TOO MUCH Got more than an eyeful

SAY IT Get a blast off your chest ❑ speak your piece ❑ spill the goods

SCARCE As hens teeth ❑ as bird droppings in a coo-coo clock ❑ as grass on a busy street ❑ as feathers on a frog (or pig) ❑ as ice water, snow cones, or Popsicles in hell ❑ as frog fangs ❑ as grass around a hog trough (or cow lick)

SCARED Boogered ❑ panic struck ❑ the living daylights out of me ❑ his heart skipped more beats than a drummer with the hiccups ❑ got the fear of God put in him ❑ into salvation and a Sunday school seat ❑ spooked ❑ trembling (or quaking) in his boots ❑ almost strangled on my heart

❏ chewing on his heart ❏ the dickens out of 'em ❏ scared half out of his wits ❏ turned my knees to Jello ❏ the bejabbers out of me ❏ got a mouthful of my own heart ❏ as a rabbit in a coyote's back pocket ❏ my backside puckered so much it bit two pounds of stuffing out of the front seat of my pickup *See also Frightened*

SCARED DOG Ran with his tail curled up so tight his hind legs were lifted off the ground. This refers to a scared dog running with his tail tucked under rather than flopping in the breeze ❏ ran like he had a can tied to his tail, which is something very scary to a dog

SCARS Hero marks ❏ battle tracks ❏ wound tracks ❏ skewer marks ❏ railroad tracks, which refers to scars from wounds that required stitches to close. E. J. Holub, the former linebacker out of Texas Tech and the Kansas City Chiefs, claimed he had had so many knee operations that the scars made him look like he'd been in knife fight with a midget.

SCARY Boogery ❏ makes your hair stand on end ❏ it'll cut the curl out of your hair or curl you hair, depending on whether or not your hair was curly to begin with ❏ a knee knocker, buckler, or trembler ❏ that would make you swallow your tobacco ❏ as the forked end of a rattlesnake tongue on the back of your hand ❏ enough to clabber a kid's blood ❏ enough to hairlip the governor ❏ a goose pimpler ❏ rates high on the pucker scale or carries a high pucker factor *See also Frightening*

SCARY MOVIE A white knuckler

SCATTERED To all the corners of Texas

SCHOOL Wisdom house

SCORPION Stinging lizard ❏ vinegroon, which is a large scorpion that smells like vinegar when squashed

SCOUNDREL Lower than a snake's belly (or navel) ❏ old buzzard ❏ stump sucker ❏ old galoot *See also Ruthless*

SCRATCHING Like a hen in a barnyard

SCRATCHY As burlap sheets or asbestos undershorts

SCREAM *See Squealed*

frying pan into the fire ❑ traded the devil for a witch ❑ put his boot, sock, and foot in his mouth ❑ bought a pig in a poke ❑ ripped his britches ❑ messed in his mess kit

Perhaps the best Screwed up is you kicked to the clock. This is a reference to the 1962 AFL Championship between the Dallas Texans and the Houston Oilers. Prior to the overtime coin toss, Dallas coach Hank Stramm instructed Abner Haynes to kick to the clock if Houston won the toss and elected to receive. Haynes carried out his instructions while a national TV audience listened in. The only problem was Dallas won the toss. When the referee asked Haynes to repeat his choice he said again, "We'll kick to the clock." The referee explained he could call the kickoff or which end zone he would defend, but not both. "We'll kick," replied a flustered Haynes. Houston Captain Al Jameson lost no time in proclaiming, "We'll take the wind." Thus Dallas had to give up the ball and the wind. Fortunately for ol' Abner, the Texans still won the game. Use "kicked to the clock" for screwed up and you always have a story to tell. **SEAL IT** Cauterize it ❑ nail it shut ❑ screw on the lid ❑ put it

to bed ❑ weld it shut ❑ cork the bottle

SEAMSTRESS, GOOD She keeps her thread galloping and her needles hot

SEARCH Beat the bushes ❑ fish around for ❑ with a fine toothed comb ❑ turn over all the rocks and cow patties in Texas ❑ look in all six directions. In Texas, it is said there are six directions, North, South, East, West, up to the moon, and down to hell

SECRET As a grand jury investigation ❑ as an old maid's dreams

SECRETIVE Close mouthed

SECURE Bulletproof and pig tight ❑ tied in a double knot with wet rawhide ❑ well bolted ❑ locked up tighter than a drum

SEE Lay an eye on

SEE A LOT He don't wear blinders, which means he doesn't have tunnel vision ❑ got more eyes than a peacock's tail, which is a reference to the eye-like designs in a peacock's tail

SEE YA' LATER Hasta la vista

SEEN ENOUGH Got an eyeful ❏ enjoyed about all this I can stand

SELECT *See Make a Choice*

SELF EMPLOYED If you don't try, you'll always work for the man that did

SELF RESPECT He's a legend in his own mind, which is how Hondo Crouch described himself

SELF TAUGHT Jake leg, such as "He's a jake leg mechanic."

SELL Turn it green ❏ garage sale it

SELL A LOT Does a big trade in ❏ does a land office business ❏ sells like popcorn at a country fair, beer at a baseball game, or Corny dogs at the State Fair ❏ sells like hot cakes

SEND Dispatch

SEND A MESSAGE Put a kid on a horse ❏ smoke it, referring to Indian smoke signals

SENSIBLE He's got good horse sense

SENSITIVE Thin skinned ❏ wears his feelings on his sleeve ❏ as a mule with a tick in his ear

SENSE DANGER Hearing hoofbeats or footsteps

SENTIMENTAL Would even kiss a ghost good-bye ❏ tears up at the drop of a hat ❏ even cries at sad television commercials

SEPARATED Split the blanket *See also Divorced*

SERIOUS Playing hard ball ❏ as a heart transplant ❏ as cancer ❏ as a grand jury indictment

SETTLED Ironed out the differences

SEVEN (PLAYING CARD) Wake up call, referring to leaving a wake call in a hotel for 7:00 o'clock in the morning

SEVERAL Right smart ❏ a good many

SEXY As a blonde in a Corvette convertible ❏ as a cowgirl in tight jeans

SHAKE HANDS Tangle mitts ❏ a two-fisted reunion

SHAKING Like a willow tree limb in a whirlwind ❑ like a hound dog passin' a peach pit ❑ like a wet dog ❑ like a hound dog eating razor blades ❑ so much I couldn't pour rainwater into a barrel with the head out *See also Nervous*

SHALLOW RIVER A good dew is deeper

SHARP Razor edged ❑ as a tack ❑ as a stinger ❑ as a pup's tooth ❑ as a mesquite thorn ❑ as the business end of a bumble bee

SHEEP Woolies ❑ hoofed locusts, which is a reference to sheep eating grass down to the top of the roots, like a swarm of locusts, and leaving nothing for cattle to graze on. For this reason it was widely thought that cattle and sheep could not graze on the same range until it dawned on someone that you could graze the cattle first and let the sheep eat what was left.

SHEPHERD Flockminder ❑ wooly wrangler

SHINY As an open mussel shell in the light of a Texas moon ❑ as a coon's (or deer's) eyes in a headlight beam ❑ as the bottom of a new (or clean) dish pan ❑ as a new mint penny

SHIVER A possum ran over your grave, often said when you shiver because someone scratched chalk across a blackboard

SHOCKED Could have knocked me over with a feather duster

SHOCKING As the business end of a cattle prod

SHOOK UP All jostled up inside ❑ half churned to death

SHOOT Burn some powder ❑ unravel a bullet

SHORT As a deadbeat's memory ❑ as an ant's eyebrow ❑ as the hemline of a mini-skirt

SHORT LIVED As a bottle at a barn raisin' ❑ as a pecan pie in a boardin' house ❑ as a June bug in a hen house

SHORT PERSON *See Small Person*

SHORT TIME About as long as you can hold a bear's (or bull's) tail ❑ about as long as you can hold a hot horseshoe

SHOT Leaned against a bullet going past ❑ plugged ❑ ventilated ❑ he's so full of lead his carcass would make a sinker factory

SHOTGUN Scatter gun ❑ bird gun

SHOULD Ought to, as in "You ought to pay that traffic ticket" ❑ might oughta, as in "I might oughta go to church someday."

SHOULD NOT Hadn't oughta, as in "You hadn't oughta do that " ❑ ought not, as in "You ought not to mess with a rattlesnake."

SHOULDER HOLSTER An ace in the armpit

SHUT UP Hobble your lip ❑ put a sock in it ❑ close your face gate ❑ bite down on the bit ❑ dally your tongue ❑ park your tongue ❑ put a plug in it ❑ cork it ❑ muffle it ❑ bridle your jaw ❑ tie your tongue in a square knot

SICK Down in the mouth ❑ as a poisoned pup ❑ I'd have to be dead three days to start feeling better *See also Ill and Ill, Gravely*

SIDEWAYS Slaunchways

SIGHT, IMPAIRED Couldn't see through a barbed wire (or pig) fence ❑ the only glasses

stronger than his would be a seeing eye dog

SIGHT UNSEEN Range delivered, which means something was bought and delivered to the ranch without being seen and inspected beforehand. A lot of cattle were bought sight unseen as range delivered.

SILENT She's shut up like a morning glory in the afternoon ❑ as a shadow ❑ as a mummy's tomb *See also Quiet*

SILLY Air headed ❑ fiddle footed

SILLY WOMAN Gill-flirt ❑ gillflurt ❑ jill-flirt

SILVERWARE Eatin' irons ❑ grub stakes

SIMILAR TO Akin to ❑ sort a like ❑ kindly like ❑ got the same earmarks

SIMPLE Dead easy ❑ anything easier would be against the law ❑ no hill for a stepper, no tree for a cat with a climbing gear ❑ as getting stuck in East Texas mud

SIMPLICITY Anything is simple if you got the brains, the brawn, or the bucks

SINFUL PERSON His dipping didn't take, which refers to the fact that Baptists immerse when they baptize ❑ a professional sinner ❑ it would take a ten-buggy prayer meeting to save him ❑ if you melted him down you couldn't pour him into a church pew ❑ went against his raising ❑ a deathbed Catholic, which means he'll only get religion on his deathbed *See also Bad Person, Evil Person, Immoral*

SINFUL PLACE Double fired or double barrelled sin joint ❑ palace of sin ❑ won't be long till sin's bustin' loose all over this place ❑ got sin oozing out of the floorboards (or rafters)

SINGER Crooner ❑ wailer

SINGER, GOOD Grand Ol' Opry material

SINGER, POOR He'd drive a coyote to suicide ❑ couldn't carry a tune in a corked bottle ❑ couldn't carry a tune in a box with the lid nailed shut ❑ sounds like a death rattle ❑ sounds like he's gargling with axle grease ❑ sounds like a dry axle

SINNER *See Sinful Person*

SISSY He was wet nursed till he was old enough to register

for the draft ❑ he drives a pink pickup ❑ a souper salad kind a guy ❑ limber tailed *See also Timid*

SITTING Bench rodeoing ❑ warming a chair

SIX (PLAYING CARD) Shooter, as in six-shooter

SIZEABLE *See Large*

SKELETON Bone rack

SKEPTICAL Wouldn't trust that if it was notarized by the Texas attorney general ❑ fishy eyed ❑ it takes a big biscuit to weigh a ton ❑ confidence is mighty frail ❑ he don't believe much of what he hears and only half of what he sees ❑ as a turkey in November ❑ as a fat fryer on a Sunday morning

SKILLFUL It's not the cards you get but how you play 'em that counts ❑ Sam Rayburn observed that, "Any jackass can kick down a barn, but it takes a skillful carpenter to build one."

SKIN (NOUN) Hide ❑ bark ❑ pelt

SKIN (VERB) Peel. Texas cowboys often referred to the hand who skinned the hide off a slaughtered steer as a "peeler."

SKINNED UP Lost enough hide to build a pair of snake leggins (or half sole an elephant) ❑ lost so much skin his own mother didn't know him from a fresh hide, which is hide that has recently been removed from the carcass

SKINNY He could stand under a clothesline in a thunderstorm and not get wet ❑ she could lay down under a clothesline and not get a sunburn ❑ she has to wear skies when she showers to keep from going down the drain ❑ he could crawl through the pipe on a depot stove and not get soot on a white shirt ❑ had to carry an anvil in his overalls to keep from blowing away ❑ so skinny he's almost transparent ❑ she could sit down on a quarter and you'd still be able to read "In God We Trust" ❑ built for speed rather than comfort ❑ hollow in the flanks ❑ have to stand up twice to cast a shadow ❑ he stuck out his tongue and looked like a zipper ❑ can shower in a gun barrel ❑ he'd have to run around in a shower to get wet ❑ he can run through an automatic car wash without getting wet ❑ a walking skeleton or a bag of bones ❑

had to tie knots in his legs for knees ❑ not much left but skin and bone ❑ smoke thin ❑ looks like he needs worming ❑ could hide in the shadow of a pig fence *See also Thin Person*

SKINNY AS A lizard-eating cat ❑ as a rail ❑ as a hairpin ❑ as the shadow of a barbed wire fence ❑ as the running board of a katydid ❑ as a bed slat ❑ as a dude's walking cane ❑ as a leg on a daddy long legs, which is a kind of spider with very thin legs

SKUNK Polecat ❑ stink sprayer

SLANTING Cattywhampus ❑ antigoglin ❑ out of square (or plumb) ❑ slaunchways ❑ his perpendicular is leaning toward the horizontal ❑ the purr is out of his perpendicular

SLEEP ON THE GROUND Use your belly as a cover and your back as a mattress

SLEEP SOUNDLY The snores of the righteous (or a man with a clear conscious) ❑ could sleep through a tornado (or hurricane) ❑ like a dead calf

SLICK As a watermelon seed ❑ as a greased door knob ❑ as okra ❑ as owl snot ❑ as a peeled cucumber ❑ as an eel in a barrel of oil ❏ as a greased ball bearing ❏ as a quarter dipped in mercury

SLINGSHOT Bean shooter ❏ pea shooter

SLIPPERY As a pocket full of banana pudding ❏ as a greased pig ❏ as owl grease ❏ as wet mud ❏ as a boiled onion ❏ as a dime dipped in mercury

SLOW As sucking buttermilk through a straw ❏ as molasses in January ❏ as smoke off a fresh cow patty in January ❏ as cream rising ❏ as wet gunpowder ❏ as a petrified porker ❏ as rush hour traffic in Houston ❏ as a hound dog in August

SLOW DOWN Drag your anchor ❏ throttle down ❏ drag your boots

SLOW MOVER If he was a baseball player, he'd be a human rain delay, which is how former Texas Ranger Mike Hargrove was often described because he took so long in the batters box getting ready for the pitch.

SLOW PERSON If they decide to hang me, I hope they send him to fetch the rope ❏ if he was in a race, you'd have to

time him with a calender instead of a stop watch ❏ moves slower than a milkman in a nudist colony ❏ couldn't outrun a newborn calf ❏ couldn't run fast enough to scatter the sweat on his forehead ❏ moves like he's got an anvil in his overalls ❏ he can gain weight walking ❏ he's only got three speeds, slow, slower, and petrified ❏ he couldn't keep up if he was shot out of a cannon ❏ he's dragging his tracks ❏ he's moving like his shadow is glued in place ❏ couldn't get out of the way of a funeral possession ❏ he's only got three speeds, start, stumble, and fall.

SLOW TALKER Thick tongued

SLOW WALKER He's so slow, his shadow went to sleep and he walked off and left it behind

SLOW WITTED Don't know the difference between a shotgun or a grease gun ❏ he'd try suicide with an electric razor ❏ could screw up an anvil (or a ball bearing) ❏ don't know spit from shineola ❏ if a duck had his brain it would fly west for the winter *See also Stupid, Ignorant*

SMALL Pissant sized ❑ peck-erwood sized ❑ tee ninety ❑ little bitty ❑ fryin' size ❑ as a cheap bar of soap after all the field hands have washed up ❑ as a frog fingernail ❑ about as big as the little end of nothing whittled to a point ❑ stingy in size ❑ hip pocket size ❑ pint sized ❑ half of a little bit ❑ half as big as a minute

SMALL AMOUNT Drop in the bucket (or Gulf of Mexico) ❑ a pissant's mouthful ❑ barely enough to fill a tick ❑ just a smidgen ❑ just a thimble full

SMALL HEAD Could look through a keyhole with both eyes at the same time

SMALL PERSON If he was a fish you'd have to throw him back ❑ he could take a sit down bath in a half-full dipper (or gourd) ❑ stands ankle high to a June bug ❑ knee high to a grasshopper, katydid, or Coke bottle ❑ he'd have to stand up to look a snake in the eye ❑ could take a bath in three fingers of creek water ❑ could bathe in a half-full cow track (or wagon track) ❑ could drown in a thimble or dipper ❑ runtified ❑ Pygmy sized

SMALL SPACE Ain't got room to cuss the cat without gettin' a

mouthful of fur ❑ had to hang my feet out the window to take off my boots

SMALL TOWN One-horse town ❑ a jerkwater town ❑ so small you can miss it even if you don't blink, which is slightly larger than a town which is so small you could miss it if you blinked ❑ too small to have a town drunk so everyone took turns ❑ a Saturday afternoon town, which refers to a town where everybody goes on Saturday but there isn't much going on any other time

SMART His mamma didn't raise a pretty boy but she didn't raise a dumb one either ❑ he may have been born at night but it wasn't last night ❑ smarter than a tree full of owls ❑ a high domer ❑ razor sharp brain ❑ got a mind like a steel trap ❑ Dallas oilman Ray E. Hubbard once said, "Anybody that's got money can hire somebody who's smart to make them money. It's the son of a gun that hasn't got any money that has to be smart." *See also Intelligence*

SMART AS A thermos bottle. A thermos bottle is smart be-cause it knows how to keep coffee hot and iced tea cold with out ever making a mistake ❏ as a bunkhouse rat ❏ as a whip ❏ as a tree full of owls

SMELLED Winded ❏ scented

SMELLS BAD Like fresh branded hair ❏ like horse sweat ❏ like sheep herder's socks ❏ stronger than a wolf's den ❏ worse than a wet dog, horse, or buffalo ❏ like he fell off a manure wagon ❏ like a packing house in July ❏ like he's got a goat under each arm and a dead fish in his back pocket ❏ smells like he works in a minnow factory ❏ all the flies stay on her side of the pickup ❏ like a goat pasture ❏ like the underside of a saddle ❏ like he camped out in the stock pens *See also Odor, Bad*

SMELLS GOOD Makes my mouth water like a patio fountain in a Mexican restaurant ❏ makes me drool like a wolf scenting a stray calf

SMILE Stretch your lips ❏ like a possum eating yellow jackets (or persimmons) *See also Grin*

SMILES Like a ten-year-old pickpocket

SMOKING Like a wet wood fire ❏ like a cook stove with

the flue closed ❏ like a burning tire

SMOOTH As a hickory branch without the bark ❏ as a baby's bottom ❏ as polished ivory ❏ as silk

SMOOTH TALKER Flannel mouth ❏ silver tongued, cotton mouthed

SNEAKY As a hound stealing eggs or smoke house meat ❏ back prowler

SNORES LOUD Like a rip saw running through pine knots. A saw makes a lot of noise cutting through a knot in a pine board.

SNUFF Sneeze powder

SOARED Like a flying squirrel ❏ like a runaway kite ❏ like an eagle on an updraft

SOBER As a watched puritan ❏ as a watched preacher ❏ as a judge in court ❏ he's got a hangover conscience

SOFT AS A baby's backside ❏ as a Tyler rose petal ❏ a calf's ear ❏ as a summer breeze

SOFT DRINK Cold drink ❏ soda water ❏ soda pop ❏ sody water

SOIL *See Land*

SOLD OUT He wanted it more than I did so I sold it to him, which implies someone was willing to pay more than you thought it was worth

SOLEMN As a frizzled chicken in a norther

SOLUTION, TEMPORARY Tide over, as in "Eat a snack to tide you over till supper."

SOOTHED Salved over ❑ tarred over

SORE A gall

SORE (ADJECTIVE) I'm like an old window, full of panes ❑ stove up ❑ crippled up ❑ got a hitch in my get along ❑ hobbled ❑ as a scalded pup ❑ feel like I was chewed up and spit out *See also Injured*

SORE THROAT Had hemp fever ❑ feel like I had a long drop on a short rope

SOUND, OMINOUS Like a beer bottle whistling through the foggy smoke of a honky tonk

SOUND, SWEET Like notes picked on a golden guitar

SOUND, THUD Like an ear of corn dropped into an empty wagon ❑ like a mule kicking a bale of hay

SOUR Curdled ❑ enough to pucker a pig

SPADES (PLAYING CARD SUIT) Shovels

SPACIOUS Lots of breathing room

SPANK Tan his hide ❑ warm his britches ❑ ruffle his rear end

SPARSE Slim pickens

SPEAK FRANKLY Call a spade a spade ❑ shoot from the hip

SPEAK UP Say your piece ❑ air your mind

SPECIALTY Stock in trade ❑ long suit ❑ money crop

SPEECH Lyndon Johnson said there are two kinds of speeches, the Mother Hubbard kind which covers everything but touches nothing and the French bikini kind which touches only the important parts

SPEECHLESS The cat that got his tongue was a wildcat

SPENDS A LOT She could exceed an unlimited budget ❑ if Visa (or any other credit card) ever starts a Hall of Fame, she'll be a charter member

SPINNING Like a weather vane in a whirlwind ❑ like a dog with a clothespin (or snappin' turtle) on his tail

SPIT, ACCURATE Could drown a housefly at ten paces. Any small flying critter like wasp, mosquito, yellow jacket could be substituted

SPITEFUL He wears dirty underwear to spite his mother in case he's in an accident

SPLIT EVENLY Went halves

SPLIT OPEN Like a watermelon dropped on a sidewalk

SPREAD OUT Like a sneeze through a crocheted handkerchief

SPRINGTIME Calf time ❑ struttin' time ❑ between hay and grass

SPREAD FAST Like a wind-whipped prairie fire ❑ like gossip at a church meeting, quilting bee, or ladies club

SPURS Gut hooks

SQUAT Hunker down ❑ set down on your haunches

SQUATY BODY *See Body, Squaty*

SQUEAK Like a rusty gate hinge ❑ like a bad speedometer cable ❑ like an old barn door ❑ like he had 20,000 miles on a 10,000-mile set of brakes

SQUEALED Like a mashed cat ❑ like a baby pig caught under a gate ❑ like a stuck pig ❑ caterwalled ❑ war hooped ❑ like a calf in hailstorm ❑ squalled

SQUEAMISH Lily livered

STABBED Skewered

STABILIZE Keep the boat from rocking

STALLED Hemmed and hawed ❑ spent half an eternity kicking dirt clods and spitting tobacco juice ❑ spit on his hands so much he washed off his fingernails

STALLING Spittin' on the handle ❑ you're just pitching cards in a hat

STAMINA Got plenty of bottom ❑ for a cowboy he can ride all day and dance all night ❑

for a farmer he can plow all day and play dominos all night ❏ for housewives she can clean house all day and two-step all night

STAND STILL Drag your rope ❏ ground hitch yourself ❏ freeze or petrify your shadow

STAND UP Put the forked end down ❏ put the spur end down ❏ hoist your carcass

STANDARD *See Common*

STARCHED SHIRT Fried shirt ❏ boiled shirt

STARE Fix eyeballs ❏ that would freeze a cat ❏ shootin' bullets with his eyes ❏ could stare a hole in an oak tree ❏ so hot it would make an ice cube feel feverish

START Pull the starter rope ❏ turn the crank ❏ pull the cork ❏ pit your bird ❏ kick the lid off ❏ strike up the band ❏ pull the gate ❏ the ball's open ❏ hit 'em north ❏ commence to cut loose with ❏ crank it up ❏ fire it up *See also Begin*

START EARLY *See Left Early*

START SLOW You gotta learn to ride before you can do any cowboying ❏ which is a cowboy version of "you have to walk before you can run"

START TROUBLE He dug up the hatchet or he glued the arrow back together, which refer to making peace with the Indians by burying the hatchet or breaking a symbolic arrow

STARVING Getting narrow at the equator ❏ feeling mighty hollow ❏ got my belt cinched to the last notch ❏ my stomach is so shriveled it couldn't chamber a single red bean ❏ stomach is so empty I'm gonna start echoing when I talk ❏ a bowl of red beans would look like a T-bone steak *See also Hungry*

STAY AWAY Distance is safer than armor plating ❏ if you ain't in gun range you can't get shot

STAY AWHILE Stake your horse ❏ sit a spell ❏ stall your stock ❏ pitch camp ❏ hole up here awhile ❏ ground hitch yourself ❏ lite and hitch

STAY CLOSE Stick to him like rosin on a ball or tar on a road

STAY WARM Sleep by the fire, kitchen stove, or depot stove

STAY WITH HIM Camp on his shirt tail

STAYED TOO LONG Frazzled (or wore out) your welcome

STEAL Thieving ❏ ruslin' ❏ using a sticky rope ❏ brand blotter *See also Crook, Thief*

STEAMY As a fat hog scalding for scraping

STEER Bovine ❏ horned devil ❏ Lyndon Johnson said, "Steers are bulls that lost their social standing."

STEP LIVELY Like a rooster in a bed of mesquite coals ❏ like a barefoot boy in a cactus patch

STICK TO IT Ride it out ❏ hang in there

STICKS Like a goathead to a horse's tail ❏ like ivy to a courthouse wall ❏ like manure to a horse blanket ❏ like a burr to a cow's tail ❏ like a postage stamp ❏ like stink to manure ❏ like snot on a wall ❏ like ugly to a buck toothed woman ❏ like manure (or mud) to a boot ❏ like a tick to a hound dog's ear

STICKS OUT Like a sore thumb at a drummer's convention

STICKY As a blacktop road in July

STIFF AS A new rawhide rope ❏ as a new baseball glove ❏ as a frozen (or petrified) rope ❏ as a starched shirt ❏ as a bois d'arc two by four ❏ as an ironing board ❏ as a table leaf ❏ as an ax handle *See also Rigid*

STILL As a sack of flour ❏ as a frozen snake ❏ as a wetting sow ❏ if he don't move soon someone is gonna do an autopsy on him

STINGER Business end of a bumble bee (or any other critter with a stinger)

STINGY Would skin a flea for the hide and tallow ❏ tight fisted ❏ tight as the bark on a hickory (or bois d'arc) tree ❏ sets in the shade of a tree to save the shade of his porch *See also Cheap, Frugal*

STOMACH Grub chamber ❏ table muscle

STOMACH, LARGE Beer bellied, pot bellied, stove bellied ❏ grass bellied ❏ kettle bellied ❏ if the way to his heart is through his stomach, it'll be a long trip

STOMACH, STRONG Fireproof innards ❑ cast iron innards, asbestos lined belly ❑ you could cook chili in his stomach if you could get him to lay still over the fire

STOP Put the brakes on or set the brakes ❑ pull back on the whoa reins ❑ hold your horses ❑ hang up the fiddle ❑ check it ❑ head 'em off at the pass ❑ nip it in the bud ❑ close the candy store ❑ call off the dogs

STORM CELLAR Fraid hole

STOVE Lizard scorcher

STRAIGHT AS A fire poker ❑ as the crow flies ❑ as bois d' arc fence posts ❑ as a gut with a pup pulling on it ❑ as a bee-line ❑ as a movie star's teeth ❑ as a wagon tongue ❑ as a plumb line ❑ as a guitar string

STRANGE As a three-dollar bill ❑ as a brassiere in a boy's shower ❑ as a sidesaddle on a sow

STRANGE PERSON He's not tightly wrapped ❑ he's three pickles short of a full barrel ❑ his calves don't suck the right cows ❑ not playing with a full

deck ❑ his porch light is on but no one is home ❑ he's cross threaded ❑ his plumb line is crooked ❑ his elevator stops a few floors short of the top ❑ he's drawing water in a bottomless bucket *See also Idiot, Stupid*

STRANGER We've never howdied

STRAW Broomweed ❑ scarecrow stuffing

STRAYED Flew the track ❑ off the range, out of the pasture ❑ wandered off the reservation

STREETS, CROOKED If you aren't careful, you'll run down the battery in your car honking at your own tail lights

STRIKE *See Hit*

STRIP Chuck your clothes ❑ shuck yourself

STRIPPER Passion peeler ❑ clothes shucker. An acquaintance who married an ex-stripper claimed he had to get rid of their refrigerator because every time she opened the door and the light come on, she started shuckin' herself. Of course, that wasn't too much of a problem until the preacher paid a visit and asked for a glass of ice water

STRONG As battery acid ❑ as a buzzard's breath ❑ as a straight flush ❑ as four acres of garlic

STRONG ARMED He could throw a rock through an automatic car wash without getting it wet ❑ he could throw a pork shop past a hungry coyote

STRONG PERSON Could squeeze naphtha out of moth balls ❑ he even had muscles in his hair ❑ he could shot-put an anvil across Palo Duro canyon ❑ could knock the white out of the moon ❑ could tear up an anvil with a tooth pick ❑ packs quite a whallop ❑ could break a trace chain with his teeth ❑ could tie a bow knot in an iron horseshoe (or crow bar) ❑ he plows through stumps ❑ he could turn a posthole (or gopher hole) inside out with one yank

STRONG WILLED Muscle minded

STUBBORN Thick headed ❑ bull headed ❑ set in his ways ❑ hard nosed ❑ as a mule (or a government mule) ❑ would take 10 yoke of ox to move him off his position ❑ you can ex-

plain it to him but you can't understand it for him

STUCK Bogged down ❑ the best four-tree horse team in all creation couldn't budge it

STUDY Get posted on ❑ bone up on

STUFFED Like a Republican (or Democratic) ballot box

STUPID In a battle of wits he'd be an unarmed man ❑ he'd use a shotgun to hunt flying fish ❑ off his mental reservation ❑ if you put his brain in a grasshopper, it would hop backwards ❑ if brains were ink, he couldn't dot an "i" ❑ don't know his butt from a waterin' hole ❑ dim witted as a possum ❑ his IQ is about half his boot size ❑ if he remade the Texas Chainsaw Massacre he'd use Weedeaters ❑ he don't like good cattle, fast horses or pretty women, which, according to famous Texas rancher W.T. Waggoner, means there is something wrong with his head. At the very least, he's stupid. *See also Dumb, Idiot, Ignorant, Uneducated*

STURDY Built like a brick outhouse

SUCCEED Make good or make room ❏ A famous Texan offered this advice for success, "If you wish to be successful in life, be temperate and control your passions. If you don't, ruin and death is the inevitable result." Those words came from John Wesley Hardin, one of the most ruthless gunfighters Texas ever produced. However, he said those words after spending 20 years in prison and becoming a lawyer.

SUCCEEDED It went according to prayer, which is how then A&M head coach Paul "Bear" Bryant described his team's upset of TCU in 1958.

SUCCESSFUL Doing a land office business

SUCCESSFUL, SOMEWHAT Made it to the fast lane but I can't get it out of second gear

SUCTION, GOOD Could pull the chrome off a bumper hitch ❏ could pull the wax out of your ears ❏ could pull a golf ball through a garden hose ❏ A friend once claimed she had a vacuum cleaner that could suck a cat through a key hole. She also claimed she had a badly skint up cat to prove it.

SUCTION, POOR Wouldn't pull a man's hat off a kid's head

SUFFERED Like a centipede with athlete's foot

SUICIDE Punched his own ticket to hell

SULKING Fawmching, which is one of the made up Texas words

SULLEN As a mule in a mud bog ❏ as an ox in a bar ditch

SUNDAY Go to meetin' day

SUNNY Had a shower of sunshine

SUPERFICIAL *See Person, Superficial*

SUPERIOR Top drawer ❏ a cut above ❏ cooked on the front burner. In many early model stoves the front burner produced the highest, most consistent heat, thus food cooked on the front burner was usually better

SUPERSTITIOUS NOTION An old wives tale

SUPERVISOR *See Boss, Leader*

SURE THING Lead pipe cinch ❑ you can bet your boots (or firstborn child) on it ❑ you can take that to the bank and draw interest on it ❑ as sure as hell's hot and a Popsicle is cold *See also Certain, Fact, Guaranteed*

SURPRISED As a young pup with his first porcupine ❑ didn't think I'd ever see the day ❑ that blew up her dress ❑ could have knocked me over with a hummingbird feather ❑ I put the bucket down the well and brought up a skunk ❑ that'll set your hair. After a hog is slaughtered, it is boiled in hot water which stands the hair on end - or sets it - to make scraping easier.

SURPRISED OATH Well I'll be a second cousin to a monkey, which replaces "monkey's uncle" since no real Texan would want to be that closely related to any primate.

SURPRISED TO SEE Look what the cat drug in

SURPRISING That'll make the back of your dress roll up like a runaway window shade ❑ as a bolt of lightning out of a blue sky. Although lightning normally occurs in association with storms, there have been lots of instances when it suddenly comes out of a perfectly blue sky. There is no greater surprise, especially if the bolt hits you.

SURRENDER Holler calf rope (or uncle) ❑ I've enjoyed all this I can stand ❑ run up a white flag

SURVIVOR He keeps his head above water

SUSPICIOUS There's a fox in the chicken coop ❑ the stove is cold but the woodpile is shrinking, implying someone is stealing wood ❑ he found tracks in his front yard, implying that another man had been prowling around with his wife

SUSPICIOUS AS A goat (or calf) eyeing a new gate

SWEATING So much it took the whole family to help her get her panty hose on ❑ like a plow mule ❑ like a pig ❑ like a fox in a forest fire ❑ like a fish out of water ❑ like a polar bear on the equator ❑ like a tallow candle

SWEET As a watermelon's heart ❑ as a grandmother's kiss ❑ would cause a cavity in an elephant's tusk (or ball bearing)

SWEET PERSON A spoonful of honey (or a sugar cube) wouldn't melt in her mouth

SWEETWATER Texas actually has three towns with names that mean sweet water. Sweetwater, Texas is located West of Abilene just a little less than half way between Dallas and El Paso. Agua Dulce, pronounced ag-wa-dulse which is Spanish for sweet water, is located in South Texas not far from Corpus Christi. Mobeetie, which is Indian for sweet water, is a small town in the Texas Panhandle northeast of Amarillo.

SWIM Like a water lizard being chased by a cottonmouth ❑ Swimming on your back is referred to as "reading the bible" style. Also, Texans don't dog paddle, they "hound crawl"

SWINDLED I got sheared like a spring lamb ❑ he sold me a bill of goods

Dog TIRED

TAKE Carry, as in "Carry that with you"

TAKE A BREAK Sit in the shade a spell ❑ shade up

TAKE A CHANCE Run the rapids ❑ play turtle, which implies that a turtle only makes progress when his neck is out ❑ you can't steal second base and keep one foot on first

TAKE ACTION It's time to plow ❑ shoot or give up the gun ❑ work or hold the light ❑ paint or get down from the ladder ❑ pee or get off the pot ❑ haul off as in "Haul off and get to work" ❑ thinking ain't doing. A steer in a pen full of cows can think about it. Texan Trammell Crow, often called the nation's landlord, has said, "There is as much danger in doing nothing as doing something."

TAKE A LOOK Climb the windmill and eyeball the pasture

TAKE CHARGE Take the bit in your mouth ❑ take the bull by the tail and face the situation

TAKE CORRECTIVE ACTION Don't worry about how the barn caught fire, worry about how to put it out

TAKE FOR GRANTED You don't miss the water till the well runs dry

TAKE IT EASY In the shadow of the moon ❑ shade up in the heat of the day

TAKE TURNS Swap about

TALK Jaw ❑ chew the fat ❑ shoot the breeze ❑ verbal lather ❑ speak your piece ❑ auger ❑ cuss and discuss ❑ chin music ❑ parlay ❑ shoot the bull ❑ jaw work

TALKER Chin wagger

TALKS A LOT They call her hurricane mouth, she talks 75 words a minute with gusts to 100 ❑ she'll bend your ear into a bow knot ❑ could talk water into a boil at 20 paces ❑ tongue is plum frolicsome ❑ ain't exactly hogtied when it comes to making chin music ❑ cackles like a hen ❑ slack in the jaw ❑ windy mouthed ❑ can talk the hide off a longhorn bull ❑ oiled tongue ❑ long winded ❑ faucet mouth ❑ runs off at the mouth ❑ words leak right out of his mouth ❑ couldn't give a single word answer to a judge asking for a plea ❑ has verbal diarrhea ❑ runs off at the mouth ❑ tongue wags at both ends ❑ she could talk the legs off an iron stove ❑ she could talk a wagon out of a ditch ❑ had to have her tongue re-treaded ❑ could talk the ears off a wooden Indian ❑ could talk the hide off a gila monster (or longhorn steer)

TALKS BIG Mouth fighter ❑ he always seems to have the ammunition to shoot off his mouth ❑ augers a big hole in the wind ❑ all gurgle, not guts

TALKS FANCY Using words that run about eight to the pound ❑ uses a big crop of words

TALKS FAST Waggin' his chin ❑ talks a blue streak ❑ talks fast but listens slow ❑ tongue runs like a machine gun (or machine gun) ❑ tongue runs faster than a Singer sewing machine

TALKS WITHOUT THINKING He's like a cat-fish, all mouth and no brains ❑ he puts his mouth in motion before his mind is in gear ❑ shoots from the lip ❑ shoots off his mouth ❑ got hoof in mouth disease ❑ must be your rear end talking cause your mouth knows better ❑ keeps a sock in

his mouth so his foot will be warm when he sticks it in

TALL His feet caught fire and his boots burned plumb up before he smelled the smoke ❑ walked into a snow drift and his boots froze off before he even knew his feet were cold ❑ wears his pockets high ❑ a long tall drink of water ❑ when he stands up you look him in the belly button ❑ lean and lanky ❑ long tall snuff dipper ❑ built high above his corns ❑ the sky comes up to his collar bone ❑ need a step ladder to look him in the eyes ❑ a real menace to low flying air-craft and high flying birds

TALL AS A widow woman's weeds ❑ a giraffe's navel ❑ the Alamo door

TAME As a lap dog ❑ as yesterday's dishwater ❑ if he was a dog he wouldn't bite a biscuit

TANGLED UP Like a bushel basket of clothes hangers ❑ like a pickle barrel full of loose fish hooks

TANTRUM Hissey, hissey fit, conniption fit

TASTE, BAD Would gag a maggot ❑ tastes like the sole of a two-year-old boot with the manure still on ❑ like wall-

226

paper paste ❑ like week-old dishwater ❑ half as good as hog slop ❑ like stump (or branch) water ❑ even a hog (or hungry dog) wouldn't eat it

TASTE, GOOD Handy to swallow ❑ tickles my tonsils

TAX EVASION You'll never hear him say "I declare"

TEACH Learn, as in "He had to learn his dog how to hunt birds."

TEACH A LESSON Break him from sucking eggs

TEACHER Live dictionary ❑ wisdom bringer ❑ school marm. There is an old saying which goes those that can, do, those that can't, teach which is a slur against one of the bravest classes of folks on earth, considering the challenges of life in our modern schools. A better saying would be those that can, teach, those that can't, get a job.

TEACHER, INCOMPETENT Couldn't teach first grade reading at Rice University

TEASED Pulled my leg plumb out of the socket

TEENAGE Growing up years ❑ parental plague

TEETH Nut crackers ❑ meat grinders

TEETH MISSING Bite hole

TELEPHONE POLE Highline pole

TELL A SECRET Let the cat out of the bag, wallet, or water

TELL A STORY Spin a yarn ❑ tell a tale

TELL IT ALL Wring it out

TEMPER *See Quick Tempered*

TEMPERAMENTAL Touchy as a teased snake

TEMPT Bait the hole

TEMPTING As a fresh painted bench (almost anything newly painted can be substituted) ❑ as a country pond to a tired mallard ❑ as a lump of sugar to a horse

TENDER As an old maid's heart ❑ tender as a grandmother's bosom

TENDERFOOT Skim milk cowboy ❑ no more a cowboy than hell is a storage shed for black powder (or rocket fuel) ❑ soda fountain puncher ❑ couldn't cut a lame cow out of the shade of a scrub oak tree ❏ never been closer to a horse than a mounted cop ❏ never been closer to a horse than a milk wagon ❏ never been closer to a cow than an encyclopedia picture *See also Cowboy, Poor and Inexperienced*

TENSE Wound tighter than an eight-day clock ❏ taut nerves ❏ his slack is twisted into a knot ❏ wound up so tight a tornado couldn't stick a straw in me. In actual practice, tornados have been know to skewer fence posts and telephone poles with straw.

TEQUILA Ta-kill-ya ❏ Mexican milk ❏ cactus juice ❏ worm medicine

TERRAIN, ROUGH Horse killing country. In the early days of Texas the terrain was said to be OK for men and dogs but hell on women and horses.

TERRIBLE Turrable

TEST See what kind of warp his backbone has ❏ a gut check

TESTIFIED Swore a paralyzed (or petrified) oath

TEXAN Never ask a man where he's from. If he's from Texas he'll tell you. If he isn't, you wouldn't want to embarrass him.

TEXAS John Steinbeck said in *Travels with Charley*, "Texas is a state of mind. Texas is an obsession. Above all, Texas is a nation in every sense of the word." ❏ Robert Ruark said, "Texas is what you are, not what you were or might be" ❏ Carl Sandberg said, "Texas is valor and swagger." *See also Friend, Heaven*

TEXAS PANHANDLE Skillet handle country

THANK YOU Much obliged ❏ muchas gracias

THANKFUL Shore much obliged

THAT'S A FACT That's the name of that tune

THICK As molasses in winter ❏ as bunkhouse chili ❏ as Red River mud

THIEF Would steal anything that isn't too hot or too heavy to carry ❏ no watermelon patch is safe when he's around ❏ careless about which horse he saddles ❏ a brand blotter ❏ nobody can give him lessons on sneaking or thieving ❏ what he wouldn't steal a hound dog pup wouldn't carry off ❑ keep your latch string on the inside when he's on the prowl ❑ you'd keep your horse in a high fence if he was your neighbor ❑ he never missed a loop no matter whose calf he threw at ❑ he'd swipe flies from the web of a crippled spider *See also Criminal, Crook, Stealing*

THIEF, EXPERT He'd steal the saddle off a nightmare ❑ he could steal the hubcaps off a moving car & he could steal the fillings out of your teeth while you were eating corn on the cob

THIEF, PETTY Chicken larceny is his long suit

THIN As hen skin ❑ as a fiddle string ❑ as a mashed snake ❑ as a rail ❑ looks like a nightcrawler with the guts flung out *See also Skinny*

THIN PERSON Narrow gauge ❑ stingy built ❑ gant up ❑ skin poor ❑ lean flanked ❑ looks basined out ❑ looks like he needs worming ❑ his shadow has holes in it ❑ if he drank a Big Red, he would look like the world's biggest thermometer *See also Skinny*

THINK Pronounced thank ❑ scratch your jaw ❑ use your head for something besides a hat rack

THINK ABOUT IT Study on it ❑ chew on it awhile

THINK ALIKE You're readin' my mail

THINK AHEAD Once the manure is in the milk, it's too late to grab the cow's tail, which refers to a milk cow swishing manure into the milk ❑ don't close the barn door if the mare is already out because she might come home

THIRSTY Enough to spit cotton ❑ enough to drink water from a cow (or wagon) track ❑ enough to drink branch water ❑ to suckle a she bear ❑ could drink enough to lower the water level in the Brazos River a half a foot ❑ enough to drink sheep dip, which is a brand of English whiskey ❑ have to prime my mouth to spit. When Pat Neff ran for governor of Texas, part of his platform included favoring prohibition and he promised to take away all the alcohol and make the state so dry Texans would have to prime themselves to spit.

THOUGHT Racked my brain ❑ figured ❑ studied on it ❑ ciphered on it

THREATEN I'll knock your eyeballs out of their sockets ❑ your scalp is in serious jeopardy ❑ there will be a new face in hell for breakfast tomorrow ❑ gonna put something on you Ajax won't take off ❑ I'll cloud up and rain on your parade ❑ gonna pull you through a knot hole so you can relive your birth ❑ gonna knock you cross-eyed ❑ I'm gonna beat the stuffing out of you and tell God you fell off a horse ❑ you better not pee into the wind, pull the mask off the Lone Ranger, or mess with me ❑ I'm gonna dot your eyes ❑ gonna stomp a mud hole in you ❑ gonna hit you so hard your teeth will decore your Adam's apple on the way down out of your mouth ❑ I'll live to wet on your grave ❑ you'll draw back a nub (or bloody stump)

THREATEN, MATERNAL If you can't listen, you can feel, referring to kids who can't listen can feel a spanking ❑ I'll peck you on the head like a mama bird

THRILLED *See Excited, Happy*

THROW Pronounced thow, chunk, as in "Chunk me the TV guide."

TIE A kiss for your sister. But even a kiss for your sister can be nice. When the Baylor Bears tied for their first conference football championship in half a century, their coach, Grant Teaff, said, "...when you haven't kissed your sister in fifty years, it can be mighty nice."

TIED Hobbled ❑ hog tied

TIGHT AS The eyelet holes in a woman's corset ❑ the skin on a sausage ❑ bee's wax ❑ as a 38 bra on a 44 frame ❑ as paper on a wall ❑ as a fiddle string ❑ as bark on a bois d' arc tree ❑ as a snare drum ❑ as a cinch on a fat horse ❑ as a fat lady's stockings ❑ as Dick's hat band ❑ as a drum ❑ as a wood tick in a dog's tail ❑ as lockjaw ❑ as a block in a vise ❑ skin on a catfish

TIGHT GRIP Like a redskin holding a jug of redeye ❑ like a cowpoke holdin' the reins of a pitchin' horse ❑ like a tick on a pup's ear ❑ like a kid with a silver dollar

TIGHT JEANS *See Jeans*

TIGHTEN UP Cinch your slack ❑ draw the knot closer ❑ shorten your stake rope

TIMBER A pine curtain. East Texas, the piney woods section of the state, is located behind the pine curtain

TIME CONSUMING That'll take longer than it did for Noah's flood to dry ❑ that'll take a spell to tend to ❑ you'll be a long time doing it ❑ you could waltz across Texas before you could get that done

TIME ENOUGH There is always time for one more dance

TIME, EXACT Straight up, as in "It's straight up 6:00 o'clock."

TIME, INDEFINITE A spell, as in "Sit a spell." Also used for awhile.

TIME ISN'T RIGHT It's too wet to plow

TIME TO LEAVE Wet on the fire and call the dogs or pour the coffee on the fire and call the dogs

TIMELESS As Buddy Holly's music

TIMID A handwringer ❑ weak kneed ❑ he wouldn't knock a hole in the wind ❑ as a whipped pup ❑ he'd rather stay home and do the milking ❑ he may make a lover, but

he'll never make a fighter ❑ as a lamb ❑ panty waist ❑ sissy britches ❑ a shy dog don't get no biscuits ❑ afraid of his own shadow ❑ his moist palms are developing mildew *See also Sissy*

TIRED Pronounced tared ❑ ran out of rocket fuel ❑ burned all my wood (or coal) ❑ feel like an empty shuck ❑ got an axle draggin' in the dirt ❑ give out ❑ worn to a frazzel ❑ dog tired ❑ been through the wringer and hung out to dry ❑ a might wilted ❑ feel like I pumped a hand car across Texas ❑ my main spring has run down ❑ my get up and go got up and went to Dallas (any Texas town name can be substituted) ❑ so give out he's making three tracks ❑ winded ❑ his tongue is hangin' out like a piggin string *See also Weary*

TIRED AS A cat (or mule) that walked a mile in East Texas mud

TIRESOME As a nagging woman or a barking dog

TOBACCO Tobaccer

TOGETHER We're in the same boat (or canoe) ❑ we're hitched to the same wagon ❑ singing off the same song sheet ❑ plowin' the same row ❑ we're on the same trail

TOGETHER, SECRETLY They got lost in the same place together

TOILET SEAT Commode saddle

TOMORROW Manana. Texans describe Old Mexico as the land of manana.

TONGUE-TIED His tongue got caught on his eye teeth and he couldn't see what he was saying

TOOTH BRUSH Molar mop ❑ ivory tickler ❑ enamel scrubber

TOOTHLESS Slick gummed

TOTAL PRICE Including tax, title, and license. Although this phrase is generally used to indicate total price of an automobile, it is often used for total price of anything

TOUCHY Raised on sour milk ❑ as a teased snake

TOUGH As a sow's snout ❑ leathery ❑ case hardened ❑ as callouses on a barfly's elbow ❑ as a trail drive steak ❑ hard boiled ❑ as a boot heel ❑ hard

shelled ❑ as rawhide ❑ as an old boot

TOUGH JOB It'll take a lot of river water to float that boat ❑ it'll be more challenging than putting a pair of socks on a fighting cock ❑ as tying a knot in a mountain lion's tail *See also Difficult, Hard to Do*

TOUGH PERSON When he yells scat, you better hunt your hole ❑ got fur on his brisket ❑ cut his teeth on a gun barrel ❑ might salty ❑ gritty ❑ gaunt and grizzled ❑ uses barbed wire for dental floss ❑ uses sand paper instead of soap (or toilet tissue) ❑ hunts wildcats with a switch ❑ he's even got a tattoo on the roof of his mouth

TOUGH TIMES When times are tough, Texans have to hang tough to keep Sam Houston, Bill Travis, and the rest of the boys from spinning in their graves.

TOWN, FICTITIOUS Snakenavel, Texas ❑ Possum Trot, Texas ❑ Numbnut or Nosepick, New York & Wierdsville, California ❑ Bunfuzzel, Egypt ❑ Chicky Butte, China

TOWN, SMALL *See Small Town*

TRANSFER Moving camp locations ❑ change brands

TRAPPED Like a calf in a pen ❑ like a cat up a tree ❑ like a treed possum ❑ got him roped and tied ❑ as a 50-pound catfish in a 40-gallon aquarium ❑ like a yearling in a cattle truck

TRAVEL FAST Keep the news behind you

TRAVEL TIME Windshield time

TRICKED Hoodwinked ❑ bamboozled ❑ hornswoggled ❑ pulled the wool over their eyes ❑ he took the bait like a bass taking a fancy lure ❑ double clutched him

TRIED HARD He bucked till he buckled ❑ popped a gut ❑ gave it all he had ❑ ran a good race ❑ he buckled up and buckled down

TRIVIAL It wouldn't be noticed if it was tied to the saddle of a galloping horse ❑ wouldn't get any more notice than one more frog in a stock pond ❑ in 100 years it won't make any difference

TROUBLE Got a skunk by the tail ❑ got an ox in the ditch ❑ got hell to pay ❑ your goose is cooked ❑ in a pickle ❑ my butt's in a sling ❑ in a heap of trouble ❑ there will be hell to pay ❑ knee deep in manure ❑ in deep sewage ❑ it's Katy bar the door ❑ got a long row to hoe ❑ up to my armpits in alligators and can't find the drain for the swamp ❑ got his tail in a crack ❑ got my tail (or teat) in a wringer ❑ got a skunk (or dead cat) down the well ❑ a washtub full of misery *See also In Trouble*

TROUBLE BREWING The storm clouds are gathering ❑ all ain't well in the chicken coop

TRUCK Kidney pounder

TRUE Natural fact ❑ it came from the horse's mouth ❑ got it straight from the mare's mouth

TRUST Trust everybody, but always cut the cards

TRUSTWORTHY He'd do to run the river with, which is a favorite saying of Lady Bird Johnson. It is derived from the fact that swimming a river on a horse can be dangerous so cowboys often made the run with a friend who could be trusted ❑ you can let him carry the gate key ❑ if he says a katydid can haul cotton, you

This Dog'll Hunt

can hitch him up ❏ if he says a hen dips snuff, you can look under her wing for the can

TRUTH Be sure your story is wider than it is tall ❏ spread the gospel ❏ the range word ❏ dead open fact *See Also Certain, Guaranteed*

TRY Give it a whirl ❏ dance it around the floor ❏ sling it on the wall and see if it sticks ❏ throw it in the creek and see if it floats ❏ run it up the flag pole and see if anyone salutes ❏ take a crack (or stab) at it ❏ wing it ❏ try it on for size ❏ see how your luck holds ❏ a baby coon can't sit in the den and learn to catch frogs

TRY AGAIN Squeeze off another round ❏ take another shot ❏ go back to the well ❏ reset your hat and give it another ride ❏ take a new hold ❏ take another swing around the dance floor

TRY EVERYTHING If you can't ride 'em and you can't bulldog 'em, you can always rope 'em. Bones Irvin, an assistant under Bear Bryant at A&M, said it another way for football. "Some days you can't tackle 'em and some days you can't block 'em but you can always fight 'em." ❏ run the

full length of the rope ❏ try every trick in the book

TRY HARD Give it your best shot ❏ go for the gusher ❏ do your dead level best

TRY SOMETHING NEW Plow some new ground ❏ try a new dance ❏ try dancing with a girl instead of a broom ❏ if the fish ain't biting, change bait

TURNED AROUND Spun around like a windmill in a whirlwind ❏ turned about

TURN OFF Cut off ❏ kill, as in "Kill the lights"

TUXEDO Scissor tail outfit

TWINE Strang ❏ runt rope

TWO (PLAYING CARD) Duck ❏ duet ❏ two spot

TWO-MAN JOB Double barrel chore

TWO TIMER He'd cheat on himself if he didn't think he'd get caught

TYRANT Old war horse

234

U

USELESS — as a milk bucket under a bull

UGLY AS A mud fence ❏ as homemade soup, soap, or sin ❏ as hammered mud (or manure) ❏ as second place ❏ as a cancer-eyed cow

UGLY FEMALE The tide wouldn't take her out ❏ coyote ugly, which means if you woke up with her asleep on your arm, you'd chew off your arm rather than wake her up ❏ she has to slap her legs to get them to go to bed with her ❏ she's a two sacker, which means if you put a sack on her head you ought to put on two in case one falls off ❏ she'd make a freight train take a dirt road ❏ her looks would stop a courthouse clock ❏ she'd scare night into day ❏ she'd turn a funeral procession down an alley ❏ her looks would scare a dog off a gut wagon ❏ her face would wilt knee-high cotton ❏ her looks would petrify a cat ❏ she'd scare a drunk man sober ❏ looks like something the cat drug in and the dog won't eat ❏ she looks like her makeup caught fire and someone used a fire ax to put out the blaze ❏ she's got a face built for a hackamore *See also Homely*

UGLY MALE When he was born, the doctor slapped his mother ❏ when he was a baby his mother fed him with a slingshot ❏ if you walk by him, your clothes will wrinkle ❏ looks like he left his teeth in a fruit jar at home ❏ his mother had to borrow a baby to take to church ❏ he couldn't get a date at the chicken ranch with a truck load of fryers, which refers to girls at the Chicken Ranch, one of the world's most famous whorehouses, accepting poultry in trade for their favors, which is how the place got its name ❏ whipped with an ugly stick ❏ if you look up ugly in the dictionary, you'll find his picture

UNABLE Can't cut the mustard ❏ can't do that any more than a steer can take care of a heifer

UNACCEPTABLE That dog won't hunt. Although long a popular phrase, it reached star status when used by Ann Richards in the 1988 Democratic National Convention to indicate the Republican policies were unacceptable ❏ Also I can't sit still for that ❏ that bucket won't hold no milk (or water) ❏ that boat won't float ❏ that horse won't trot

237

UNAFRAID Ain't a scared ❑ meant to worry about it but didn't have the time

UNAPPRECIATIVE He checks every tooth in the mouth of a gift horse ❑ if you gave him a horse, he'd expect you to feed it ❑ if you gave him a watch, he'd expect it to keep time

UNATTACHED Footloose and fancy free ❑ unbriddled ❑ got a loose stake rope

UNATTRACTIVE As a tow sack shirt (or skirt) ❑ a real eyesore ❑ looks like 40 miles of bad road

UNAVAILABLE Out of pocket ❑ off the range ❑ my dance card is full

UNAVOIDABLE You gotta play the hand you're dealt ❑ you gotta dance to the tune the band plays ❑ no matter how warm the sunshine is, the cat always has her kittens in the barn ❑ there are some things a man can't ride around ❑ that's the way the cow chip crumbles

UNBELIEVABLE Beats anything I ever saw or heard tell of ❑ sounds a might far fetched to me

UNCERTAIN Absolutely buffaloed ❑ don't have a clue ❑ don't have anymore an idea about that than a pig knows what day of the week it is

UNCHANGEABLE Set in concrete ❑ cast in bronze ❑ written in ink ❑ you can take the Texan out of Texas, but you can never take the Texas out of a Texan

UNCLEAR That's about as clear as Red river mud ❑ about as clear as a fog in a river bottom

UNCOMMITTED He won't stay hitched (or harnessed) ❑ he's like a grasshopper, you never know which way he'll jump ❑ Red Adaire, world famous Texas oil well fire-fighter has a sign on his desk proclaiming, "I said maybe, and that's final."

UNCOMPROMISING Dead tough no matter what the game or odds ❑ he won't bend as much as a crow bar

UNCONCERNED It's all water off a duck's back to him

UNCONSCIOUS Out like a dead cat

UNCONTROLLABLE He's a hard dog to keep under the porch □ can't check him with a 3/4 hemp rope and a bois d'arc snubbing post

UNCOORDINATED As a drunk getting out of a sunken bathtub □ as a hog on ice

UNCOUTH A nose picker □ he'd pick his nose at a state dinner □ ain't particular where he spits

UNDECIDED Straddling the fence □ the jury's still out

UNDEPENDABLE He's in and out like a dog's hind leg

UNDERSTAND Savvy □ see the light □ get your meaning □ get your drift □ 'nuff said □ comprende □ it finally soaked in □ hear tell, as in "I hear tell she's on the prowl."

UNDERWEAR Scanties □ long johns □ unmentionables □ under drawers

UNDRESSED Shucked himself

UNEDUCATED Couldn't count to 20 with both boots and his socks off □ if intelligence was leather, he would

have enough to saddle a flea (or mosquito) □ don't know gee from haw, which refers to mule team driver's terms for right (gee) and left (haw) □ couldn't pour rainwater out of a boot with the instructions printed on the heel □ don't know cow chips from computer chips □ ain't got a lick of sense *See also Dumb, Ignorant, Stupid*

UNEMPLOYED Riding with the chuck line, which refers to out-of-work cowboys riding with the chuck wagon hoping for a meal □ my spurs are rusting

UNEQUALLED Nothing could hold a candle to it

UNEXPECTED As a fifth ace □ as the flurry of a flushed covey of quail

UNFAITHFUL Bobbing around □ skating around out high □ got a lot of strings on her fiddle (or guitar)

UNFAMILIAR WITH Not too well versed in □ not posted on □ don't know as much about that as the devil does the scriptures □ it's news to me

UNFINISHED Still got some branding (or hoeing) to do

UNFRIENDLY As fire ants ❏ as a forest fire ❏ as a mule on a sawdust diet

UNHAPPY Ain't had this much fun since the hogs ate baby sister

UNIMPORTANT Don't make no never mind ❏ a no account

UNKNOWN Never saw or heard tell of it ❏ wouldn't know him if he bit me on the leg ❏ wouldn't know him from Adam (or her from Eve) ❏ don't know that anymore than a pig knows he's pork ❏ you never know when the live round will come up in Russian roulette ❏ if it ain't a mystery, it's guesswork ❏ don't know any more about that than a sow does about bikini bathin' suits

UNKNOWN AS Whistler's father ❏ as Ameilia Earhart's co-pilot ❏ as a player to be named later

UNLESS Lessen

UNLUCKY If he bought a cemetery, people would stop dying ❏ he's paying the wrong preacher ❏ he put his hat on a bed, which is a reference to the old country belief that anyone who puts his hat on a bed will have bad luck ❏ his luck is running muddy ❏ playing with a cold deck ❏ my luck come unraveled ❏ my cup is empty but my slop bucket is overflowing ❏ the flowers are blooming but they're in someone else's garden ❏ if it wasn't for bad luck I wouldn't have no luck atall ❏ fishing with the wrong bait ❏ dropped a basket full of mirrors ❏ he's snakebit. Although there are lots of snakes in Texas, bites are somewhat rare thus anyone who is snakebit is really unlucky ❏ if I bought a truck load of pumpkins in October, they'd cancel Halloween ❏ he couldn't win a bet on a football game if he had tomorrow's paper in his pocket ❏ "If I started to hell with a load of ice to sell, the damn place would freeze over before I could get there," which is a quote attributed to Temple Houston, noted attorney, gunman, and son of General Sam Houston.

UNMARKED Slick eared, which is a reference to livestock whose ears are not marked

UNNATURAL A chicken and a coyote might sleep together but the chicken will keep one eye open

UNNECESSARY As two tails on a tom cat ❑ as three horns on a steer ❑ as axle grease on a jackrabbit

UNPLEASANT As sticking your hand in a bucket of minnows

UNPREDICTABLE Can't tell what's gonna happen no more than a car-chasing dog knows what he'd do with a car if he caught it ❑ you never know which way the cat will jump ❑ you never know what the jury will say ❑ as Texas weather. Only fools and newcomers predict the weather in Texas.

UNPREPARED He's riding without a rope ❑ he's hunting with an empty gun ❑ he's hunting buffalo with a BB gun. About the only way a buffalo could die from a BB gun would be if he ate it and choked to death.

UNPROTECTED Unarmed ❑ his bulletproof vest is in the wash

UNRELIABLE He won't do to tie to ❑ he don't tote level ❑ he'll be late to his own funeral ❑ you wouldn't want to

hitch him to your wagon ❑ you couldn't trust him with the key to your wife's chastity belt *See also Untrustworthy*

UNRESTRAINED Going hog wild ❑ running with the bridle off ❑ flying like an eagle ❑ soaring free ❑ the wide open spaces are his back yard ❑ kicked off the harness, traces, or stake rope ❑ the fence is down ❑ the gate's open

UNROMANTIC Kisses with his eyes open

UNSAFE It's held together with a lick and a promise ❑ it's held together with a cobweb

UNSEEN Never laid eyes on

UNSTEADY Wobbles like a newborn colt (or calf) ❑ his knees are drunk *See also Shaky*

UNSURE *See Indecisive*

UNTOUCHABLE Couldn't touch her with a ten-foot pole

UNTRAINABLE Got the mind of an old dog, which comes from "You can't teach an old dog new tricks."

UNTRUSTWORTHY He has to have someone else call his hogs ❑ trust him as far as you can throw a bale of hay ❑ you never know where his loop will land ❑ as far as you can throw a 90-pound anvil (or a full-grown bull) ❑ don't bunk with him if you value the gold in your eye teeth ❑ trust him as far as you can throw a post hole ❑ never trust a rooster handler. This is derived from cock fighters often betting on the other man's bird then disabling his own fowl fighter so it will lose *See also Unreliable*

UNUSUAL It isn't your average garden variety ❑ beats anything I ever saw

UNWANTED I need that like a hog needs a packing house ❑ like I need a third foot ❑ like a mermaid needs a bicycle ❑ like a duck needs an umbrella ❑ like an armadillo needs an Interstate ❑ like a chicken coop needs a fox ❑ as a hailstorm to a farmer ❑ as a blown-over outhouse ❑ no more use for it than a sow has for an extra set of teats ❑ as a wart on a pretty girl's bottom ❑ as a run in your panty hose

UNWELCOME He's about as welcome as a rattlesnake in a prairie dog town ❑ as a skunk (or fire ants) at a picnic

UPPITY *See Aloof, Arrogant*

UPSET Walking mad all over ❑ pitching and squealing ❑ having a walleyed fit ❑ hopping mad ❑ fangs are itching ❑ spoiling for a fracas ❑ she gathered up her skirts and left ❑ took his ball and went home ❑ threw the cards in the fire ❑ ate the dice *See also Angry, Mad*

UPSIDE DOWN Like an Interstate possum (or armadillo) which refers to dead animals in the Interstate usually being upside down

UPSTAGED Stole his thunder and his lightning

URGENT That needs tending to

URINATE Water the grass or horses ❑ kill a tree (or some bushes) ❑ drain your crankcase, dragon, snake, or radiator ❑ see a man about a dog or a horse ❑ go see if the horse has kicked off his blanket ❑ milk a rattlesnake

USE SPARINGLY Don't burn all the kindling on one fire

USEFUL *See Handy*

USELESS As a milk bucket under a bull ❑ as a needle without an eye ❑ as teats on a boar hog ❑ as a screen door on a submarine ❑ as a saddle without a horse ❑ as a bird nest that ain't rainproof ❑ as an unloaded gun ❑ as a cable car to a cowboy ❑ as a steam engine without water ❑ a cowboy without a horse ❑ windmill without water ❑ as speaking Chinese to a jackass ❑ as wet powder ❑ as trying to rodeo on a stick horse (or rocking horse) ❑ as a side saddle on a sow ❑ as a computer in a black out ❑ as a water bucket without a well rope *See also Worthless*

USELESS PERSON Deadwood ❑ more ornamental than useful

UTOPIA Hog heaven

V

VULNERABLE — as a sittin' duck

VACILLATE Crawfish ❏ changes his mind as often as he does socks ❏ shilly shally. Sam Rayburn said, "I've found that people respect you if you tell them where you stand. If you shilly shally you'll get into trouble."

VALUABLE As a herd of pregnant racehorses ❏ worth his weight in oil leases ❏ wouldn't take a purty for it

VANDAL A terrorist on a limited budget

VARIED Checkered as in "He's had a checkered career."

VERY Powerful, as in "I'm powerful glad you weren't hurt in the accident" ❏ mighty, as in "I'm mighty happy over the election results" ❏ plumb, as in "I'm plumb proud to accept the nomination" ❏ durn, as in "I'm durn glad to see you" ❏ dead as in "He's dead in love." ❏ right, as in "Are you right sure she likes me?"

VERY FEW Precious few ❏ precious little

VICE PRESIDENT Texan John Nance Garner said it best with, "The Vice Presidency isn't worth a bucket of warm spit."

VICINITY In these parts ❏ hereabouts ❏ this neck of the woods ❏ round about

VICIOUS He don't believe in taking prisoners ❏ full of natural cussidness ❏ he's part volcano, part tornado, and all earthquake ❏ give you as much chance as a wolf would give a sucklin' lamb ❏ got snake blood in his veins ❏ a rattler would die if he bit him ❏ he'll rub cockleburs in the hair of an orphan girl ❏ rides rough shod over everybody ❏ his favorite tune is Deguello (de-gwa-lyo), which is the Mexican song signifying "no quarter will be given" that was played during the siege of the Alamo. *See also Ruthless*

VICTORY, SLOPPY Old ugly is better than old nothing, a Royalism meaning that even if you play sloppy football, a win is still better than losing

VIOLIN Fiddle, in Texas

VIRTUE Keeps him bored stiff

VIRTUOUS Pure as driven snow

VISIT Set a spell and take a load off

VOICE, LOW You could smell boot leather (or socks) on his

breath ❑ sounds like an un-
greased wooden gin screw,
which produces a low moan
when it turns

VOICE, HIGH Talks like a
mockingbird shrill ❑ like the
screech of a locomotive when
there's a cow on the tracks

VOICE, GRAVELY Sounds
like he gargled with axle
grease ❑ like a crow with the
croup

VOMIT Throw up his toenails
(or socks) *See also Sick*

VOTE Cast lots

VULNERABLE A sitting
duck, which implies that a
duck which is sitting is much
more vulnerable than one
which is flying ❑ as a trailer
house in a tornado. It seems
whenever tornados strike,
trailer houses (or mobile
homes) take the most beating
❑ as a 200-pound highline
walker on a 100-pound test
line

W

WASTING TIME — barking at a knot

WAIT Slack up on the reins ❑ hold your horses ❑ camp and make coffee

WAITRESS Biscuit shooter (or dealer) ❑ grub quarterback, which refers to a waitress picking up food from the cook and handing it off to the customer ❑ menu mamma ❑ steak (or chili) slinger ❑ tip wrangler

WALK On the boot leather express ❑ footin' it ❑ doin' a sidewalk sashay ❑ pounding the pavement ❑ legging it ❑ hoofin' it ❑ jingling his spurs ❑ moseying ❑ pi-eyeing ❑ afoot. To a cowboy, a man afoot was no man atall.

WALK FAR Used up enough leather to half sole the confederate (or Chineses) army

WALK FUNNY Like a duck out of water ❑ like a drunk roadrunner

WALK SLOW *See Slow Walker*

WANDERING Sloshing around ❑ moseyin' around ❑ strayed off the trail ❑ got saddle itch

WANT Give half of all creation for ❑ would trade all the mineral rights in Texas for it *See also Desire*

WARM As a depot stove ❑ as a grandmother's blanket ❑ as a turtle on a log ❑ hot off the griddle ❑ as a fresh biscuit ❑ as a fat woman in a feather bed

WARN Shake a rope (or big stick) at 'em ❑ send up a smoke signal

WARNING I'm gonna knock a lung out of you ❑ snatch you baldheaded ❑ get on you like stink on manure ❑ knock you into the middle of next week ❑ grab your tongue and turn you inside out ❑ grab you and tear along the dotted line ❑ skin you and tan your hide (or nail your hide to the barn door) ❑ wring your neck ❑ you better give your soul to Jesus, cause your butt belongs to me ❑ you'll cuss the day you were born ❑ if you know a prayer, nows the time to say it ❑ I'm gonna cut out your gizzard and eat it (or feed it to my dog) ❑ you better hunt a storm cellar 'cause I'm coming after you like a cyclone *See also Threaten*

WASH Warsh

WASP Mud dauber ❑ dirt dauber ❑ hornet ❑ yellow jacket ❑ stinger bringer

WASTEFUL As a trainload of lawyers going off a bridge with two empty cars. Texan Lamar Hunt, who owns the Kansas City Chiefs, once said, "My definition of utter waste is a busload of lawyers going over a cliff with three empty seats." He made the remark because of all the lawyers involved in the dispute between the national Football League and the Oakland Raiders.

WASTING MONEY Burning rocket fuel in a coal oil lamp ❑ throwing good dollars after bad ❑ might as well flush it down a toilet (or chunk it in an outhouse hole) ❑ putting a $100 saddle on a $20 horse ❑ buying pearls for a pig ❑ you're buying horse feed after the horse died ❑ you're buying hay for a mechanical bull

WASTING TIME Burning daylight ❑ whistling at the moon ❑ barking at a knot ❑ picking at a wart ❑ fishing with an empty hook ❑ might as well talk Egyptian to a pack mule ❑ putting silk stockings on a sow ❑ following a cold trail ❑ playing solitaire with a deck of 51 ❑ dilly-dallying around ❑ just chewing and

whittling ❑ arguing with a wooden Indian, which was a favorite saying of Sam Houston ❑ you're following an empty wagon waiting for something to fall off ❑ you're robbing the mail stage (or mail train.) This refers to mail carriers not usually carrying money so it would be wasting time to rob them ❑ you can kick all you want but, unless you're a mule, it won't do any good *See also Effort, Wasted*

WASTING YOUR BREATH You're hollering down a rain barrel, armadillo hole, or empty well

WATCH (NOUN) Time dispenser *See also Rolex*

WATCH (VERB) Keep tabs on ❑ keep your eyes peeled (or skinned) ❑ be on the lookout ❑ keep your weather eye open

WATER Branch water ❑ well water ❑ spring water ❑ Brazos River water

WATER, MUDDY Too thick to drink, too thin to plow, which is often said of water from the Red River

WAVING Wagging his mitt

WAXAHACHIE, TEXAS
Pronounced Wok-si-hatch-i,
not Wack-si-hatch-i or Wax-
si-hatch-i, a small town in
central Texas

WEAK Raised on skim milk
❑ paper backed ❑ built on butter ❑ couldn't lick his upper
lip ❑ limp as a dish rag ❑
panty waist ❑ couldn't pull his
hat off ❑ as a two-day-old kitten *See also Sissy, Timid*

WEAKLING A weak sister

WEALTHY *See Rich*

WEATHER, BAD We didn't
have this kind of weather
when Lyndon Johnson was
President, which is a reference to the only real Texan to
ever be President of the United
States. ❑ the weather got
wholesale ❑ the skies muddied up *See also Norther*

WEATHER, CLEARING
Breaking up ❑ fairing up ❑
moderating ❑ clearing off ❑
lettin' up

WEARY Feel like a whipped
pup ❑ could sleep on a barbed
wire fence, could sleep standing up in a snowstorm ❑ his
tongue was flapping in the
dust ❑ ready to rock on the
porch ❑ been run down, run
over, and wrung out ❑ my tail

(or dauber) is dragging in the
dirt ❑ petered out ❑ plum
tuckered ❑ played out *See Also
Tired*

WEDDING RING One-man
band

WELCOME As a pardon to a
death row inmate ❑ as Santa
Claus in an orphan's home ❑
as a cloud burst to a dry land
farmer ❑ a site for sore eyes ❑
the latch string is out for you ❑
make yourself to home

WELL DRESSED More or-
namental than useful, which
refers to the fact that someone
who is dressed up isn't ready
for work ❑ looks like the
judge set the trial date ❑ looks
like he's going to a wedding or
a preaching

WELL OFF *See Rich*

WENT BROKE Lost everything but the air in my tires ❑
lost everything but the fillings
in my teeth ❑ they took everything but the dirt under my
fingernails, which was often
said by a farmer when the
bank repossessed his land ❑
bought a one way-ticket on the
express train to financial ruin
See also Bankrupt

WENT CRAZY Spun a bearing ❑ threw a rod ❑ slipped a

cog ❑ blew a gasket ❑ warped his head

WENT TOO FAR Went to the well once too often

WENT WILD Came unbuckled ❑ broke his trace chin ❑ pitched for the moon

WESTERN SHOW Horse opera ❑ wild west show ❑ rodeo

WET As a drowned rat ❑ as a fish in water ❑ as a rooster under a drain spout ❑ as a kid in a mud puddle

WHEELER DEALER Risk runner ❑ riverboat gambler ❑ horse trader. When John Connally was asked if he was a wheeler dealer he replied, "If it means I could enter a horse trade and come out without losing, I guess I'm guilty."

WHILE Whilst

WHIPPED Like a stepchild

WHIPPING Woodshed lecture

WHISKY Coffin varnish ❑ tonsil paint ❑ tarantula juice ❑ cowboy cocktail ❑ firewater ❑ whusky ❑ gut warmer ❑ jig juice ❑ jig water ❑ glee

medicine ❑ giggle water ❑ grief remover ❑ snake bite medicine ❑ lamp oil ❑ scamper juice ❑ conversation fluid ❑ snake oil juice ❑ tornado juice ❑ spider killer ❑ redeye ❑ tongue oil *See also Champagne, Liquor, Tequila*

WHISKY, BOOTLEG It is in the barn not in bond ❑ bonded in the barn

WHISKY, STRONG Enough to make a muley cow (or jackrabbit) grow horns ❑ strong enough to make a grasshopper fight a surly wolf ❑ strong enough to draw blood blisters on a boot heel *See also Drink, Strong, Liquor, Strong*

WHISPER Funeral talk

WHITE As bleached bones ❑ as driven snow

WHITE MAN Paleface ❑ white eyes

WHO KNOWS Quien sabe (pronounced kin savvy). Any ornate brand that can't be read is said to be a quien sabe brand.

WHORE Alley bat ❑ lady of loose virtue ❑ painted lady ❑ honky tonk angel ❑ fallen angel ❑ angel flying too close to the ground

WHORE HOUSE Chamber of commerce ❑ bawdy house ❑ parlour house ❑ bordello ❑ cat house ❑ pleasure palace ❑ house of ill fame ❑ sporting house ❑ hurdy-gurdy house ❑ joy parlor ❑ Chicken Ranch, which, according to some, was the Best Little Whorehouse in Texas.

WICKED If he walked through the valley of the shadow of death, he'd fear no evil cause he'd be the meanest critter in the valley ❑ if he didn't like the tune, he'd shoot the piano player ❑ Western Union won't deliver to him because if it's bad news he shoots the messenger ❑ the devil's got a mortgage on his soul ❑ kin to a rattler on his father's side and a black widow on his mother's side *See Evil Person, Mean Person*

WIDE OPEN SPACES Where a man can switch his tail

WIDOW Widder ❑ widder woman

WIFE Running mate ❑ better half ❑ bitter half ❑ ball ❑ chain ❑ warden ❑ my kid's mama ❑ the wife ❑ the old lady

WIGGLE Like a lizard (or a frog) in a skillet ❑ like a fish on a line ❑ like a worm on a hook ❑ like a worm in a bed of Mesquite coals

WILD Running loose in the streets ❑ uncurried ❑ fuzztail ❑ as a turpentined cat ❑ bucking in eight directions at once

WILDCATTER Everett Lee DeGoyler said there were two kinds of wildcatters, the silver spoon boys and the rabbit foot boys. The silver spoon boys were the ones that had money before they got in the oil business and the rabbit foot boys made their money from oil.

WILLING Game, as in "He's game for a little poker."

WIND, COLD the breath of a glacier ❑ raw as a whip

WIND, STRONG Windmill breaker (or spinner) ❑ blowing like the inside of a NASA wind tunnel

WINDED Couldn't gather enough breath to blow out the candle on a kid's birthday cake ❑ couldn't gather enough wind to blow a smoke ring

WINDOW, OPEN Pneumonia hole

WINDOW, OPEN (ON PICKUP) Juice hole

WINNING Daylighting, which means he's putting daylight between him and all the rest

WIRE War, as in bobbed war

WIRE CUTTERS Range pliers ❑ war pliers, which refers to the range wars that were fought over wire cutting

WISE Book learned and horse smart

WITCH Broom rider ❑ broom wrangler ❑ she rides a pitchin' broom

WOMAN TROUBLE Got too many hearts in the fire

WOMANIZER Skirt (or petticoat) chaser ❑ he's AWOL - after women or liquor (or a wolf on the loose) ❑ he ain't married but his wife is ❑ he'll change everything about you but your name ❑ booby hunter

WOMEN Women folk ❑ the spare sex

WON Put another feather in his hat (or head band) ❑ struck pay dirt ❑ put another notch in his gun ❑ put another scalp on his belt ❑ he got the buckle, which refers to winning rodeo cowboys receiving trophy buckles

WON AT POKER Sheared the flock

WON BIG Raked in all the chips ❑ if you were gonna take a photo of the finish, you'd need a wide angle lens, which is a horse racing reference to the winning horse finishing far ahead of the other horses

WORDS, BIG Got double barrelled syllables ❑ two-bit words ❑ words that run about two dollars to the pound

WORK Make hay while the sun shines ❑ tend to business ❑ like a dog trying to shake off a pinching worm ❑ wore fingernails clear down to the knuckles ❑ works from can't see till can't see ❑ hard at it ❑ As Henri Castro, an early Texas colonist said, "Begin your day with labor and end it with laughter."

WORK, CASUALLY He keeps banker's hours or he's got a banker's watch, both of which imply he doesn't work all day. Since banks generally close early in the afternoon, it has long been perceived that a banker's day is short although people in the industry say it ain't so.

WORK, HARD The yeast that raises the dough ❑ nobody ever drowned in his own sweat ❑ it's better to have two tired arms than one empty stomach ❑ luck don't jump on a man sitting in the shade ❑ Bobby Layne, perhaps the most competitive football player Texas has ever produced, once said, "If a man has to work past noon, the job was too big for him in the first place." On the other hand, Lyndon Johnson said, "The more you work the luckier you get." Then, of course, there is the old country adage Hard work keeps the fences up.

WORK LATE Burn the midnight oil ❑ ride the night herd ❑ ride the sunset rounds ❑ night hawking ❑ put the sun to bed

WORKER, GOOD Top hand ❑ he strikes one match and burns daylight and midnight oil ❑ could gather all the county's crops by dark 30, which can be either 30 minutes before or 30 minutes after dark ❑ a real plow horse *See also Employee*

WORKER, POOR Does the work of two people, Laurel and

Hardy ❑ does the work of three people, Larry, Moe, and Curly ❑ bottom hand ❑ he thinks dirt under the fingernails causes cancer or he could wear his work shirt to a church social, both of which imply he didn't get dirty. On a ranch, a farm, or in the oil field, any man not willing to get dirty was worthless. *See also Employee, Worthless*

WORKING END The business end ❑ blister end. No one ever raised a blister holding a hammer by the head.

WORKS GOOD A going jesse ❑ like an automatic milking machine ❑ like a pair of $5.00 teeth

WORRIED Something is eating on me like a caterpillar on a leaf ❑ something is sleeping on my pillow with me

WORRIED AS A duck in a desert ❑ as a camel in the Klondike ❑ as a frog in a frying pan ❑ as a pig in a packing plant

WORTHLESS No account ❑ not worth didley squat (or just didley) ❑ wouldn't make good shark bait ❑ plumb no account ❑ gone to the dogs ❑ not worth a bucket of spit, which is exactly how Texan John Nance

Garner described the Vice Presidency of the United States ❑ ain't worth a crying dime ❑ good for nothing ❑ not worth a plug nickel ❑ ain't worth his feed ❑ plumb sorry *See also Useless*

WORTHLESS AND HEAVY Good for nothing but a trot line weight

WORTHLESS AS A bow without an arrow ❑ as a nail without a hammer ❑ as a canceled stamp ❑ as a four-card flush ❑ as a broken boot jack ❑ as half a hair cut ❑ as one boot ❑ as an unloaded gun ❑ a screen door on a submarine

WORTHLESS PERSON He ain't worth the oxygen he uses up ❑ ain't worth killing ❑ ain't worth the powder to blow him to hell ❑ nothing but buzzard bait ❑ never raised nothing but hell and hot air

WORTHY He's earned his saddle ❑ he's earned all he ever got ❑ he's earned his spot at the bar

WORSE OFF Jumped from the frying pan into the fire or from the skillet into the deep fryer

WOUNDED Lost enough blood to paint the back porch ❑

skewered ❑ shot up some ❑ if he was cut any worse, it would qualify as an autopsy ❑ got shish ke bobbed *See also Shot, Skinned Up*

WRAP Dally, which is derived from wrapping, or dallying, a rope around a saddle horn

WRESTLING Pronounced ras-ling

WRINKLED As an old boot ❑ as the horns on an old steer

WRITE FAST Smoke the lead ❑ scorch the paper

WRITER Ink slinger ❑ word wrangler ❑ pen pusher ❑ paper waster

WRONG You're on a cold trail ❑ you're leading the ducks to the wrong pond *See also Error, Incorrect, Mistaken*

X I T Pronounced as three separate letters, X I T, never as
"exit." Refers to the brand of
the ranch that was formed witn
the three million acres of
Panhandle land which the
state of Texas traded in return
for the building of the state
capitol building in Austin. It
has to be one of the biggest
trades in the history of the
world.

XEROX Often pronounced x-
rock in Texas, perhaps because Texans refused to
believe that a word which
starts with an x could sound
like it starts with a z.

Y

Does a 50lb sack of flour make a big biscuit? — YES

YANKEE Blue belly ❑ blue coat ❑ blue butt

YEAR-OLD Yearling

YELL Beller ❑ holler ❑ squall like a shoat ❑ blattin' ❑ yelp ❑ brayin' like a mule ❑ war hoop ❑ whopped out ❑ like a bluejay protecting her nest ❑ caterwall

YELLOW Yaller ❑ yeller ❑ as a no-passing stripe ❑ as the sun's insides ❑ as the stripe down a coward's back ❑ as a summer squash

YES Darn tootin' ❑ si ❑ is a pig's butt pork ❑ does a bear sleep in the woods ❑ is the pope Catholic ❑ is a snake's belly low to the ground ❑ does a wet horse (or dog) stink ❑ does a cat have a climbing gear ❑ does a fifty-pound sack of flour make a big biscuit ❑ does a fat man sweat ❑ does the sun set in the west ❑ does a hog love slop ❑ is a duck's butt waterproof

YOU Pronounced ya, as in "How ya doing," or "Where ya been."

YOU ALL Y'all. The national word of Texas, don't y'all know.

YOU ARE WELCOME Is replaced with "Ah, it weren't nuthin', ma'm," when a lady says thanks for a good deed

YOUNG Teeth ain't wore down much

YOUNGSTER Whipper snapper ❑ a spring chicken ❑ plumb full of vinegar ❑ hen wrangler ❑ whistle britches

YOUR Yore

YOUR TURN It's your bat (or bet)

Z

ZEBRA — a half painted horse

ZEBRA Half painted (or dressed) horse

ZIPPER, OPEN The barn door is open ❑ the corral gate is open ❑ the lid to the snake cage is open ❑ the lizard pen is open

ZOO Critter corral

Index

Index

Index

Index

Index

Index

Index

MORE REGIONAL BOOKS

100 Days in Texas: The Alamo Letters $17.95

Although many have written their version of the fall of the Alamo, the real story was actually written by the men involved. This book is a collection of surviving documents that actually trace the story of one of the epic battles in American history. Years of research have gone into compiling letters, diary entries, newspaper accounts, and official records that were written during the days of Texas revolution that pertain to the saga of the Alamo. The true story of the Alamo is told by those who knew it best, the men who fought the battle.

1-55622-131-2   Fall '89

50 Days in Texas: The San Jacinto Letters $17.95

A perfect companion to *100 Days in Texas*, this book tells the ultimate story of the winning of Texas Independence in the words of the men who lived the adventure. The battle of San Jacinto has been called the 16th most important battle in history because the American West was opened to exploration after Texas won its independence from Mexico. Read this book to discover what really happened at the battle.

1-55622-133-9   Fall '89

Exploring the Alamo Legends $17.95

As much as any other event in American history, legends and folklore tend to cloud what really occurred at the fall of the Alamo. Did Travis draw the line? Did some men actually escape? Was Sam Houston at least partially responsible, and did he cover up his involvement? These and many more questions remain for speculation. This book explores these and many other Alamo questions using exhaustive research of hard evidence. Based on logical interpretations of the evidence, some startling conclusions have finally be drawn.

1-55622-132-0   Fall '89

Forget the Alamo $17.95

Historians have long argued over whether or not the Texas freedom fighters should have defended the Alamo. Based on years of research, this historical work explores the possibility that Texas history might be different had the defenders chosen to stand and fight in one of the other San Antonio missions.

1-55622-134-7   Fall '89

Call Wordware Publishing, Inc. for names of the bookstores in your area.
(214) 423-0090

OVER TEXAS SOIL

This Dog'll Hunt was printed over Texas soil. Since it couldn't actually be printed in Texas, we took a little bit of Texas to it. A wooden box in the shape of Texas filled with dirt from the four corners of the great state was shipped to the printer. The box was sent with explicit instructions for the box to be placed under the press at the time *This Dog'll Hunt* was printed.

Wordware Publishing, Inc.'s traveling box of dirt is not a first of its kind. While LBJ was President, one of his grandchildren was born in Maryland, a fact that didn't sit well with the family. They wanted the little one to be a native Texan. The Johnsons solved their problem by placing a box of sterilized Texas dirt under the table in the delivery room. In that way, the little one could always say that he was born over Texas soil.

Now, never before offered, Wordware Publishing, Inc. will make its box of Texas dirt available to any displaced Texan who wishes to have some special event happen over Texas soil.

For more information about our Traveling Box of Texas Dirt or our miniature Texas dirt boxes, contact Wallace O. Chariton at (214) 423-0090.

Coming soon
to a bookstore near you!

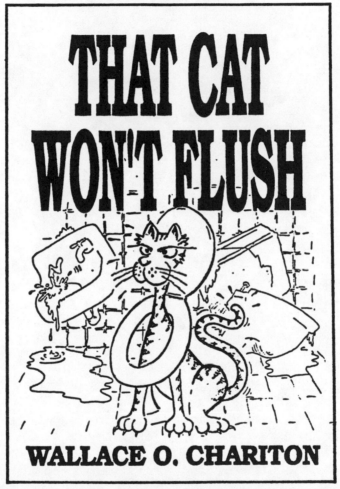

An entertaining country dictionary that begins where This Dog'll Hunt ends. Hundreds more humorous sayings in a convenient dictionary format. Available at bookstores in October 1990 or place an advance order by contacting:

Wordware Publishing, Inc.
1506 Capital Avenue
Plano, Texas 75074
Order line: 1-800-229-4949